Korean History in Maps

Korean History in Maps is a beautifully presented, full-color atlas covering all periods of Korean history from prehistoric times to the present day. It is the first atlas of its kind to be specifically designed for students in English-speaking countries. There is a map for each era in Korean history, showing every major kingdom or polity that existed on the Korean peninsula, and maps are also included for topics of additional historical interest, including each major war that took place. In addition, the atlas contains chronologies, lists of monarchs, and overviews of the politics, economy, society, and culture for each era which are complemented by numerous photos and full-color images of artifacts, paintings, and architectural structures. This fascinating historical atlas is a complete reference work and unique teaching tool for all scholars and students of Korean and East Asian history.

Korean History in Maps

From Prehistory to the Twenty-first Century

EDITED BY

Michael D. Shin

CONTRIBUTORS

Lee Injae

Owen Miller

Park Jinhoon

Yi Hyun-Hae

CAMBRIDGE
UNIVERSITY PRESS

University Printing House, Cambridge CB2 8BS, United Kingdom

Cambridge University Press is part of the University of Cambridge.

It furthers the University's mission by disseminating knowledge in the pursuit of education, learning and research at the highest international levels of excellence.

www.cambridge.org
Information on this title: www.cambridge.org/9781107490239

First published 2014
Reprinted 2016

Printed in the United Kingdom by Bell and Bain Ltd, Glasgow

A catalogue record for this publication is available from the British Library

Library of Congress Cataloguing in Publication data

ISBN 978-1-107-09846-6 Hardback
ISBN 978-1-107-49023-9 Paperback

To our students and our teachers

Contents

Preface and Acknowledgments

Michael D. Shin

Even in the second decade of the twenty–first century, the majority of students enter college, unable to find Korea on a map of the world. Though virtually all of them are familiar with China and Japan, they have little knowledge or even awareness of the peninsula that lies between them. Part of the reason is the lack of historical connections with Korea. The West first came into direct contact with the country only in the mid nineteenth century. Two wars – the first Sino-Japanese War and the Korean War – brought the country to the attention of a greater number of people. However, the country, despite its geopolitical importance during the Cold War, remained largely unknown. With its rapid industrialization, South Korea has become an export-oriented economy whose products, including textiles, cars, and electronics, are sold throughout the world. Though some brands such as Samsung and LG have been fixtures in Western households, few consumers know that these products are from South Korean companies – a stark contrast to their familiarity with Japanese ones. In this century, the situation seems to be changing as more and more people are becoming familiar with its cuisine and popular culture.

One of the tasks of Korean Studies has been to raise knowledge of the country to a level commensurate with its importance in world history and in the world today. Though many general histories of Korea have been published in the past two decades, there has not been an atlas specifically tailored to the needs of students in English-speaking countries interested in Korean history. The aim of this book is not just to enable students to find Korea on a map but also to provide the basic geographic information necessary to study Korean history. It is meant to complement the textbooks currently used in undergraduate and graduate classes on Korean history. Full-color maps show the territorial boundaries of all polities that have existed on the Korean peninsula, and there are images of artifacts and historic sites for each period of Korean history. To enhance its usefulness to students, this book also has concise overviews and chronologies for each period, as well as lists of monarchs and basic statistics for periods where sufficient sources exist.

Though the production of an atlas may seem to be a straightforward process, Korean history poses difficulties that Chinese and Japanese history do not. Some students will be aware that the territorial borders, names, and the ethnic composition of historical polities in and around the Korean peninsula have been sources of controversy in East Asia. For instance, since the turn of the century, China has claimed that the northern kingdom of Goguryeo was part of Chinese history, as well as the kingdom of Balhae. The issue of Korea's historical borders is a very explicit and extreme instance of how the work of history is inherently political, an issue that can even lead to diplomatic conflict in the region. In general, our approach was to try to find a consensus that the majority of scholars could agree upon. We hope to have provided material to help students learn about such issues and debates rather than taking a particular side.

This book was truly a collaborative effort. Most obviously, this is a book with many authors. Owen Miller of SOAS handled the sections on prehistoric Korea and did some parts of the section on the Joseon period; Yi Hyun-Hae of Hallym University wrote all the text in the section on the Joseon (Old Joseon) period. Lee Injae of Yonsei University wrote the overviews of Baekje and Silla in the Three Kingdoms Period section; Park Jinhoon of Myongji University wrote the Goguryeo overview and the sections on the Northern and Southern States Period and the Goryeo Period. Michael D. Shin of the University of Cambridge wrote the sections on the modern period, as well as some parts of the Joseon-period section. Owen Miller did the translations of texts that were originally written in Korean. Each author provided suggestions on the images to accompany his or her text and checked successive drafts of the atlas, including commenting on other sections.

We also received a tremendous amount of help from many colleagues, without whom this book would not exist. A number of experts were invited to Cambridge to consult on matters ranging from the accuracy of maps to the selection of images for each section. Seo Insun, a graduate student in archaeology at the University of Paris X Nanterre, provided advice and guidance on prehistoric Korea. Yi Tae-jin, emeritus of Seoul National University, gave extensive comments on the premodern sections of the book that helped to make it both more accurate and more cohesive. Oh Jinseok of Pai Chai University compiled the statistics that we used for most of the tables and charts in the book and gave us a thorough overview of the sources for statistical data and their limitations. Na Hee-La of Gyeongnam Naitonal University of Science and Technology gave detailed comments on the sections on the ancient period. Im Kihwan of Seoul National University of Education did a thorough review of the Goguryeo section. Song Kiho of Seoul National University, the director of its university museum, provided invaluable advice on the maps in the Balhae section and generously allowed us to use some of his photographs. The Joseon-period section was challenging to do because of its length and the amount of information in it. Detailed comments and advice from colleagues who are specialists on the period – Ko Dong-Hwan of the Korea Advanced Institute of Science and Technology (KAIST), Choi Yoonoh of Yonsei University, and

James B. Lewis of the University of Oxford – saved us from many potentially embarrassing errors. Charles Armstrong of Columbia University, Jae-Jung Suh of Johns Hopkins University, and Suzy Kim of Rutgers University reviewed the section on North Korea. We also discussed the atlas with and received help from other colleagues, such as Bruce Cumings of the University of Chicago, Hong Sung-Chan of Yonsei University, Jun Seung-Ho of the Academy of Korean Studies, Albert Park of Claremont-McKenna College, Park Tae-gyun of Seoul National University, Peter Kornicki of the University of Cambridge, and Mark Selden of Binghamton University and Cornell University, The book's chief designer, Joon Mo Kang, was in many ways another "author" of this text. He not only designed the entire book but also made all the charts, diagrams, and maps. Working closely with the contributors, he pushed us to create a book that is more useful and ambitious in clarity and visual impact than we had originally planned.

Finding all the images for the book proved to be more difficult and time-consuming than we had expected, and we are grateful for all the help we received from various individuals and institutions. Most of all, we wish to thank Oh Youngchan, a former curator at the National Museum of Korea, who now teaches at Ewha Womans University. We were fortunate that he was spending a year as a visiting curator at the British Museum when we began this project. He provided invaluable advice and contacts and even helped us to navigate the paperwork necessary to acquire the rights to the images from museums throughout South Korea. Jung Jieun of the National Museum of Korea processed the paperwork and was very helpful in allowing us to download the images we requested. Park Sook-Hee, the Head Librarian of the Kyujanggak Archives' Reference Services, was generous with her time in helping us to locate old maps and other images. Seo Hyunju of the Northeast Asian History Foundation and Nayoung Chung of the Dokdo Research Institute helped us to acquire images of Dok Island (Dokdo). Joo Sung-jee, also of the Northeast Asian History Foundation, provided valuable assistance with the images of Goguryeo tomb murals. Choi Inho of the Seoul Museum of History helped us acquire additional maps of Dok Island. Jae-Hyun Choi of the Bank of Korea generously provided us with photographs of South Korean currency. Henny Savenije gave us permission to use images from his personal collection of maps. Eric Luhrs, Digital Initiatives Librarian of Lafayette College, generously allowed us to use images from their collection of colonial–era postcards for free. Closer to home, the late Mark Blackburn, Head of the Department of Coins and Metals of the Fitzwilliam Museum at the University of Cambridge, took the time to show us their collection of Korean coins, the largest in Europe, and let us use the images we needed. The museum's collection of celadon and the Cambridge University Library's collection of old European maps were also helpful resources. David Heather gave us permission to use an image from his vast collection of North Korean posters. Daniel Brennwald, Charlie Crane, Robert Koehler, Eric Lafforgue, and Kernbeisser gave us discounted rates on their photographs or let us use them for free.

Because of the time and expense involved, it is rare to have the opportunity to make a historical atlas. This project would not have been possible without funding from the Academy of Korean Studies (AKS) under its "Curriculum and Teaching Materials for Global Korean Studies" program. The amount of funding allowed us to work for three years to create an atlas with few compromises. Five anonymous reviews of the manuscript arranged by the AKS contained many useful comments. Generous donations from Mr. and Mrs. I.H. Cho and Mr. M. Kim helped to cover the printing costs and enabled us to undertake extra work that improved the final product. The atlas was also made possible by the institutional support provided by Robinson College, which has provided a home for Korean Studies at the University of Cambridge. The dedicated staff of the college handled the accounts and provided housing for guests, technical support, and catering for all related events. Owen Miller, one of the authors of this book, was the first post-doctoral associate for the grant project who was hired at Robinson to handle logistical details and administrative work, as well as all sorts of behind-the-scenes tasks. He was followed by two able successors, Gian-Marco Bussandri and Stefan Knoob. Thanks are due to Michèle Tumber, Julia McCarthy, Cathie Howell, and Shirley Young in the College Office and Christine James, Kara Sheehan, Lianne Stroud, Amy Brown, Michael Howley, and Emma Webb in the Conference and Catering Office – who all made sure that everything ran with cheerful efficiency. The book's chief designer worked with two assistant designers, Susie Choi and Sung Hun Jung, and he would also like to thank Sue Park for help with map design, Jesse Senje Yuan for help with map design and Chinese characters, and Seulgi Ho for help with chart design. David Miao of HOUSE, a digital post–production studio in New York City, did all the color correction, with assistance from Nicole N. Kim, and enabled us to stay on schedule with his quick work. Graduate student assistants, Ji-yoon An and Youngchan Justin Choi, were helpful, and two former undergraduate students, Laura Leung-How and Gian-Marco Bussandri, did a very thorough job of proofreading the entire manuscript. Lucy Rhymer, our editor at Cambridge University Press, has been an enthusiastic supporter of our project and skillfully guided it to completion. The anonymous reviews undertaken at the Press' request were helpful, giving us fresh perspectives on the material. Thanks are especially due to Claire Wood, an Editor at the Press, and two Production Editors, Vania Cunha and Joanna Breeze, for helping us to prepare the manuscript for the printer. Noel Robson, a designer at the Press, looked over all the images and provided valuable advice that helped us to fine–tune the design.

Though so many people contributed to the book, all errors are, of course, the responsibility of the authors. Last but not leaset, we want to thank all the family, friends, and colleagues – too many to name here – who provided support to us, in both tangible and intangible ways. The romanization of Korean terms follows the Revised Romanization system of the South Korean Ministry of Culture that was adopted in the year 2000; exceptions have been made for names of people and places that already have a widely accepted spelling in English-speaking countries, such as Pyongyang and Syngman Rhee. Japanese terms have been romanized according to the Revised Hepburn system, and Chinese terms have been romanized in pinyin.

RUSSIA

CHINA

Hoeryeong ●
Seonbong ●
Najin ●

NORTH
HAMGYEONG

Mt. Baekdu ▲

Cheongjin ●

Hyesan ●

YANGGANG

Manpo ●
Ganggye ●
Chosan ●

JAGANG

Gimchaek ●
Dancheon ●

SOUTH
HAMGYEONG

Sinuiju ●

NORTH
PYEONGAN

Hamheung ●

Anju ●

SOUTH
PYEONGAN

Suncheon ●

○ Pyongyang

Wonsan ●

Nampo ●

GANGWON

Goseong ●

Sariwon ●

NORTH
HWANGHAE

Sokcho ●

SOUTH
HWANGHAE

Haeju ●

38°

Gaeseong ● ● Panmunjeom

GYEONGGI

Chuncheon ●

Gangneung ●

Incheon ● ○ Seoul

GANGWON

Ulleung

Dok

Suwon ●

GYEONGGI

Wonju ● Pyeongchang ●

NORTH
CHUNGCHEONG

Cheonan ●

SOUTH
CHUNGCHEONG

Cheongju ●

Andong ●

● Sejong
Daejeon ●

NORTH
GYEONGSANG

Pohang ●

Jeonju ●

Daegu ● Gyeongju ●

NORTH JEOLLA

Ulsan ●

SOUTH
GYEONGSANG

Gwangju ●

Changwon ● Busan ●

SOUTH JEOLLA

Mokpo ●

Yeosu ●

KOREA STRAIT

Tsushima

JAPAN

● Jeju City

JEJU

● Fukuoka

| ○ Capital | ◉ Metropolitan cities | ● Major cities | ○ Special autonomous city | Provincial boundaries | The 38th parallel | Ceasefire line |

Capitals   Major cities

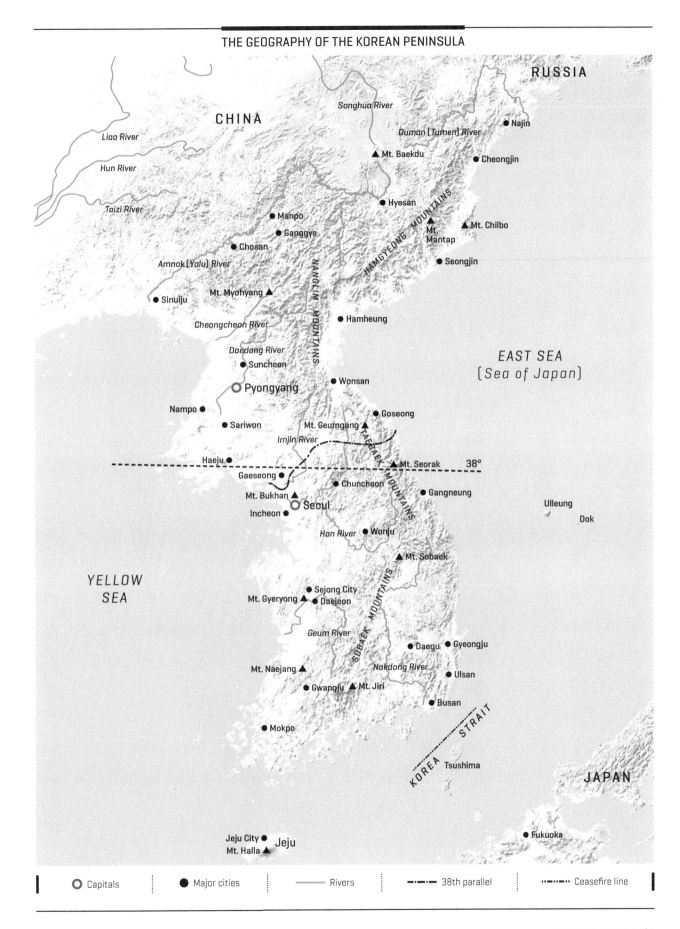

Neolithic comb-pattern pot
excavated at Amsa-dong, Seoul.
(National Museum of Korea)

1
PREHISTORIC KOREA

Bronze rattle
from the 3rd century BCE.
Excavated at Daegok-ri,
South Jeolla province.
(National Museum of Korea)

The prehistoric era spans the period from the earliest hominid inhabitation on the peninsula, some time before 200,000 BP, up to the first recorded polities that emerged between the seventh and third centuries BCE. The Paleolithic peoples of the Korean peninsula were nomadic and subsisted on what they could gather and hunt; from the Neolithic period, people began to live a more settled life, and primitive agriculture developed. The Bronze Age saw the first signs of significant social differentiation such as dolmen tombs containing luxury objects, and the transition from the Neolithic to the Bronze Age was marked by a change from pottery incised with various patterns to a plain style.

The Peopling of the Korean Peninsula

Existing evidence shows that hominids populated the Korean peninsula by at least 200,000 years BP, but many archaeologists believe that early humans were living on the peninsula as long ago as 500,000 BP. Modern humans (*Homo sapiens sapiens*) began to populate the Korean peninsula around 30,000–40,000 years ago, replacing or intermingling with the earlier inhabitants. Recent genetic evidence suggests that there were two distinct paths by which modern humans migrated to the peninsula, one from the north and one from the south.

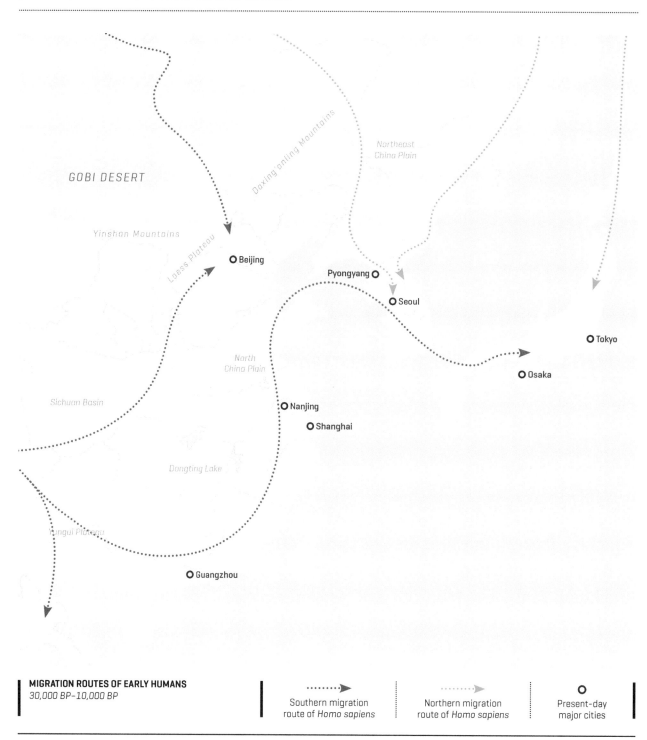

MIGRATION ROUTES OF EARLY HUMANS
30,000 BP–10,000 BP

• • • ▶ Southern migration route of *Homo sapiens*

· · · ▷ Northern migration route of *Homo sapiens*

O Present-day major cities

The Paleolithic Era | *Approximately 200,000 BP–8,000 BP (6,000 BCE)*

The Paleolithic period on the Korean peninsula is characterized by the use of stone tools. As in other parts of the world, finds of such tools show a progression over thousands of years from large rough tools to smaller and more delicate ones. The inhabitants of Paleolithic Korea were hunter-gatherers who relied on foraging for edible plants. They are thought to have lived a nomadic life in small bands, setting up temporary camps or living for brief periods in caves. The warming climate at the end of the last ice age brought about changes in the mode of human life on the Korean peninsula, as elsewhere, and marked the beginning of a transition to the Neolithic period.

Hand axe
excavated at Juwol-ri, Gyeonggi province.
Length: 235mm.
[Yonsei University Museum]

Obsidian burin
[chisel-type implement]
excavated at Seokjang-ri, South Chungcheong province. Length: 39mm.
[Yonsei University Museum]

Stone scraper
excavated at Jungnae-ri, South Jeolla province.
Length: 155mm.
[Yonsei University Museum]

Stone tool with tanged point
excavated at Wolpyeong, South Jeolla province.
Length: 71mm.
[Yonsei University Museum]

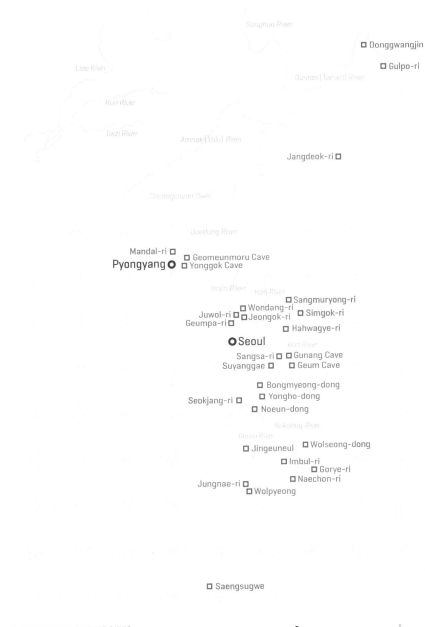

Songhua River

☐ Donggwangjin

☐ Gulpo-ri

Liao River

Duman (Tumen) River

Hun River

Taizi River

Amnok (Yalu) River

Jangdeok-ri ☐

Cheongcheon River

Daedong River

Mandal-ri ☐
☐ Geomeunmoru Cave
Pyongyang ◯ ☐ Yonggok Cave

Imjin River · Han River

☐ Sangmuryong-ri
☐ Wondang-ri
Juwol-ri ☐ ☐ Jeongok-ri ☐ Simgok-ri
Geumpa-ri ☐
☐ Hahwagye-ri

◯ Seoul

Han River

Sangsa-ri ☐ ☐ Gunang Cave
Suyanggae ☐ ☐ Geum Cave

☐ Bongmyeong-dong
Seokjang-ri ☐ ☐ Yongho-dong
☐ Noeun-dong

Nakdong River

Geum River
☐ Jingeuneul ☐ Wolseong-dong
☐ Imbul-ri
☐ Gorye-ri
Jungnae-ri ☐ ☐ Naechon-ri
☐ Wolpyeong

☐ Saengsugwe

MAJOR PALEOLITHIC SITES

☐
Sites of
excavations

◯
Present-day
major cities

The Neolithic Era | *8,000 BCE–2,000 BCE*

The Neolithic period is marked by two major developments: the appearance of pottery and the development of ground rather than chipped stone tools. The earliest pottery of the Korean peninsula was characterized by raised or stamped decoration. This later tended to be replaced by incised decoration, typified by *jeulmun* or "comb-pattern" pottery. The people of the Neolithic era also made adornments and symbolic items such as necklaces and small animal figures or human faces. Settled life began in this period, and villages of earth-pit houses dating from this period have been discovered all over the peninsula. People continued to subsist by foraging and hunting, but another major development was the beginning of agricultural cultivation. Archaeological evidence suggests that people were cultivating millet and rice in this period.

Comb-pattern earthenware pot
excavated at Nongpo-dong, North Hamgyeong province.
(National Museum of Korea)

Polished stone axes
excavated at Hupo-ri in North Gyeongsang province.
(Gyeongju National Museum)

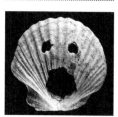

Shell depicting a human face
excavated from a shell midden at Dongsam-dong in Busan.
(National Museum of Korea)

Liao River
Songhua River
Dumon (Tumen) River
◇ Gulpo-ri
◇ Nongpo-dong
Hun River
Taizi River
Amnok (Yalu) River
Cheongcheon River
◇ Sinam-ri
Daedong River
◇ Cheongho-ri
Geumtan-ri ◇
Gungsan-ri ◇ ◎ Pyongyang
Imjin River
Jitam-ri ◇
Han River ◇ Osan-ri
◇ Kyo-dong
Seoul
Si Island ◇ ◎◇ Misa-ri
Oi Island ◇ ◇ Amsa-dong
Han River
Nakdong River ◇ Hupo-ri
Geum River ◇ Songjuk-ri
◇ Gyewha Island ◇ Imbul-ri
◇ Sinam-ri
Suga-ri ◇ ◇ Dongsam-dong
Daeheuksan Island ◇
Sangnodae Island ◇◇ Yeondae Island
Song Island ◇ ◇ Yokji Island

MAJOR NEOLITHIC SITES

◇ Sites of excavations

◎ Present-day major cities

The Beginning of the Bronze Age | *2,000 BCE–300 BCE*

The earliest signs of the beginning of the Bronze Age were actually the appearance of dolmen tombs and a plain pottery style called *mumun* beginning in the early second millennium BCE. The first evidence of bronze artifacts in Korea can be dated to the thirteenth century BCE, indicating the arrival of bronze wares and later bronze technology from northern China. Ceremonial bronze objects such as mirrors and rattles were also used in the later Bronze Age. During this period, people began to live in larger villages, and it is thought that chiefs began to rule over groups of people in the mid-Bronze Age.

Plain earthenware pot
excavated at
Songgung-ri, South
Chungcheong province.
(Buyeo National Museum)

Stone cist burial
excavated at
Songgung-ri, South
Chungcheong province.
(National Museum of Korea)

***Geompa*-style bronzeware**
discovered in
Namseong-ri, South
Chungcheong province.
4th–3rd centuries BCE.
(National Museum of Korea)

MAJOR BRONZE AGE SITES

△ Early Bronze Age sites

○ Present-day major cities

YAN

Shenyang ◯   ● Lianhuapu

Mt. Baekdu ▲

Taizi River

Amnok [Yalu] River

● Wujintang

▲ Mt. Qianshan

◯ **Wanggeomseong**

Liaodong
Peninsula

JOSEON

● Sejung-ri

Daedong River

◉ **Wanggeomseong**

● Taeseong-ri

● Unseong-ri

● Seoksan-ri

◯ Seoul

QI

● Namseong-ri

JIN
[SAMHAN]

Joseon [Early Period]	Joseon [Later Period]	◯ Proposed locations of Joseon capitals	● Archaeological sites	◯ Present-day cities	Border of present-day Liaoning province

2

JOSEON AND EARLY STATE FORMATION

A monument purported to be the **tomb of Dangun**, mythical founder of Joseon. National Treasure no. 174. Constructed by the North Korean government in 1994. Gangdong County, Pyongyang. (Eckart Dege)

With the spread of bronze culture from China, the first state developed in the Korean peninsula, now called "Old Joseon" to distinguish it from the later kingdom with the same name. By the early fourth century BCE, the time of the Warring States period in China, it developed into a state that was a major player in international politics. The first reference to a country called "Joseon" was in the Chinese text *Guanzi*, which was compiled in the year 26 BCE. The Joseon era is commonly divided into two periods. The Early Period lasted from the seventh to the fourth century BCE, and the Later Period began in 300 BCE with the introduction of iron culture and ended in 108 BCE with its conquest by the Han Dynasty.

The tomb of Gija, a semi-mythical figure who supposedly brought Chinese civilization to Joseon and ruled the country after Dangun. Located in Pyongyang and probably constructed during the Joseon period. (Lafayette College)

International Relations and Trade

According to the *Guanzi*, Joseon had relations with the state of Qi on the Shandong Peninsula in the seventh century BCE, during China's Spring and Autumn Period. By at least the late fourth century BCE, it developed into a major player in international politics in Northeast Asia. For instance, when the country battled with the Chinese state of Yan for regional supremacy, the rulers of the two states agreed to address each with the title "king." After Wiman seized the throne in the Later Period, King Jun and his followers moved to the southwest of the peninsula, resulting in the expansion of bronzeware production and trade networks. The major products of Joseon included patterned animal hides and fur clothes, and it also handled some of the trade between Chinese states and polities further south in the Korean peninsula, such as Jinbeon, Imdun, and Jin. Through this trade, it acquired iron tools and the raw material for bronze production. When tensions developed with Han China in the late second century BCE, King Ugeo seized control of all land and overseas trade routes to China in order to profit from the trade as an intermediary. When the Yemaek people requested the protection of the Han dynasty, China responded by establishing the commandery of Canghai in 128 BCE. Its aim was to put pressure on Wiman Joseon, but it was not particularly effective and was abandoned after three years. Wiman Joseon's iron technology was already developed to a considerable degree, and it attempted to form ties with the Xiongnu tribes to the north.

Culture

During the seventh to fourth centuries BCE, a distinctive Bronze Age culture emerged in the northeast that was different from that of the Yellow River basin. It was marked by the use of mandolin-shaped bronze daggers. Areas associated with Joseon have a high concentration of mandolin-shaped bronze daggers, Misongni-style earthenware, and dolmen-style tombs. As a theocratic society, religious authority in Joseon was an important way of controlling and uniting the members of the group. Large dolmen tombs were constructed for the heads of the individual polities, and they were buried with the bronze weapons and ceremonial items that they owned in life. It seems that various ceremonies were conducted near the tombs and that they played a central role in achieving communal unity.

In the Later Period, a distinctive metal culture blossomed in the Daedong River basin, and it was characterized by the use of "slender bronze daggers." Slender bronze dagger culture spread throughout the Korean peninsula and even reached as far as the Japanese archipelago and the coast of what is now Russia's Maritime Province. Since iron tools gradually began to be used in this time, archaeologists view this period as the early Iron Age. Joseon artisans began to apply iron-making techniques to the making of bronzes to produce even more exquisite and high-quality bronzeware. When King Ugeo blocked trade routes in the second century BCE, there was a sharp decline in bronze production in the southwest of the peninsula.

Earthenware pot in the Misongni style. Misong-ri, North Pyeongan province.

Politics

Joseon was a confederation that united many independent polities. Most of these polities were situated on the Liaodong peninsula and the northwest part of the Korean peninsula. There is debate over the location of the political center of Joseon in the Early Period, with some claiming Liaoxi and others arguing for modern-day Pyongyang, but the most likely location is Liaodong. After the state of Yan attacked Joseon in the early third century BCE, it moved its political center from Liaodong to Pyongyang. This marked the beginning of the Later Period. There are various theories about where the border between Yan and Joseon was located, including the Cheongcheon River and the Liao River, but the Amnok (Yalu) River is the most likely. In the *Weilüe*, a text written during the fourth century CE, it is recorded that the ruler of Joseon began to use the title of "king" around the year 320 BCE. In the second century BCE, a man named Wiman, who was originally from Yan, carried out a coup and took the throne himself. Initially, Wiman Joseon maintained amicable relations with the Han Dynasty and was able to strengthen itself with the support of Han's more advanced technology. It subjugated neighboring polities such as Jinbeon and Imdun and gradually expanded its influence to the Yemaek region. Han launched an invasion in 109 BCE, and Wiman Joseon fell the following year when a faction who wanted to surrender assassinated King Ugeo.

Knife money from the state of Yan discovered in Yongyeon-dong, North Pyeongan province. Evidence that trade existed between Joseon and Yan. (National Museum of Korea)

In Northeast Asia, the greatest number of dolmens can be found in or near the Korean peninsula. Approximately 35,000 have been found in North and South Korea. There are three main types of dolmen. The "table-type" dolmen consists of four stone slabs arranged in the shape of a cube, covered by a large capstone, and this type is mainly found in the north. The "*go*-board type" dolmen is made of a large stone placed over a pile of small stones. The "capstone-type" dolmen consists simply of a capstone put on top of an underground stone cist. It is the most common type of dolmen and can be found all over the Korean peninsula.

TYPES OF DOLMEN

Table-type

Go-board type

Unsupported capstone type

DOLMEN SITES
7th–2nd centuries BCE

Table-type dolmen site

Go-board-type dolmen site

Present-day major cities

Joseon Culture | *Bronze Daggers*

During the seventh–fourth centuries BCE, Joseon developed its own bronze culture which is characterized by the mandolin-shaped (Liaoning-style) bronze dagger. This cultural sphere can be subdivided into at least four areas, each with its own characteristic tomb culture, pottery, and bronzeware. After the center of Joseon moved southward to the Daedong River in the third century BCE, a new bronze culture developed characterized by the slender bronze dagger. The slender dagger culture spread to other parts of the Korean peninsula and was transmitted as far as the Japanese archipelago and the coast of what is now Russia's Maritime Province.

**Mandolin-shaped
bronze dagger**
from Gangshang tombs,
Liaoning province, China.

BRONZE DAGGER SITES
7th–2nd centuries BCE

▲ Slender
dagger site

▲ Mandolin-shaped
dagger site

○ Present-day
major cities

Slender bronze daggers
discovered in Daegok-ri
in South Jeolla province.
[National Museum of Korea]

**Coarse-patterned
bronze mirror**
dating to slender dagger
period. Discovered in
Namseong-ri, Ansan.
[National Museum of Korea]

The Han Commanderies

Reconstructed Lelang lacquerwares.
Some were found in tombs in the Pyongyang region.
[National Museum of Korea]

Han Dynasty gold belt buckle,
1st century CE.
Discovered in a Lelang tomb at Seogam-ri, Pyongyang.
[National Museum of Korea]

After the fall of Wiman Joseon, Han China established four commanderies within its former sphere of influence. It set up the commandery of Lelang in the territory that had been directly controlled by Wiman Joseon. It then established the commanderies of Zhenfan and Lintun in Jinbeon and Imdun, two polities that had been under Wiman Joseon's control. In the Yemaek region, Han established a fourth commandery named Xuantu. The territory of Xuantu covered the land routes that connected major polities from the central Yalu River basin to the Liaodong peninsula. Around 82 BCE, both Zhenfan and Lintun were abolished, and in 75 BCE, Xuantu was forced to move to the Hun River basin by the resistance of the Goguryeo people, leaving only the commandery of Lelang. For a while, Lelang continued to rule over parts of the former commanderies of Zhenfan and Lintun, but this was abandoned in 30 CE. Around 203–204 CE, the powerful Gongsun clan of Liaodong took control of Lelang and founded a new commandery named Daifang in part of the former Zhenfan commandery. These two commanderies continued under Chinese control, but the era of the Han commanderies ended when Lelang fell to Goguryeo in 313 CE.

THE HAN COMMANDERIES

Xuantu (Hyeondo)

Lintun (Imdun)

Lelang (Nangnang)

Zhenfan (Jinbeon)

Cities at the time

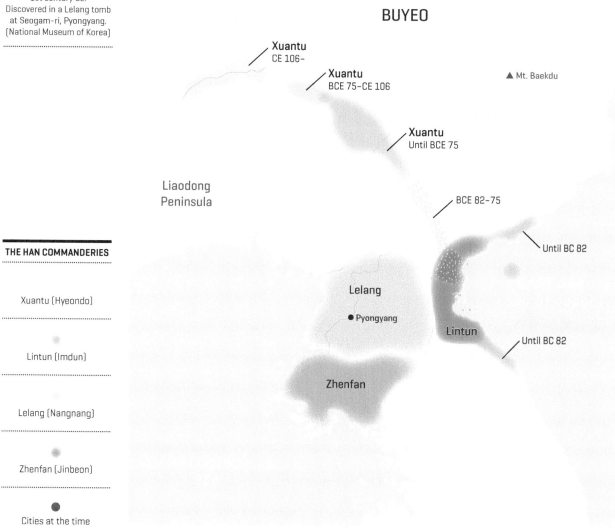

BUYEO

Xuantu
CE 106–

Xuantu
BCE 75–CE 106

▲ Mt. Baekdu

Xuantu
Until BCE 75

Liaodong
Peninsula

BCE 82–75

Until BC 82

Lelang

● Pyongyang

Lintun

Until BC 82

Zhenfan

Agriculture in Early Korea

The beginning of agricultural cultivation in the prehistoric era was such a momentous event in human history that it is known as the "Neolithic Revolution." From around 3,500 BCE, people on the Korean peninsula began to engage in a primitive form of millet cultivation. Recent discoveries have suggested that people in the Han River and Geum River basins were already cultivating rice, in addition to millet, in the Neolithic period. Agriculture was mainly done by the technique of slash–and–burn farming, and the primary tools were stone axes, hoes, and *ddabi* (a plow–like tool). After they were cleared, fields could be cultivated for two to three years but then had to be left fallow for more than ten years.

By the Bronze Age, a variety of crops were regularly cultivated, including millet, sorghum, soybeans, red beans, wheat, barley, and rice. After the seventh and eighth centuries BCE, paddy–field agriculture began to spread in the southern and central regions, while the fallow period for dry–fields decreased to five to ten years. This was when the Korean tradition began of the coexistence of these two different forms of agriculture. As the fallow periods became shorter, stone farming tools gradually disappeared, and a variety of wooden tools, including spades, hoes, and *ddabi*, began to develop. Even in the Bronze Age, bronze was mainly used to make weapons and ritual implements. Archaeological sites excavated in the last ten years have revealed that the majority of Bronze Age paddy fields were divided into rather small sections of around ten square meters in order to facilitate easy irrigation and draining. In the case of dry fields, the shapes of furrows and ridges were diverse and complex because of the inefficiency of wooden farming tools and the lack of labor power.

Excavated ridges and furrows dating to the late Bronze Age in Daepyeong–ri, near Jinju, South Gyeongsang province. [Gyeongsang National University Museum]

Bronzeware with engraved depiction of a farmer plowing. Treasure no. 1823. Discovered in Daejeon. [National Museum of Korea]

In the Samhan and Three Kingdoms periods, farming technology continued to develop with the use of iron tools and of draft animals. While the exact timing varied according to region, wooden farming tools generally began to be replaced by iron ones in the first century BCE, and by the fourth–fifth centuries CE, iron sickles, spades, hoes, and pitchforks were widely used. The use of oxen began first in Goguryeo, and by the fifth century CE, the ox–plow was used in Baekje and Silla as well. Iron tools made plowing easier and more efficient, thus greatly improving the fertility of the soil and the efficacy of weeding. As a result, it was possible to reduce significantly the amount of time that fields were left fallow. If the fallow period continued for more than three years, the grass would become too well rooted, making it impossible to use a plow. Thus, the introduction of the ox–plow meant that Korean agriculture had already reached the stage in which fields were left fallow for only one or two years. In addition, the size of a field was now more than ten times larger than it had been in the Bronze Age, and fields were reorganized into long, stepped paddies to make them easier to plow. The development of agricultural techniques also provided an impetus for the centralization of political power, as the state monopolized the manufacture of iron tools, mobilized labor for large-scale public works, and expanded the area of land under cultivation. There are various theories about when Korean agriculture began to move beyond the stage of fallow-field farming, but it is clear that it remained widespread until the end of the Later Silla period.

The Samhan Confederations

The fall of Wiman Joseon and the establishment of the Han commanderies had a major influence on the central and southern regions of Korea, leading to the dissolution of the Jin state and the formation of many small statelets. These small-scale polities had an average population of 10,000–15,000 people and were far smaller in both population and territory than the later Three Kingdoms. The *Dongyi* (Eastern Barbarians) chapter of the Chinese text *Records of the Three Kingdoms* contains the names of around seventy statelets existing in the mid-third century. These statelets formed the regional confederacies of Mahan, Jinhan and Byeonhan, thus giving rise to the name Samhan (Three Han). The Chinese character *Han* first appeared in the *Records of the Three Kingdoms*. The Samhan were, ethnically and culturally, the direct descendants of the peoples of the slender bronze dagger culture. They later merged and developed into the kingdoms of Baekje, Silla, and Gaya.

Lelang and other Chinese-controlled areas served as a conduit for the spread of advanced technology and new culture and exerted great influence on the political and economic development of the peninsula. The international trade network connecting the Chinese mainland with the Korean peninsula and the Japanese archipelago had stagnated during the final years of Wiman Joseon, but it was now revived and expanded further. The Chinese luxury goods and advanced technology imported through Lelang stimulated demand for trade in the southern statelets. The Jinhan and Byeonhan regions produced large quantities of iron that played an important role in promoting international trade. Iron was exported to Lelang, the Japanese archipelago, Mahan, and Dongye, and it was made into ingots for distribution. The ingots were also used as a form of currency when other goods were traded. The development of long-distance trade accelerated the spread of iron weapons and tools and thus promoted the growth of political authority. The leaders of the Samhan statelets already exercised their power on the basis of their military and economic might rather than their religious authority. Evidence for this is found in the fact that the tombs of the chiefs of the Jinhan and Byeonhan statelets contained dozens of iron arrowheads and iron spears.

Han Dynasty bronze mirror
excavated in Yangdong-ri, in what was
once part of the Byeonhan confederation.
(Gimhae National Museum)

Han Dynasty bronze tripod cauldron (*ding*)
excavated from a tomb at Yangdong-ri,
South Gyeongsang province. Clear evidence of
the active trade between the southern Korean peninsula
and Han China during the Samhan period.
(Gimhae National Museum)

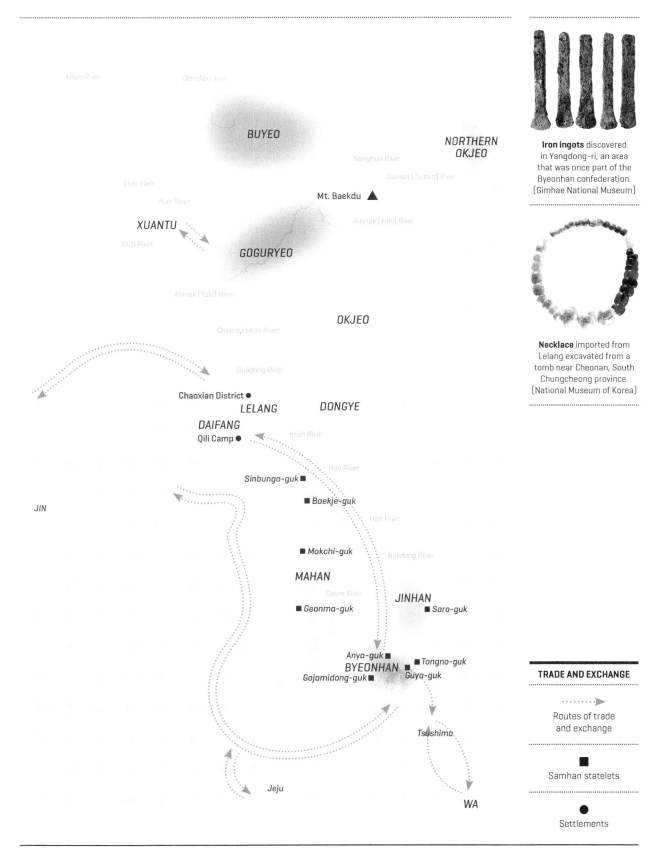

Xiliao River

Dongliao River

BUYEO

NORTHERN
OKJEO

Songhua River

Duman (Tumen) River

Mt. Baekdu ▲

XUANTU

Liao River

Hun River

Taizi River

GOGURYEO

Amnok (Yalu) River

Amnok (Yalu) River

OKJEO

Cheongcheon River

Daedong River

Chaoxian District ●

LELANG   DONGYE

DAIFANG
Qili Camp ●

Imjin River

Hun River

Sinbungo-guk ■

■ Baekje-guk

Han River

JIN

■ Mokchi-guk

Nakdong River

MAHAN

Geum River   JINHAN

■ Geonma-guk   ■ Saro-guk

Anya-guk ■
BYEONHAN   ■ Tongno-guk
Gojamidong-guk ■   Guya-guk

Tsushima

Jeju

WA

Iron ingots discovered
in Yangdong-ri, an area
that was once part of the
Byeonhan confederation.
(Gimhae National Museum)

Necklace imported from
Lelang excavated from a
tomb near Cheonan, South
Chungcheong province.
(National Museum of Korea)

TRADE AND EXCHANGE

⋯⋯▷
Routes of trade
and exchange

■
Samhan statelets

●
Settlements

CHRONOLOGY OF JOSEON AND EARLY STATE FORMATION

EARLY PERIOD
Seventh–Fourth Century BCE

SEVENTH CENTURY BCE: Joseon is recorded as having diplomatic relations with the state of Qi on the Shandong peninsula.

320 BCE APPROX.: The ruler of Joseon takes the title of king for the first time.

LATER PERIOD
300 BCE–108 BCE

THIRD CENTURY BCE: The Yan army invades the west of Joseon.

195 BCE: Wiman flees the state of Yan and arrives in Joseon where he is made responsible for the defense of the western border.

194–180 BCE: Wiman mounts a coup against King Jun of Joseon, defeating him and establishing the new dynasty of Wiman Joseon.

128 BCE: The Han Dynasty establishes the commandery of Canghai.

126 BCE: Han abolishes the commandery of Canghai.

109 BCE: Wiman Joseon attacks Han territory in the Liaodong peninsula. Emperor Wu of Han responds by sending a force of 60,000 soldiers to attack Wiman Joseon.

108 BCE: Although Joseon resists the Han attack for a year, it is finally defeated when King Ugeo is killed by a faction in his own court.

THE HAN COMMANDERIES AND THE SAMHAN CONFEDERATIONS
108 BCE–Early Fourth Century CE

108 BCE: The Han Dynasty establishes the commanderies of Lelang, Zhenfan and Lintun in the former area ruled by Wiman Joseon.

107 BCE: Han establishes the commandery of Xuantu in regions formerly subject to Wiman Joseon.

FIRST CENTURY BCE: Dissolution of the Jin state in the southern part of the Korean peninsula and emergence of the Samhan statelets.

82 BCE: The Zhenfan and Lintun commanderies are abolished.

75 BCE: The Xuantu commandery moves to the Hun River basin.

25 CE: Wang Diao kills the Lelang governor and establishes his own regime.

203–204 CE: The Gongsun clan takes control of the Lelang commandery and creates the new commandery of Daifang to the south of Lelang.

237–239 CE: The commanderies of Lelang and Daifang come under the control of the Chinese state of Wei.

313 CE: Goguryeo attacks and conquers the commandery of Lelang.

CHINA
221 BCE–206 BCE: Qin
206 BCE–220 CE: Han

JAPAN
14,000 BCE–300 BCE: Jōmon period
400/300 BCE–250 CE: Yayoi period

Dongliao River

Songhua River

GOGURYEO

Duman (Tumen) River

Liao River

▲ Mt. Baekdu

Hun River

Taizi River

O Gungnaeseong

Amnok (Yalu) River

Cheongcheon River

Daedong River

O Pyongyangseong
(Pyongyang)

Imjin River

Han River

O Seoul

SILLA

Danghangseong ●

TAEBAEK MOUNTAINS

Ulleung

Dok

SOBAEK MOUNTAINS

O Ungjin

Sabi O

Geum River

Nakdong River

O Geumseong

BAEKJE

WA

TAMNA
(JEJU)

| O Capitals | ● Cities at the time | O Present-day capital |

3

THE THREE KINGDOMS PERIOD

Goguryeo	Baekje	Silla	Gaya
37 BCE–668	18 BCE–660	57 BCE–935	42–562

After the fall of Joseon, the statelets on the Korean peninsula underwent a series of conquests and consolidations that led to the formation of three kingdoms. Goguryeo conquered Biryu, Northern Okjeo, and Buyeo and occupied the northern part of the peninsula and what is now Manchuria. Baekje emerged from the Mahan region and conquered neighboring polities in the southwest. Silla emerged in the Jinhan region and expanded to occupy the southeast portion of the peninsula, conquering the Gaya confederation. The lack of a unified dynasty in China gave the peninsula some breathing room to absorb Chinese influence and yet to develop its own civilzation. This period was characterized by the shifting alliances among the three kingdoms as they battled each other for supremacy on the peninsula and defended their countries against invasions from China. Eventually, Silla allied with Tang China and was able to defeat Baekje in 660 and then Goguryeo in 668. Tang had designs on conquering the whole Korean peninsula, but in 676, Silla drove out the Tang army and united the peninsula under one government for the first time.

Goguryeo

Tomb of King Dongmyeong, founder of the state of Goguryeo. National Treasure no. 36. Reconstructed by North Korea in 1993. Located near present-day Pyongyang. [Eckart Dege]

According to legend, Goguryeo was founded by a Buyeo prince named Jumong, who ran away to found a new kingdom. It emerged out of tribes that existed within the Yemaek region, and it was the first of the three kingdoms to develop into an advanced polity. It is known for its martial prowess, and it is credited with driving the Han commanderies out of the Korean peninsula and with protecting it from later Chinese invasion.

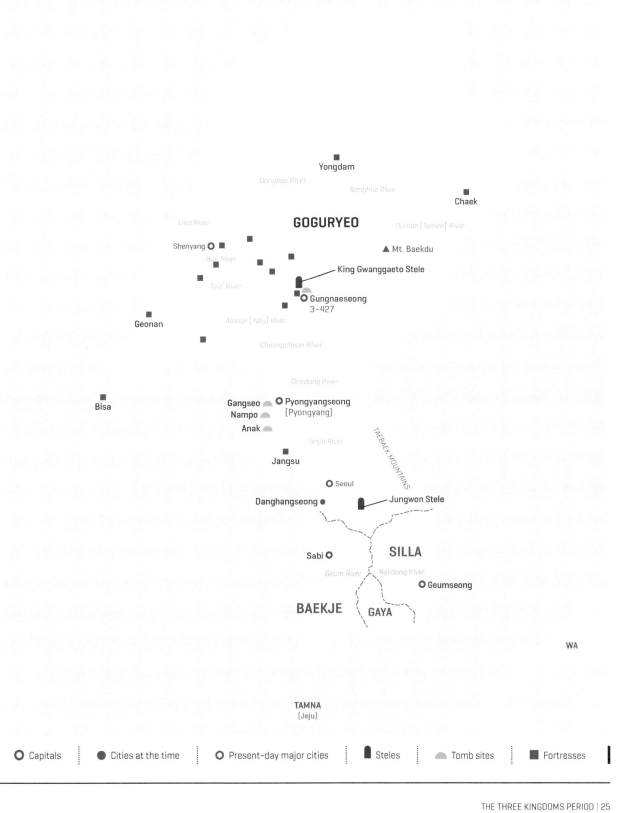

Yongdam

Dongliao River

Songhua River

Chaek

Liao River

GOGURYEO

Duman (Tumen) River

Shenyang

▲ Mt. Baekdu

Hun River

King Gwanggaeto Stele

Taizi River

○ Gungnaeseong
3–427

Geonan

Amnok (Yalu) River

Cheongcheon River

Daedong River

Bisa

Gangseo ○ Pyongyangseong
Nampo (Pyongyang)
Anak

Imjin River

Jangsu

○ Seoul

Danghangseong ●

Jungwon Stele

TAEBAEK MOUNTAINS

Sabi ○

SILLA

Geum River *Nakdong River*

○ Geumseong

BAEKJE **GAYA**

WA

TAMNA
(Jeju)

| ○ Capitals | ● Cities at the time | ○ Present-day major cities | Steles | Tomb sites | ■ Fortresses |

Portrait of an official named Jin in the Deokheung–ri tomb. The tomb is National Treasure no. 156. Discovered in 1976 in Nampo, South Pyeongan province. (Northeast Asian History Foundation)

Society

The royal Go family and the five main aristocratic clans held high positions and dominated political life. Most aristocrats lived in the capital; they had their own armies and embarked on campaigns for foreign conquest, playing a leading role in wars. Most commoners were independent cultivators who had to pay taxes to the government, serve in the military, and were mobilized as labor for public works projects. However, the livelihood of the peasantry was insecure as a result of constant warfare and the instability of agricultural production. The government tried to prevent the collapse of poor peasants and operated a relief system called the *jindaebeop* in order to maintain state finances and the country's defences. Slaves and those of low-born status came from prisoners of war and commoners who had fallen into ruin. Under the strict penal code, those who plotted treason or instigated a rebellion were burned at the stake and then beheaded, while those who surrendered to the enemy or were defeated in battle were put to death. According to the custom of the Goguryeo ruling class, if an older brother died, his younger brother would marry his widow and support her family. Another custom was for a man to spend a fixed period of time in his wife's household after marriage.

Culture

The Goguryeo people were known for their martial qualities and also to have enjoyed dancing, music, and drinking. The *geomungo*, a zither-type instrument, was invented in the late Goguryeo period. In the early period, tombs were usually made with piled stones, but they gradually developed into stone-chamber tombs that often contained murals. Tomb murals usually depicted scenes of everyday life, but in later periods, they became more abstract and depicted symbolic subjects as in the Painting of the Four Guardian Deities. It is thought that Chinese influence led to the early adoption of Chinese characters, and in the capital, a Confucian academy was established to teach the Confucian classics and history. In the provinces, schools were built to teach writing and martial arts to youth. In its early years, it compiled a 100-volume history called the *Yugi*, but no copies have survived to the present day. Buddhism was first introduced to the Korean peninsula through Goguryeo; many monasteries were established and Buddhist sculptures were created. The science of astronomy developed in Goguryeo, and astronomical charts were created showing the various constellations. The Joseon star chart *Cheonsang yeolcha bunya jido*, made in the year 1396, was based on a Goguryeo astronomical chart.

Gilt-bronze standing Buddha. National Treasure no. 119. Discovered in Uiryeong, South Gyeongsang province. According to its inscription, it was originally made in Goguryeo in 539 CE, making it one of the oldest extant Buddhist images in Korea. (National Museum of Korea)

Economy

Goguryeo's economy was based on agriculture, but most farmland had to be left fallow for a year or more because composting methods were not developed. Food production was insufficient since the climate was cold and since the kingdom's territory was mainly located in mountainous areas. Stone and wood tools were used, but from the fourth century, iron tools and ox plowing gradually became more common. Iron technology developed, and iron production became very important. Fishing, livestock raising, and hunting were also important parts of the Goguryeo economy. The aristocracy had large landholdings and owned many slaves, and they also mobilized the peasants under their control to cultivate their land. By participating in wars, aristocrats could increase the number of slaves and the amount of land they owned. On the other hand, because of constant warfare and a high tax burden, many peasants ended up becoming slaves. Trade was mainly conducted with the Northern and Southern Dynasties of China and with nomadic tribes in the north.

Politics

According to the *History of the Three Kingdoms*, the mythical founder of Goguryeo was Jumong, who established the kingdom in 37 BCE, but it actually existed even earlier. After Joseon was conquered by Han China, the Goguryeo people formed their own polity in the Liaodong area. They later joined forces with a group that moved south from Buyeo, developing into a confederated kingdom which was sometimes called "Goryeo." It then subjugated a number of neighboring statelets and moved its capital from the Huanren region to Gungnaeseong on the banks of the Amnok (Yalu) River. Goguryeo attacked the Han commanderies, expanding into the Liaodong Peninsula. Goguryeo's history became a series of struggles with Chinese states and other northern groups. In the late first century, the kingship became hereditary. By the fourth century, it developed into a centralized aristocratic state. During the reigns of Gwanggaeto and Jangsu in the fifth century, it expanded southward to the Han River region and northward to the plains near the Xinganling Mountain range. Weakened by wars with Sui and Tang and by internal conflict, the kingdom fell to the combined forces of Silla and Tang in 668.

After unifying China, the Sui dynasty wanted to bring neighboring states into its sphere of influence. Goguryeo launched a preemptive attack on Sui in 598, and the subsequent Chinese invasion ended in failure. Sui commenced another invasion in 612 that was also unsuccessful.

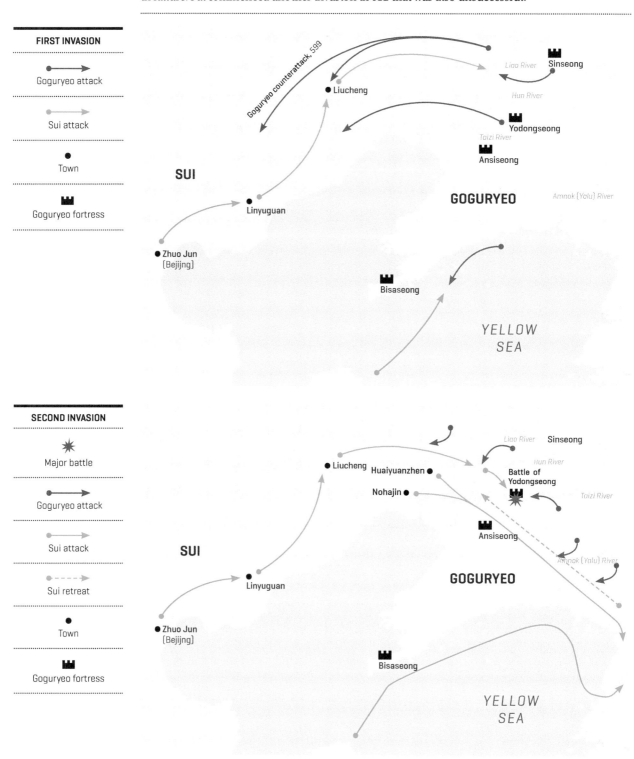

FIRST INVASION

Goguryeo attack

Sui attack

● Town

♜ Goguryeo fortress

Gogoryeo counterattack, 599

Liucheng

SUI

Linyuguan

● Zhuo Jun [Bejijng]

Liao River

Sinseong

Hun River

Yodongseong

Taizi River

Ansiseong

GOGURYEO

Amnok (Yalu) River

Bisaseong

YELLOW SEA

SECOND INVASION

✳ Major battle

Goguryeo attack

Sui attack

Sui retreat

● Town

♜ Goguryeo fortress

Liucheng Huaiyuanzhen ●

Nohajin ●

SUI

Linyuguan

● Zhuo Jun [Bejijng]

Liao River Sinseong

Hun River

Battle of Yodongseong

Taizi River

Ansiseong

GOGURYEO

Amnok (Yalu) River

Bisaseong

YELLOW SEA

After the Tang dynasty succeeded the Sui, the second Tang emperor also tried to bring Goguryeo under its control, launching an unsuccessful attack in 645. Goguryeo repelled a second invasion in 662 with victories by the general Yeon Gaesomun.

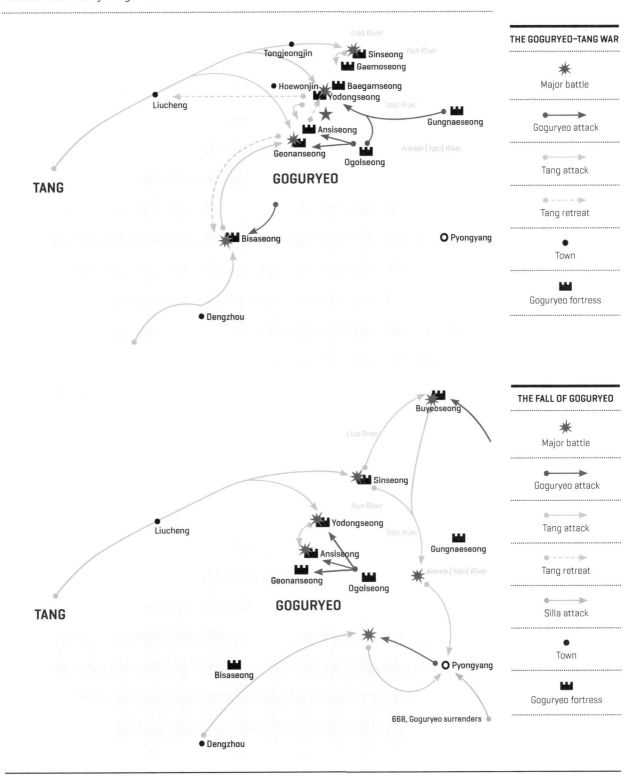

THE GOGURYEO–TANG WAR

✴ Major battle

➝ Goguryeo attack

➝ Tang attack

⇢ Tang retreat

● Town

🏰 Goguryeo fortress

THE FALL OF GOGURYEO

✴ Major battle

●➝ Goguryeo attack

➝ Tang attack

⇢ Tang retreat

➝ Silla attack

● Town

🏰 Goguryeo fortress

CHRONOLOGY OF GOGURYEO

82 BCE: The Goguryeo people drive out the armies of the Han commanderies of Lintun and Zhenfan.

75 BCE: The Goguryeo people attack the Han commandery of Xuantu.

37 BCE: According to the *History of the Three Kingdoms*, Jumong (King Dongmyeong) establishes the kingdom of Goguryeo at Jolbon.

3 CE, TENTH MONTH: The Goguryeo capital is moved from Jolbon to Gungnaeseong.

20, THIRD MONTH: The tomb of King Dongmyeong is constructed.

55, SECOND MONTH: In order to guard against Han attacks, ten fortresses are built in the Liaoxi region.

194, TENTH MONTH: A grain loan system called the *jindaebeop* is established.

244, EIGHTH MONTH: A Wei army under the command of General Guanqiu Jian invades Goguryeo. The capital Gungnaeseong falls.

259, TWELFTH MONTH: The invading Wei army is defeated at Yangmaenggok.

263: The Goguryeo monk Ado enters Silla to spread Buddhism.

313, TENTH MONTH: Goguryeo destroys the former Han commandery of Lelang.

324, SEVENTH MONTH: Goguryeo sends iron shields and targets to Japan.

342, ELEVENTH MONTH: Former Yan invades Goguryeo.

357, TENTH MONTH: The Anak Tomb No. 3 is constructed.

371, TENTH MONTH: The Goguryeo army suffers a heavy defeat in a war with Baekje. King Gogugwon dies in battle.

372, SIXTH MONTH: A state Confucian academy called the Taehak is established.
MONTH UNKNOWN: Goguryeo officially adopts Buddhism.

373: A legal code is promulgated.

375, SECOND MONTH: The first Buddhist monasteries on the Korean peninsula are constructed – Chomun Temple and Ibullan Temple.

400: A 50,000-strong Goguryeo military force defeats the united armies of Baekje, Gaya, and Japan to save Silla.

408, TWELFTH MONTH: The Deokheung-ri tomb and its murals are completed.

414, NINTH MONTH: The stele of King Gwanggaeto is erected.

427: The capital is moved south to Pyongyang.

449: The Jungwon Stele is erected.

475, NINTH MONTH: Goguryeo captures the Baekje capital and kills the Baekje king, Gaero.

595, FIFTH MONTH: The monk Hyeja travels to Japan and becomes the teacher of Prince Shōtoku.

598, SIXTH MONTH: Sui attacks Goguryeo with an army of 300,000 and is repulsed.

610, THIRD MONTH: The monk Damjing brings paper, ink, and the waterwheel to Japan.

612, SEVENTH MONTH: General Eulji Mundeok destroys an invading Sui army at the Battle of Salsu.

613: Third invasion by Sui repulsed.

614: Goguryeo repulses the last invasion by Sui.

631: An envoy from Tang destroys the Gyeonggwan, a memorial commemorating Goguryeo's victory over Sui.

642: Yeon Gaesomun kills King Yeongnyu and takes control of the government.

643, THIRD MONTH: Taoism comes to Goguryeo from Tang.

645, NINTH MONTH: The commander of Ansi Fortress, Yang Manchun, defeats an invading Tang army sent by Emperor Taizong.

658: Tang attacks Goguryeo.

666: Death of Yeon Gaesomun leads to internal strife.

668, NINTH MONTH: Goguryeo surrenders to the allied armies of Silla and Tang. Fall of Goguryeo.

CHINA
206 BCE–220 CE: Han
265–420: Jin
420–589: Southern and Northern Dynasties
581–618: Sui
618–907: Tang

JAPAN
400/300 BCE–250 CE: Yayoi period
250–538: Kofun period
538–710: Asuka period

MONARCHS OF GOGURYEO

37BCE–19BCE	King Dongmyeong	[東明王 동명왕]
19BCE–18CE	King Yuri	[琉璃王 유리왕]
18–44	King Daemusin	[大武神王 대무신왕]
44–48	King Minjung	[閔中王 민중왕]
48–53	King Mobon	[慕本王 모본왕]
53–146	King Taejo	[太祖王 태조왕]
146–165	King Chadae	[次大王 차대왕]
165–179	King Sindae	[新大王 신대왕]
179–197	King Gogukcheon	[故國川王 고국천왕]
197–227	King Sansang	[山上王 산상왕]
227–248	King Dongcheon	[東川王 동천왕]
248–270	King Jungcheon	[中川王 중천왕]
270–292	King Seocheon	[西川王 서천왕]
292–300	King Bongsang	[烽上王 봉상왕]
300–331	King Micheon	[美川王 미천왕]
331–371	King Gogugwon	[故國原王 고국원왕]
371–384	King Sosurim	[小獸林王 소수림왕]
384–391	King Gogugyang	[故國壤王 고국양왕]
391–413	King Gwanggaeto	[廣開土王 광개토왕]
413–491	King Jangsu	[長壽王 장수왕]
491–519	King Munjamyeong	[文咨明王 문자명왕]
519–531	King Anjang	[安臧王 안장왕]
531–545	King Anwon	[安原王 안원왕]
545–559	King Yangwon	[陽原王 양원왕]
559–590	King Pyeongwon	[平原王 평원왕]
590–618	King Yeongyang	[嬰陽王 영양왕]
618–642	King Yeongnyu	[榮留王 영류왕]
642–668	King Bojang	[寶臧王 보장왕]

THE FOUR GUARDIAN DEITIES

Digitally enhanced images from a mural in the Gangseo Middle Tomb located in Daean, South Pyeongan province.

Blue Dragon (Cheongnyong).
[Northeast Asian History Foundation]

White Tiger (Baekho). [Northeast Asian History Foundation]

Black Tortoise-Serpent (Hyeonmu).
[Northeast Asian History Foundation]

Red Phoenix (Jujak). [Northeast Asian History Foundation]

Baekje

Gilt-bronze incense burner.
6th–7th centuries CE.
National Treasure no. 287.
From the site of a Buddhist
temple near Buyeo, South
Chungcheong province.
[Buyeo National Museum]

According to legend, Baekje was established when Soseono, the wife of Goguryeo's Jumong, left with her two sons Biryu and Onjo to found a new kingdom. It developed out of one of the Mahan statelets in the Han River area. It conquered its neighbors and established its rule over the entire territory of Mahan. It reached its peak at the end of the third century and the early fourth century and was later defeated by the Silla-Tang alliance in the seventh century.

THE KOREAN PENINSULA IN THE LATE 4TH TO EARLY 5TH CENTURIES

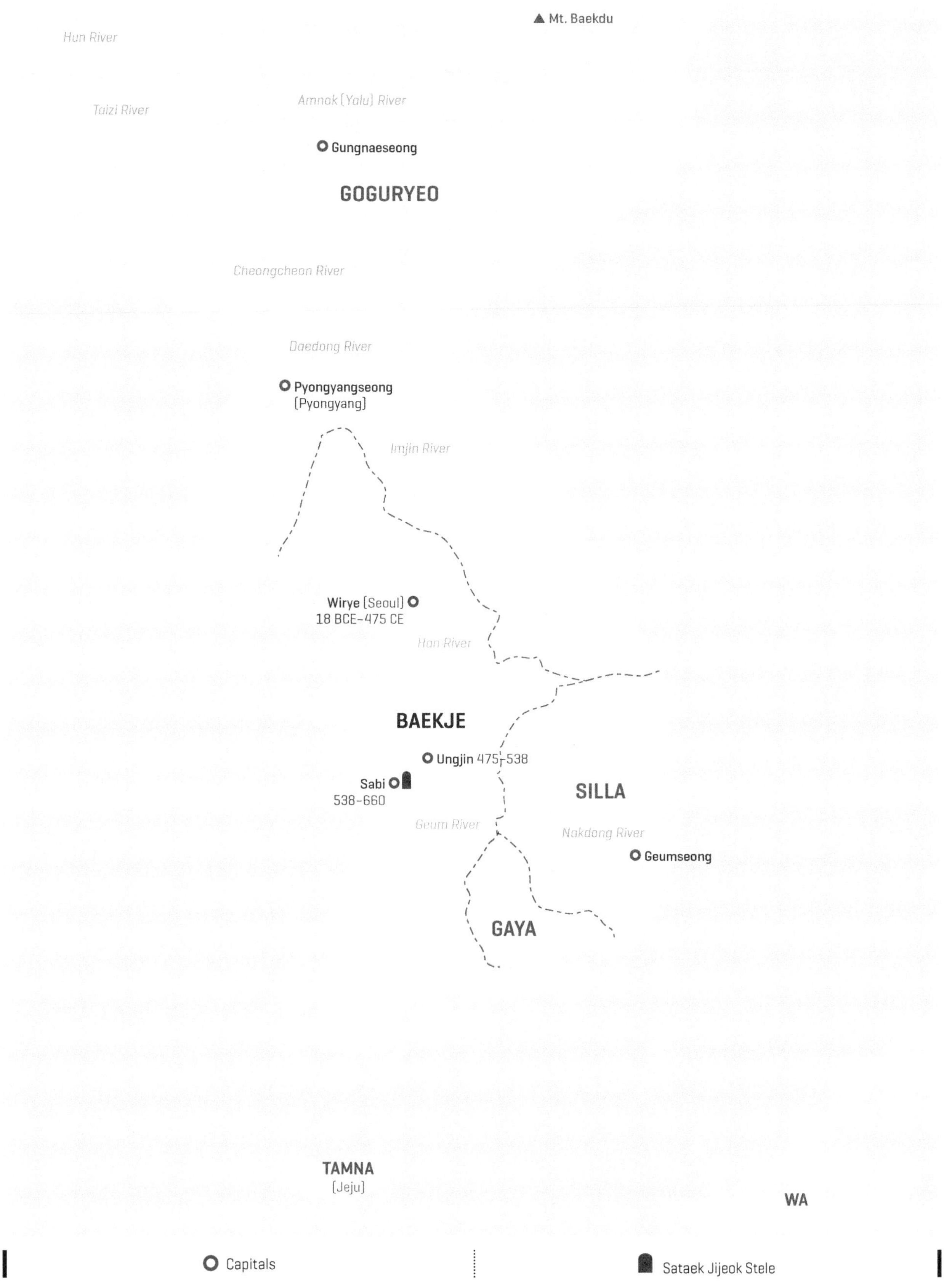
Mt. Baekdu
Hun River
Amnok (Yalu) River
Taizi River
Gungnaeseong
GOGURYEO
Cheongcheon River
Daedong River
Pyongyangseong
(Pyongyang)
Imjin River
Wirye (Seoul)
18 BCE–475 CE
Han River
BAEKJE
Ungjin 475–538
Sabi
538–660
SILLA
Geum River
Nakdong River
Geumseong
GAYA
TAMNA
(Jeju)
WA
Capitals
Sataek Jijeok Stele

Gungnamji, an artificial pond probably first constructed during the reign of King Mu. Historic Site no. 135. Located in the former Baekje capital of Buyeo, South Chungcheong province. [Christophe Chenevier]

Culture

Baekje appointed official educators in the Chinese Five Classics, medicine, and astronomy. Buddhism was widely accepted as a religion and a relatively high level of philosophical understanding was achieved. The grandest of its Buddhist monasteries was Mireuk Temple. One of its most famous Buddhist sculptures is the Buddha triad carved into a rock cliff at Seosan. The seven-branched sword, sent to Japan as a gift in the late fourth century, made from steel, and engraved with inlaid gold letters demonstrated an advanced degree of metallurgy. In the early Hanseong period, tombs were constructed in the stone-mound style similar to that of Goguryeo. During the Ungjin period, stone-chamber tombs with a tunnel entrance or brick-chamber tombs became common. The Sataek Jijeok Stele and the inscriptions in the tomb of King Muryeong are considered to be valuable sources for understanding Baekje culture. Baekje engaged in frequent cultural exchanges with the Southern Dynasties of China and with the Liang Dynasty in particular. They requested copies of the classics and the dispatch of artisans, painters, and experts in poetry. It also played an important role in transmitting this culture and thought to the Yamato state, contributing to the formation of the culture of the Asuka period.

Economy

Little is known about the economy of Baekje. Agriculture developed early in the country, and rice cultivation and irrigation facilities had already been introduced during the Samhan period. The state seems to have granted the right to collect taxes of a parcel of land to the royal family, members of the aristocracy, and other elites; it was an institutional mechanism to support the ruling class and establish the state's control over land and the peasantry. Handicraft production such as weaving and dyeing also developed. Since metallurgy was developed, they made weapons, gold crowns, gold and silver ornaments, and Buddhist statues. Taxes were collected in rice, cloth, and silk thread and were adjusted according to the year's harvest. Baekje engaged in lively trade with southern China and the Japanese. It transferred products and technologies such as horses, silkworms, weaving, and brewing to Japan. Yeongam and Danghangseong were known to be thriving trading ports.

Society

The highest social class in Baekje consisted of the royal family, who had the surname Buyeo, and an aristocracy made up of eight clans, including the Hae, Yeon, and Hyeop families. Having had contact with China from early on, they enjoyed reading the Chinese classics and histories and were proficient in reading literary Chinese. The aristocracy had a deliberative council called the Jeongsaam that elected the ministers called *sangjwapyeong*. In terms of language and customs, it is thought that Baekje was generally similar to Goguryeo. The Baekje people put great emphasis on cultivating martial spirit and enjoyed archery and horse riding. Another point of similarity with Goguryeo was the severity of its criminal code. Traitors, murderers, and deserters were beheaded, while thieves had to pay back twice the value of what they stole and were also banished. Chinese records from the period suggest that Baekje attire was stylish and refined.

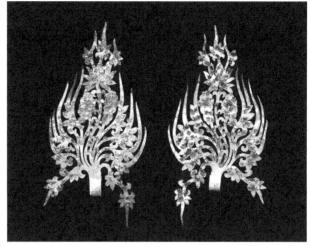

Gold crown ornaments from the tomb of King Muryeong in Gongju, South Chungcheong province. National Treasure no. 154. These ornaments were part of the king's crown which was more ornate than that for the queen consort. (National Museum of Korea)

Rubbing of the epitaph on the **Sataek Jijeok Stele**. (National Museum of Korea and Buyeo National Museum)

Politics

The Baekje state was established in the lower reaches of the Han River by refugees from Goguryeo of Buyeo descent. The capital of the country was moved twice, and thus its history is divided into three periods. The Hanseong Period (18 BCE–475 CE) was a time of growth; the Ungjin Period (475–538) began when attacks by Goguryeo forced the kingdom to move its capital to the Geum River area; it was a period of retreat and then resurgence. During the Sabi Period (538–660), it experienced a golden age of culture but suffered its downfall at the hands of its rival Silla.

In the late third century during King Goi's reign, Baekje developed into a centralized political structure consisting of six ministers and sixteen official ranks. Directly under the king, a prime minister was appointed with the title *sangjwapyeong,* while elections were held for the six ministers every three years. The Namdang was an important political organ in which the king sat and handled state affairs. After the capital moved to Sabi, the central administration was reorganized into twenty-two offices with twelve inner offices (*naegwan*) and ten outer offices (*oegwan*). The country was divided into five provinces (*bang*), and the capital city had five departments called *sang, ha, jeon, hu,* and *jung* (*obu*). Each province was divided into ten counties (*gun*) and was ruled by a governor (*bangnyeong*) and vice-governor (*bangjwa*). Each county had three military commanders in charge of 700–1,200 soldiers.

CHRONOLOGY OF BAEKJE

CHINA
206 BCE–220 CE: Han
265–420: Jin
420–589: Southern and Northern Dynasties
581–618: Sui
618–907: Tang

THE HANSEONG PERIOD
18 BCE–475 CE

18 BCE: Onjo establishes his capital at Wiryeseong, founding the state of Baekje, according to the *History of the Three Kingdoms*.

6 BCE: Mahan sends an envoy to Baekje; the borders between the two countries are set.

5 BCE, FIRST MONTH: The capital is moved to Hansan.

8 CE, TENTH MONTH: Baekje annexes Mahan.

9 CE, FOURTH MONTH: The two remaining fortresses loyal to Mahan surrender to Baekje.

33, SECOND MONTH: In the southern regions, rice cultivation is introduced for the first time.

125, SEVENTH MONTH: Baekje sends five generals to help Silla fight against a Mohe invasion.

132, SECOND MONTH: Construction of Mt. Bukhan Fortress.

221, FIFTH MONTH: Floods cause severe damage in mountain regions in its eastern regions.

222, THIRD MONTH: The government issues an order to promote agriculture.

247, FIRST MONTH: Sacrifices are made to the spirits of heaven and earth at the Namdan Altar.

255, NINTH MONTH: Baekje's attack on Silla's Bongsan Fortress fails.

260, FIRST MONTH: The central government system of six ministers and sixteen official ranks is introduced.
SECOND MONTH: Regulations for officials' attire are set.

371, WINTER: With 30,000 men under his command, the Baekje king attacks the Goguryeo fortress of Pyongyangseong, killing King Gogugwon of Goguryeo.
UNKNOWN MONTH: The capital is moved to Hansan.

372, FIRST MONTH: Tribute is sent to Eastern Jin. For the first time, the kingdom has diplomatic relations with a Chinese state under the name Baekje.
NINTH MONTH: A seven-branched sword is given to the King of Wa.

377, TENTH MONTH: The Baekje king attacks Goguryeo's Pyongyangseong Fortress with 30,000 men.

384, NINTH MONTH: Marananta of Eastern Jin brings Buddhism to Baekje.

392, SEVENTH MONTH: King Gwanggaeto of Goguryeo invades Baekje.

397, FIFTH MONTH: Diplomatic relations are established with Wa (Japan).

399, EIGHTH MONTH: Baekje forms an alliance with Wa and invades Silla.

425, MONTH UNKNOWN: Arrival of an envoy from Song (Liu Song).

472, SECOND MONTH: Envoys are sent to Northern Wei to appeal for aid against the southern advance of Goguryeo.

475, NINTH MONTH: The capital Hanseong falls to an invasion by King Jangsu of Goguryeo.
TENTH MONTH: The capital is moved to Ungjin.

THE UNGJIN PERIOD
475–538 CE

479, THIRD MONTH: Tribute is sent to the Southern Qi Dynasty.

493, THIRD MONTH: The Baekje king requests a bride from Silla. The daughter of Ichan Biji is sent.

498, EIGHTH MONTH: The king visits Mujin province in order to subjugate the island of Tamna (modern-day Jeju Island).

501, TWELFTH MONTH: King Dongseong is killed by an assassin sent by Baek Ga.
MONTH UNKNOWN: Baek Ga raises a rebellion at Garim Fortress but is captured and beheaded.

513, SIXTH MONTH: Baekje sends Confucian scholar Eunyang to Japan.

525: Construction of the tomb of King Muryeong.

526, MONTH UNKNOWN: The monk Gyeomik travels to India.

538, SPRING: The capital is moved to Sabi. The name of the country is changed to Nam Buyeo (Southern Buyeo).

JAPAN
400/300 BCE–250 CE: Yayoi period
250–538: Kofun period
538–710: Asuka period

THE SABI PERIOD
538–660 CE

552, TENTH MONTH: Norisachigye, a Baekje aristocrat, introduces Buddhist images and sutras to Japan for the first time.

556, MONTH UNKNOWN: Prince Hye returns from Japan.

579: Jihye supervises the painting of the mural of Fifty-Three Buddhas at Anheung Temple.

595: The monk Hyechong travels to Japan and becomes a teacher to Prince Shōtoku.

607, THIRD MONTH: Yeon Munjin and Wang Hyorin are dispatched to Sui to ask for the subjugation of Goguryeo.

634, THIRD MONTH: The Gungnamji pond is created.

640, MONTH UNKNOWN: The king's son enters the Tang state academy.

642, SEVENTH MONTH: Baekje attacks Silla, capturing forty fortresses.

654, TENTH MONTH: The Sataek Jijeok Stele is created.

660, THIRD MONTH: The Tang army begins its invasion of Baekje.
SEVENTH MONTH: Gyebaek is defeated and killed at the Battle of Hwangsanbeol by General Gim Yusin of Silla. King Uija surrenders to the allied Tang–Silla forces. Fall of Baekje.

661, FIRST MONTH: A Baekje restoration movement emerges centered on Juyu Fortress.

663, NINTH MONTH: Fall of Juyu Fortress, the last refuge of the Baekje restoration army.

MONARCHS OF BAEKJE

18BCE–28CE	King Onjo	[溫祚王 온조왕]
28–77	King Daru	[多婁王 다루왕]
77–128	King Giru	[己婁王 기루왕]
128–166	King Gaeru	[蓋婁王 개루왕]
166–214	King Chogo	[肖古王 초고왕]
214–234	King Gusu	[仇首王 구수왕]
234	King Saban	[沙伴王 사반왕]
234–286	King Goi	[古爾王 고이왕]
286–298	King Chaekgye	[責稽王 책계왕]
298–304	King Bunseo	[汾西王 분서왕]
304–344	King Biryu	[比流王 비류왕]
344–346	King Gye	[契王 계왕]
346–375	King Geunchogo	[近肖古王 근초고왕]
375–384	King Geungusu	[近仇首王 근구수왕]
384–385	King Chimnyu	[枕流王 침류왕]
385–392	King Jinsa	[辰斯王 진사왕]
392–405	King Asin	[阿莘王 아신왕]
405–420	King Jeonji	[腆支王 전지왕]
420–427	King Gu-isin	[久爾辛王 구이신왕]
427–455	King Biyu	[毘有王 비유왕]
455–475	King Gaero	[蓋鹵王 개로왕]
475–477	King Munju	[文周王 문주왕]
477–479	King Samgeun	[三斤王 삼근왕]
479–501	King Dongseong	[東城王 동성왕]
501–523	King Muryeong	[武寧王 무령왕]
523–554	King Seong	[聖王 성왕]
554–598	King Wideok	[威德王 위덕왕]
598–599	King Hye	[惠王 혜왕]
599–600	King Beop	[法王 법왕]
600–641	King Mu	[武王 무왕]
641–660	King Uija	[義慈王 의자왕]

Silla

Silla crown made from
gold and jade, 5th century CE.
National Treasure no. 191.
Excavated from the Great Tomb
of Hwangnam tomb in Gyeongju,
North Gyeongsang province.
[National Museum of Korea]

The mythical founder of Silla was Bak Hyeokgeose, who supposedly emerged from an egg near a well when the heads of six chiefdoms gathered to select a king. It emerged from Saro, one of the statelets of the Jinhan confederation. It survived numerous attacks from Goguryeo and Baekje and ultimately conquered the other two kingdoms in the seventh century through an alliance with Tang China.

Hun River

Taizi River

Amnok [Yalu] River

O Gungnaeseong

GOGURYEO

Cheongcheon River

Daedong River

O Pyongyangseong
[Pyongyang]

Imjin River

Hun River

Haseulla ●

O Seoul   **SILLA**

Siljik ●

● Danghangseong

● Jeokseong

Geum River

● Sabeol

Ungjin O

Sabi O   Nakdong River

BAEKJE   O Geumseong

Daeyaseong ●   ▮

Geumgwan ●

TAMNA   **WA**
[JEJU]

O Capitals   ● Major cities at the time   O Present-day major cities   ▮ Steles of King Jinheung

Stone brick pagoda at the site of Bunhwang Temple, Gyeongju. Early 7th century. National Treasure no. 30. One of the four main temples of the Silla kingdom. [Christophe Chenevier]

Society

Social position was determined by the hereditary bone-rank system which was as strict as the caste system of India. The bone-rank system divided the elites into two groups: those with "bone-rank" and those with "head-rank" status. Bone-rank status was for the royal family which was further divided into sacred-bone and true-bone groups, and there were six levels of head-rank status. After the death of Queen Jindeok in 654, sacred-bone status was eliminated. Head-rank status was for the aristocracy which was originally divided into six levels with head-rank six being the highest and head-rank one being the lowest. But as a result of social change, head-ranks three to one lost their significance as status categories. The political and social influence of the true-bone group was tremendous, and they monopolized the ministerial positions in the central government. With their scholarly knowledge and administrative skills, people of head-rank six served the king and were active in politics, but they could not advance into positions as ministers or provincial magistrates.

Economy

From its early years, Silla built reservoirs such as *byeokgolji* and *sije*, and in years of famine, the government would grant tax exemptions or open up the state granaries to provide relief to the people. As its territory expanded, Silla devoted much effort to maintaining its labor force and improving its productivity. From early on, Silla built and operated roads in important locations such as the Gyerip Pass and Jungnyeong Pass. In 490, the kingdom was able to open a commercial district in the capital and sell products from all over the kingdom. The government encouraged the use of the ox-plow in 502, and the practice of burying retainers with a deceased aristocrat was forbidden in an effort to prevent a reduction in the number of laborers.

Politics

Both the *History of the Three Kingdoms* and the *Memorabilia of the Three Kingdoms* divided Silla history into three periods, though there were differences between the two. According to the former text, the first period was from 57 BCE to 654 CE, the second from 654 to 780, and the last from 780 to 935. According to the latter, the first period was from 57 BCE to 514 CE, the second from 514 to 654, and the third from 654 to 935. The *History of the Three Kingdoms* claimed that Silla was established in 57 BCE by Bak Hyeokgeose. It was originally one of the minor states of the Jinhan confederation. At first, three different clans – Bak, Seok, and Gim – took the throne in turns, but later, the throne became the hereditary possession of the Gim clan. The title of the Silla monarch was initially *geoseogan,* then *chachaung* (shaman), and *isageum* (elder)*,* but it changed to *maripgan* in 417 and then to *wang* (king) in 503. Silla introduced a legal code during the reign of King Beopheung. A bureaucratic hierarchy was established according to a system of official ranks and attire; this was called the "bone-rank" system. Some sources indicate that there was a deliberative council called the Hwabaek that consisted of aristocrats of true-bone status with the rank of *daedeung*; important matters of state had to be passed by unanimous agreement. As part of the effort to strengthen the institutions of its rule, the government created the *hwarang* youth corps during the reign of King Jinheung. By the reign of Queen Jindeok, the central government, provincial administration, and the military were all rapidly expanded. The growth of the state in this period was a significant factor that enabled Silla, which had started out as the weakest of the Three Kingdoms, to unify the peninsula.

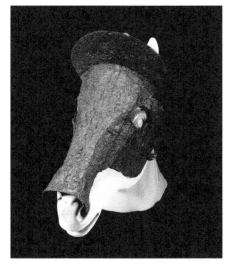

Iron horse armor from the 5th century CE. Excavated from tomb no. 65, Sara-ri, Gyeongju. [Gyeongju National Museum]

A stone structure called the **Cheomseongdae,** located in Gyeongju. Constructed during the reign of Queen Seondeok. National Treasure no. 31. [Zsinj–Wikipedia]

Culture

Because of its geographical location, Silla was the last of the Three Kingdoms to be influenced by Chinese culture; as a result, it developed its own particular culture. The Chinese writing system was introduced to Silla, but because of the differences in linguistic structure, two separate languages came to be used. To mitigate problems caused by this situation, Silla developed systems for writing the indigenous language using Chinese characters such as *idu* and *hyangchal*, and they were used to write a form of poetry called *hyangga*. It seems that Confucian ethics were promoted in Silla, judging from writings such as the Five Secular Injunctions (*Sesokogye*) by the Buddhist monk Wongwang. Buddhism was adopted as the state religion during the reign of King Beopheung, and it received strong support from the royal family and became popular as a religion devoted to the protection of the country. Buddhist monasteries were established around the capital and all over the country, and kings were given Buddhist-style posthumous names. Silla produced sophisticated Buddha sculptures such as the Gilt-Bronze Seated Maitreya that South Korea has designated National Treasure no. 83. The gold crowns, ornaments, and glassware discovered in Silla burial mounds demonstrate the excellence of Silla's handicrafts.

CHRONOLOGY OF SILLA

CHINA
206 BCE–220 CE: Han
265–420: Jin
420–589: Southern and Northern Dynasties
581–618: Sui
618–907: Tang

57 BCE, FOURTH MONTH: Bak Hyeokgeose founds the state of Silla on the basis of six villages within the Jinhan confederacy, according to existing historical sources. The initial name of the country is Seorabeol.

39 BCE: The Byeonhan confederation surrenders to Silla.

37 BCE: The Silla capital Geumseong is built at modern-day Gyeongju.

32, SPRING: A surname is conferred upon the people of each of the six villages. A system of seventeen official ranks is established.

57: The first king from the Seok clan comes to the throne.

65, THIRD MONTH: Gim Alji is born in the forest to the west of Geumseong. The name of the forest is changed to Gyerim (Chicken Forest) and becomes another name for the country.

102, EIGHTH MONTH: The statelets of Eumjeupbeol, Siljikgok and Apdok surrender to Silla.

108, FIFTH MONTH: The statelets of Biji, Dabeol and Chopal are defeated and annexed to Silla.

138, SECOND MONTH: The Jeongsadang (Hall of Political Administration) is established in the capital.

156, SECOND MONTH: Opening of Gyerimnyeong Road through the Sobaek Mountains.

158, THIRD MONTH: Opening of Jungnyeong Road through the Sobaek Mountains.

185, FIRST MONTH: The title *gunju* (martial lord) is used for the first time.

236, SECOND MONTH: The king of the Golbeol state surrenders to Silla.

245, TENTH MONTH: Goguryeo invades Silla's northern frontier region.

249, SEVENTH MONTH: Construction of the Namdang in the southern part of the palace.

251, FIRST MONTH: First deliberation on the affairs of state in the Namdang.

262: The first king of the Gim clan ascends the throne.

283, NINTH MONTH: Baekje attacks the Silla frontier and lays siege to Goegokseong Fortress.

392, FIRST MONTH: Silseong is sent to Goguryeo as a hostage.

330, MONTH UNKNOWN: Completion of the first reservoir with an embankment of 1,800 *bo* in length.

381, MONTH UNKNOWN: An envoy is sent to Former Qin.

417: The first king with the title *maripgan* ascends the throne.

429: Construction of the Sije reservoir.

469, FIRST MONTH: The names of the administrative districts of Gyeongju are set.

487, THIRD MONTH: The government orders provincial offices to make repairs to main trunk roads.

490, THIRD MONTH: Opening of the first market in the capital.

502, SECOND MONTH: Provincial and county officials are ordered to promote agriculture, and the use of ox-plows begins.

503, TENTH MONTH: The name of the country is confirmed as Silla, and monarchs now take the Chinese title of king (*wang*).

504, FOURTH MONTH: A law concerning proper mourning attire is promulgated.

512, SIXTH MONTH: General Gim Isabu subjugates the statelet of Usan on Ulleung Island.

514, FIRST MONTH: A secondary capital is established at Asichon. Posthumous titles for kings are used in Silla for the first time.

517, FOURTH MONTH: Establishment of the Department for Military Affairs (Byeongbu).

520, FIRST MONTH: A legal code is promulgated.

528: Adoption of Buddhism as the state religion.

531, FOURTH MONTH: Creation of the office of *sangdaedeung*.

532: The king of Geumgwan Gaya surrenders to Silla.

553, SECOND MONTH: The construction of Hwangnyong Temple begins.

554, SEVENTH MONTH: King Seong of Baekje attacks Gwansanseong Fortress and is killed.

566, THIRD MONTH: The construction of Hwangnyong Temple is completed.

576: Establishment of the Hwarang.

581, FIRST MONTH: Establishment of the Ministry of Personnel (Wihwabu).

MONARCHS OF SILLA

583, FIRST MONTH: Establishment of the Department of Ships.

589, THIRD MONTH: The monk Wongwang travels to Sui to study Buddhism.

634: The construction of Bunhwang Temple is completed.

636: The monk Jajang travels to Tang to study Buddhism.

640, FIFTH MONTH: The king sends his sons to Tang and asks that they be admitted to the state academy.

642, SEVENTH MONTH: King Uija of Baekje launches a major attack on Silla.

643, NINTH MONTH: Silla sends an envoy to Tang to request assistance.

645, THIRD MONTH: The nine-story pagoda of Hwangnyong Temple is built.

648: Gim Chunchu goes to Tang to request assistance in the war against Baekje.

651, SECOND MONTH: The Royal Secretariat (Pumju) is reorganized as the Chancellery Office (Jipsabu).

655: Goguryeo joins forces with Baekje and the Mohe tribes to attack the northern border of Silla. Tang China attacks Goguryeo.

660: General Gim Yusin defeats General Gyebaek. Fall of Baekje.

667: Silla launches an all-out attack on Goguryeo.

668: The combined forces of Silla and Tang occupy Pyongyang Fortress. Fall of Goguryeo.

57BCE–4CE	Hyeokgeose	〔赫居世 혁거세〕
4–24	Namhae Chachaung	〔南解次次雄 남해 차차웅〕
24–57	Yuri Isageum	〔儒理尼師今 유리 이사금〕
57–80	Talhae Isageum	〔脫解尼師今 탈해 이사금〕
80–112	Pasa Isageum	〔婆娑尼師今 파사 이사금〕
112–134	Jima Isageum	〔祇摩尼師今 지마이사금〕
134–154	Ilseong Isageum	〔逸聖尼師今 일성이사금〕
154–184	Adalla Isageum	〔阿達羅尼師今 아달라이사금〕
184–196	Beolhyu Isageum	〔伐休尼師今 벌휴이사금〕
196–230	Naehae Isageum	〔奈解尼師今 내해이사금〕
230–247	Jobun Isageum	〔助賁尼師今 조분이사금〕
247–261	Cheomhae Isageum	〔沾解尼師今 첨해이사금〕
261–284	Michu Isageum	〔味鄒尼師今 미추이사금〕
284–298	Yurye Isageum	〔儒禮尼師今 유례이사금〕
298–310	Girim Isageum	〔基臨尼師今 기림이사금〕
310–356	Heulhae Isageum	〔訖解尼師今 흘해이사금〕
356–402	Naemul Maripgan	〔奈勿麻立干 내물마립간〕
402–417	Silseong Maripgan	〔實聖麻立干 실성마립간〕
417–458	Nulji Maripgan	〔訥祗麻立干 눌지마립간〕
458–479	Jabi Maripgan	〔慈悲麻立干 자비마립간〕
479–500	Soji Maripgan	〔炤知麻立干 소지마립간〕
500–514	King Jijeung	〔智證王 지증왕〕
514–540	King Beopheung	〔法興王 법흥왕〕
540–576:	King Jinheung	〔眞興王 진흥왕〕
576–579:	King Jinji	〔眞智王 진지왕〕
579–632:	King Jinpyeong	〔眞平王 진평왕〕
632–647:	Queen Seondeok	〔善德女王 선덕여왕〕
647–654:	Queen Jindeok	〔眞德女王 진덕여왕〕
654–661:	King Muyeol	〔太宗武烈王 태종무열왕〕
661–681:	King Munmu	〔文武王 문무왕〕

Gaya

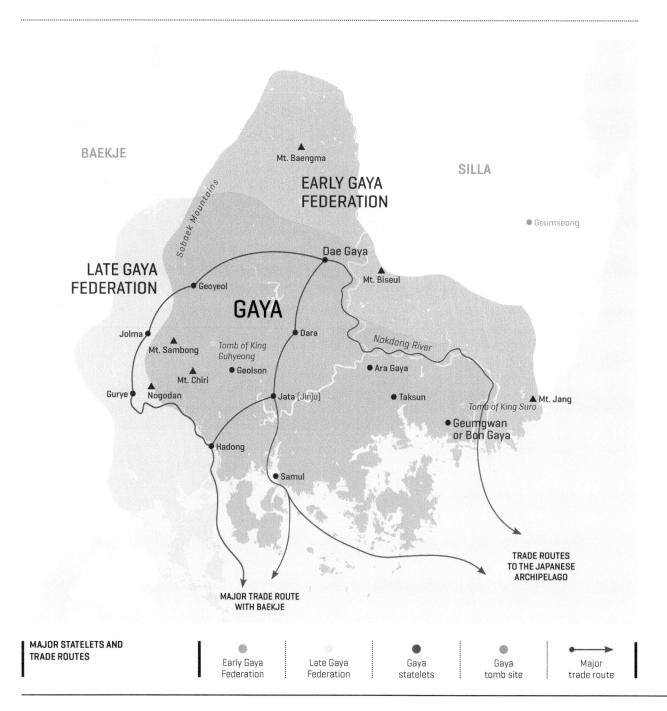

BAEKJE

SILLA

Mt. Baengma ▲

EARLY GAYA FEDERATION

● Geumseong

Soboek Mountains

Dae Gaya

LATE GAYA FEDERATION

Mt. Biseul ▲

● Geoyeol

GAYA

Jolma ●

● Dara

Mt. Sambong ▲

Tomb of King Guhyeong

Nakdong River

● Ara Gaya

Mt. Chiri ▲

● Geolson

Gurye ● ● Nogodan ▲

Jata (Jinju) ●

● Taksun

Mt. Jang ▲

Tomb of King Suro

● Geumgwan or Bon Gaya

● Hadong

● Samul

TRADE ROUTES TO THE JAPANESE ARCHIPELAGO

MAJOR TRADE ROUTE WITH BAEKJE

MAJOR STATELETS AND TRADE ROUTES

●	○	●	●	●→
Early Gaya Federation	Late Gaya Federation	Gaya statelets	Gaya tomb site	Major trade route

Duck-shaped pottery vessels from Byeonhan or early Gaya.
(Gimhae National Museum)

Gaya Federation

Gaya was a group of small polities located in the Nakdong River basin, between the Silla and Baekje states. It is generally thought that Gaya developed from the Byeonhan confederation sometime in the first century CE, with the emergence of a statelet called Guya under King Suro. By the third–fifth centuries neighboring Baekje and Silla, which themselves had emerged from the earlier Mahan and Jinhan confederations, were becoming centralized states, but Gaya remained a loose collection of polities ruled by individual "kings." Although these statelets, which were based around walled-towns, sometimes warred with one another, they were also able to form a federation that was dominated first by Geumgwan Gaya or Bon Gaya "Original Gaya" and later by Dae Gaya "Great Gaya." The wealth of the Gaya statelets came from their deep involvement in maritime trade and their importance as centers of iron-working. They had extensive contacts by sea with the commanderies of Lelang and Daifang as well as with polities in the Japanese islands, forming a key intermediary in the trade in high-value goods from the Chinese states. However, Gaya's strategic location also meant that it became embroiled in the wars between Silla and Baekje. In 400 CE, this ongoing conflict saw both Yamato mercenaries and Goguryeo troops intervening on Gaya territory. The federation was much weakened by these wars but the individual Gaya statelets continued to exist throughout the fifth century until they were finally subjugated in the sixth century by an ascendant Silla.

MONARCHS OF GAYA

GEUMGWAN GAYA

1st. King Suro [首露王 수로왕]
2nd. King Geodeung [居登王 거등왕]
3rd. King Mapum [麻品王 마품왕]
4th. King Geojilmi [居叱彌王 거질미왕]
5th. King Isipum [伊尸品王 이시품왕]
6th. King Jwaji [坐知王 좌지왕]
7th. King Chwihui [吹希王 취희왕]
8th. King Jilji [銍知王 질지왕]
9th. King Gyeomji [鉗知王 겸지왕]
10th. King Guhyeong [仇衡王 구형왕] 521–532

DAE GAYA

1st. King Ijinasi [伊珍阿豉王 이진아시왕]
2nd. King Geumnim [錦林王 금림왕]
3rd. King Haji [荷知王 하지왕]
4th. King Gasil [嘉悉王 가실왕]
5th. King Inoe [異腦王 이뇌왕]
6th. King Doseolji [道設智王 도설지왕] –562

Iron breastplate and helmet
from Gaya. Excavated at Goryeong,
North Gyeongsang province.
(National Museum of Korea)

Trade Routes in the Three Kingdoms Period | *4th–7th centuries*

Though their expansionist policies often led to conflict, trade was active among the Three Kingdoms. Overland and maritime trade routes connected the peninsula with the Silk Road, and there is evidence suggesting that Goguryeo envoys might have travelled as far as western Asia. At a time when there was little direct trade between China and Japan, the Three Kingdoms served as an intermediary between the two.

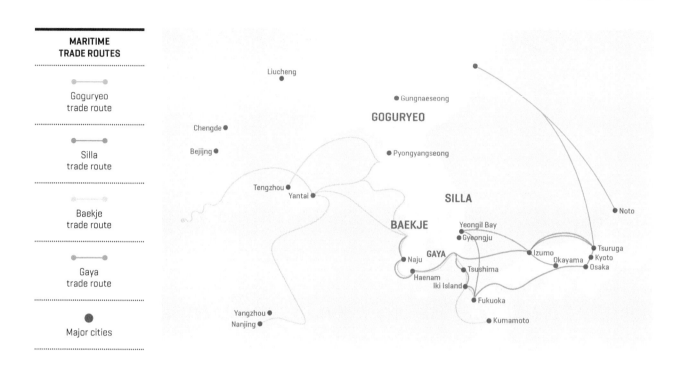

MARITIME TRADE ROUTES

Goguryeo trade route

Silla trade route

Baekje trade route

Gaya trade route

● Major cities

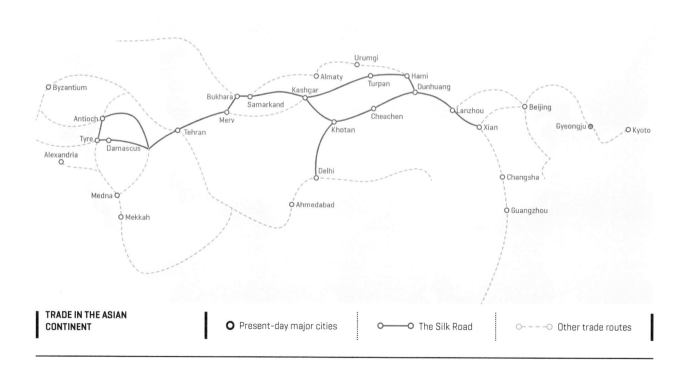

TRADE IN THE ASIAN CONTINENT   ○ Present-day major cities   ○—○ The Silk Road   ○- - -○ Other trade routes

The "Unification" Wars

The final stage in the struggle for dominance among the three kingdoms began with Silla's formation of an alliance with Tang China. In 660, they launched an invasion of Baekje, which fell soon after its defeat in the Battle of Hwangsanbeol. King Muyeol of Silla died in 661, but his successor, King Munmu, conquered Goguryeo in 668, bringing the Three Kingdoms Period to an end.

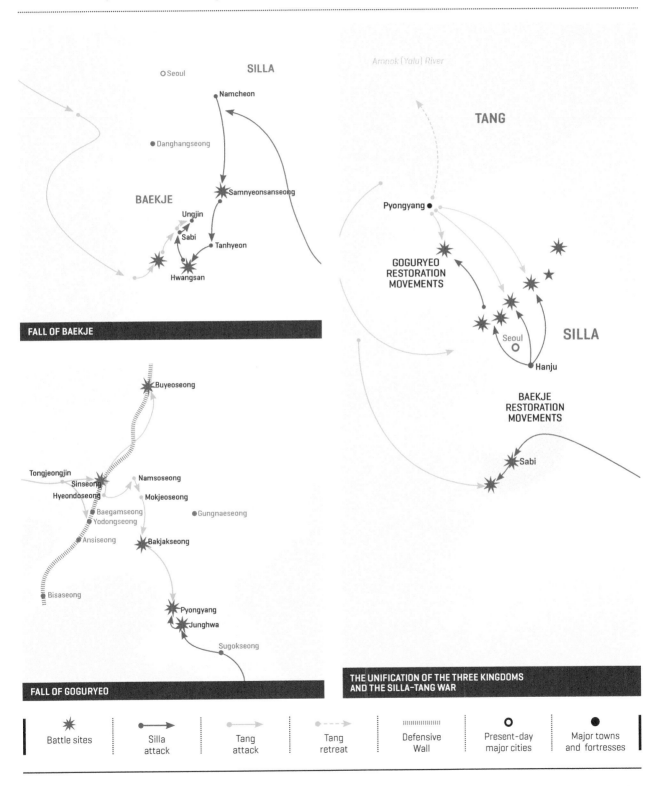

FALL OF BAEKJE

FALL OF GOGURYEO

THE UNIFICATION OF THE THREE KINGDOMS AND THE SILLA–TANG WAR

| ✳ Battle sites | ●→ Silla attack | →→ Tang attack | - -→ Tang retreat | ⫼⫼⫼ Defensive Wall | ○ Present-day major cities | ● Major towns and fortresses |

The Spread of Buddhism | *1st–8th centuries*

Centuries after Buddhism emerged in India, the Mahayana school was introduced to China in the first century CE. It seems to have reached the Korean peninsula in the third century during the Three Kingdoms Period. Goguryeo was the first of the kingdoms to adopt Buddhism as its official state ideology in the year 372, and Silla followed in 528. Baekje introduced Buddhism to Japan in 552.

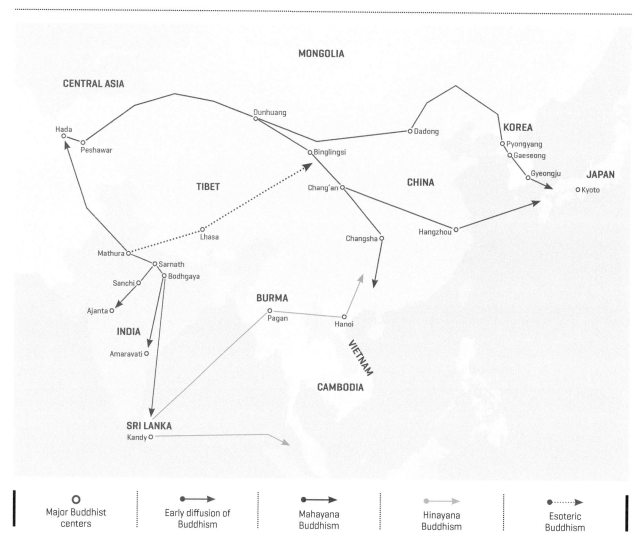

The Stele of King Gwanggaeto

The stele of King Gwanggaeto was erected in the year 414 by his son, King Jangsu. It is located in Ji'an in Jilin province, near what is presumed to be his tomb. It is approximately 6.34 meters (20.8 feet) in height with an inscription on all four sides totaling 1,802 characters. The text can be roughly divided into three sections. The first contains a description of the foundation myth of Goguryeo and the genealogy of Gwanggaeto. The second describes his conquests and achievements while the third recorded the king's instructions for the maintenance of his tomb. Forgotten after the fall of Goguryeo, it was rediscovered in the late nineteenth century, and a Japanese military officer made the first rubbing of the stele's inscription in the 1880s. It is now enclosed within a pavilion built by the Chinese authorities.

King Gwanggaeto Stele. Located in the city of Ji'an, China near the Amnok (Yalu) River. Early 20th century photograph. (National Museum of Korea)

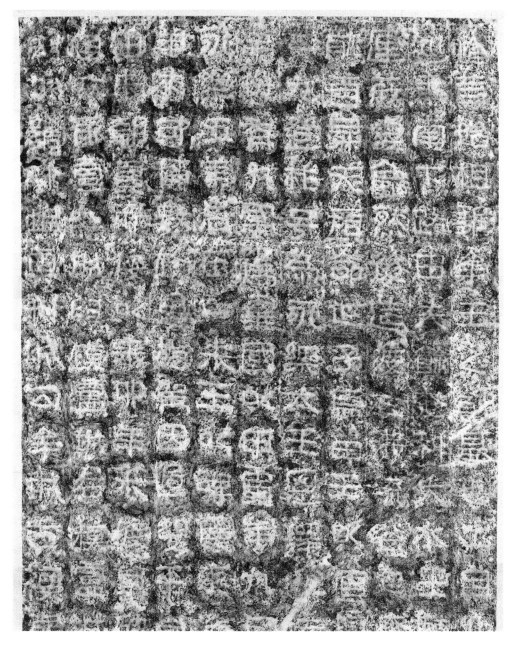

Detail of a **charcoal rubbing of the stele inscription.** (National Museum of Korea)

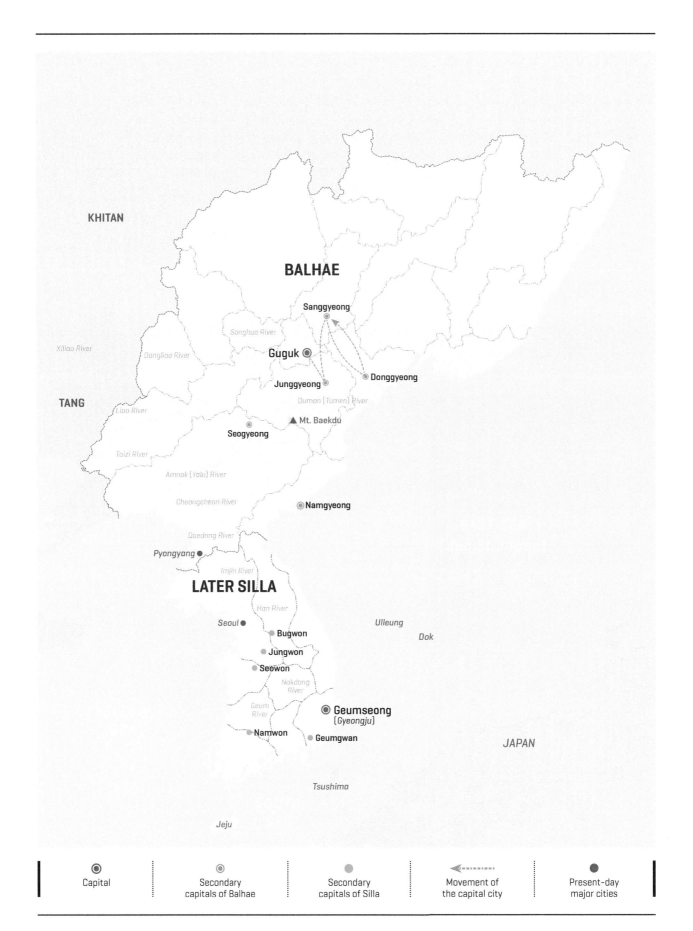

KHITAN

BALHAE

Sanggyeong

Songhua River

Xiliao River

Dongliao River

Guguk

Junggyeong

Donggyeong

TANG

Liao River

Duman (Tumen) River

Taizi River

▲ Mt. Baekdu

Seogyeong

Amnok (Yalu) River

Cheongcheon River

Namgyeong

Daedong River

Pyongyang

Imjin River

LATER SILLA

Han River

Seoul

Ulleung

Bugwon

Dok

Jungwon

Seowon

Nakdong River

Geum River

Geumseong
(Gyeongju)

Namwon

Geumgwan

JAPAN

Tsushima

Jeju

◎	◎	●	◄-----	●
Capital	Secondary capitals of Balhae	Secondary capitals of Silla	Movement of the capital city	Present-day major cities

4

THE NORTHERN AND SOUTHERN STATES PERIOD

Later Silla	Balhae
668–918	698–926

Silla allied with Tang China to defeat the other two kingdoms and brought the Three Kingdoms Period to an end in 668. It now occupied all of the central and southern parts of the peninsula, as well as part of the northern regions. Refugees from Goguryeo formed a new kingdom called Balhae that encompassed much of Goguryeo's former northern territory. Because of the existence of these two states, this era is known as the "Northern and Southern States Period." Both countries were conquered in the early tenth century soon after the fall of the Tang Dynasty.

Later Silla

The Sacred Bell of King Seongdeok, also known as the "Emille Bell." Cast in 771. National Treasure no. 29. It is the largest extant bronze bell in Korea. (Gyeongju National Museum)

After forming an alliance with Tang China, the kingdom of Silla defeated Baekje in 660 and Goguryeo in 668. Silla then drove the Tang forces out of the peninsula in 676, achieving a complete unification. The country in this period is called "Later Silla" or, because it defeated the other two kingdoms, "Unified Silla." Because of the existence of Balhae to the north, this period is called the "Northern and Southern States period."

BALHAE

Cheongcheon River

Daedong River

Pyongyang ○

HANSAN

SUYAK

Imjin River

Han River

■ SAKJU
[Chuncheon]

■ MYEONGJU
[Gangneung]

Seoul ○

HANJU ■

BUGWON
[Wonju]

HASEO

JUNGWON
[Chungju]

SEOWON
[Cheongju]

UNGCHEON

■ UNGJU
[Gongju]

Geum River

■ SANGJU

SABEOL

Nakdong River

JEONJU ■

WANSAN

NAMWON

⊙ Geumseong
[Gyeongju]

SAMNYANG

CHEONG

■ YANGJU

■ GANGJU
[Jinju]

GEUMGWAN
[Gimhae]

■ MUJU
[Gwangju]

MUJIN

Cheonghaejin ●

Tsushima

| ⊙ Capital | ○ Present-day major cities | ■ Provincial capital | ⬠ Secondary capital | –·–·– Provincial borders |

Anapji Pond. Historic Site no. 18. An artificial pond in the former Silla capital, thought to have been constructed in 674. Many significant artifacts have been excavated from the pond, including Buddhist sculptures, wooden writing strips, and a rare wooden boat. [riNux–Flickr]

Economy

Through the unification of the three kingdoms, the economy of Silla underwent substantial growth since it now commanded far more territory and population. Taxes were reduced to around one-tenth of the harvest, and two more markets opened in the capital of Gyeongju because of the increase in population and economic production. The royal family and aristocracy enjoyed a luxurious lifestyle thanks to their large landholdings, their ownership of slaves, livestock farms, and islands, and the general increase in agricultural productivity. Trade was active with Tang China and Japan, and even Muslim merchants came to Silla to trade. The Silla merchant Jang Bogo (787–846) controlled maritime trade in East Asia, using his garrison at Cheonghaejin as a base. On the other hand, the peasantry faced economic difficulties because agriculture still involved fallow farming and because of the various burdens they had to bear such as taxes, land rent, and military service. Peasant life became even more difficult toward the end of the Later Silla period with the revival of the stipend village system (*nogeup*) and the expansion of the landholdings of the true-bone aristocracy.

Society

After the unification of the Three Kingdoms, the true-bone aristocrats, the group with the highest social status, continued to monopolize privileged status in politics, the economy, and society. Aristocrats of head-rank six studied Confucianism and took trips to China to develop their scholarly knowledge and administrative skills. They then moved into official positions and offered advice to the king. But they could not rise to the highest ranks of the aristocracy. On the other hand, for people of head-rank one to three, their rank no longer had any meaning, and they became equivalent in status to commoners. After the unification, members of the former ruling classes of Baekje and Goguryeo were given official ranks and absorbed into the Silla elite. Refugees from the former Baekje and Goguryeo kingdoms were assigned to serve alongside Silla people in one of the nine divisions of the central army.

Politics

After the unification of the Three Kingdoms, Silla developed into an absolute monarchy based on its strong military and enhanced economic power. It created a centralized political system with a strong bureaucracy; in the provinces, it established five secondary capitals (*sogyeong*) and divided the country into nine provinces (*ju*). The central army was organized into nine divisions, and the provincial army consisted of ten garrisons. Two of the garrisons were stationed in Hansan province, and the remaining eight provinces had one garrison each. As royal authority was strengthened, the power of the true-bone aristocrats declined. However, from the mid-eighth century, their political and economic influence grew, and the struggle among the aristocrats intensified for control of the throne. As royal authority declined and the ability of the central government to maintain control over the countryside weakened, local gentry (*hojok*) emerged in the provinces as a new political force. In the end, Gyeon Hwon (867?–936) founded the state of Later Baekje in the former territory of Baekje, and Gungye (?–918) established the state of Later Goguryeo in the area once ruled by Goguryeo, thus marking the beginning of the Later Three Kingdoms period.

Tortoise base stone. National Treasure no. 25. Base of a monument at the tomb of King Muyeol in Gyeongju. The tablet containing an inscription has been lost. Photograph from the late 1930s.

Roof-end tile with monster face. Later Silla period, Gyeongju. (Gyeongju National Museum)

Culture

Later Silla combined the cultures of Baekje and Goguryeo with its own to form the foundation for a Korean national culture. Buddhism and traditional beliefs formed the core of the dominant culture. Building on the introduction of Buddhism in the Three Kingdoms period, Silla studied Chinese Buddhism and developed a deeper understanding of its thought. The most important developments in Buddhism in this period were the "One Mind" philosophy of Wonhyo (617-686) and the "Flower Garland" philosophy of Uisang (625-702). The Buddhist monk Hyecho (704-787) travelled around India and Central Asia and afterwards wrote a record of his travels called the *Wang ocheonchukguk jeon* (Story of a Journey to the Five Indian Kingdoms). Toward the end of the Later Silla period, the Chan (Kor. Seon, Jap. Zen) school of Buddhism became popular and played an important role in developing regional culture under the sponsorship of the emerging local gentry. Many statues of Buddha were produced that demonstrate the outstanding artistry of this period, including the famous cave grotto Buddha of Seokguram. The understanding of Confucianism also deepened in this period. Efforts were made to propagate Confucian ideas through the establishment of a Confucian academy called the Gukhak and the introduction of a system for selecting government officials based on their understanding of the Confucian classics. Many Confucian scholars came from aristocrats of head-rank six. One of the most important writers of the period was Gim Daemun, who wrote the *Hwarang segi* (Annals of the Hwarang) and the *Goseungjeon* (Lives of Eminent Monks).

Bulguk Temple | *751–774*

Bulguk Temple was one of the main state temples of the Later Silla period. A temple was first built on the site in 528; it was rebuilt beginning in 751, and construction was completed in 774. The South Korean government designated it as Historic Site no. 502, and it was designated a World Heritage Site by UNESCO in 1995. The entrance to the temple has a staircase with thirty-three steps – corresponding to the thirty-three steps to enlightenment in Buddhism. The stairs are called bridges, symbolizing the movement from the secular world to the realm of Buddha.

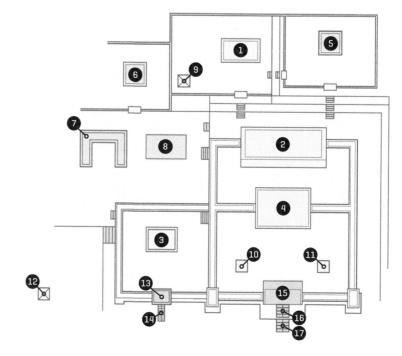

Postcard of the front of **Bulguk Temple** from the 1930s; photo probably taken in the 1910s. [Lafayette College]

Seokga Pagoda and Dabo Pagoda

In this period, most temples had two identical pagodas in front of the main hall. One of the distinctive features of the temple is that it has two pagodas of different styles in its main compound. Seokga Pagoda, representing Sakyamuni, is more typical of pagodas from its period, having a simple design. Dabo Pagoda, representing Prabhutaratna, has an elaborate design that was not common at the time. The two pagodas depict a scene from the Lotus Sutra where Sakyamuni explains the sutras to his disciple Prabhutaratna, who is also known the Buddha of Many Treasures. Seokga Pagoda is also called the Shadowless Pagoda (Muyeongtap) because of the legend of Asadal and Asanyeo. The image of Dabo Pagoda appears on the ten-won coin in South Korea.

10. Seokga Pagoda. National Treasure no. 21. Constructed around 751. Photograph from the late 1930s.

11. Dabo Pagoda. National Treasure no. 20. Believed to have been built in 751, during the reign of King Gyeongdeok. Photograph from the late 1930s.

10.   11.

The Structure of the Temple

As its name suggests, the temple is meant to represent the world of Buddhism. The stairs to the temple are called bridges because crossing them signifies a passage from the secular to the Buddhist world. Another unique feature of the temple is the division of its grounds into distinct spaces. The most important areas are associated with a particular Buddha and sutra, each representing an aspect of the Buddhist worldview.

	BUILDING	BUDDHIST FIGURE	ASSOCIATED SUTRA
4.	Hall of Great Enlightenment	Sakyamuni	Lotus Sutra
3.	Hall of Supreme Bliss	Amitabha	Amitabha Sutra
1.	Vairocana Buddha Hall	Vairocana	Avatamsaka Sutra
5.	Avalokitesvara's Shrine	Avalokitesvara	Lotus Sutra

Though Silla and Balhae engaged in little trade with each other, both were actively involved in trade with neighboring countries. Silla served as an intermediary in trade between Tang China and Japan, and its merchants handled goods from as far as Southeast Asia and sometimes had contact with Arabian traders. Thanks to advances in shipbuilding technology and navigation, the volume of maritime trade increased significantly in this period. Trade was conducted both through direct trade and through envoys on diplomatic missions.

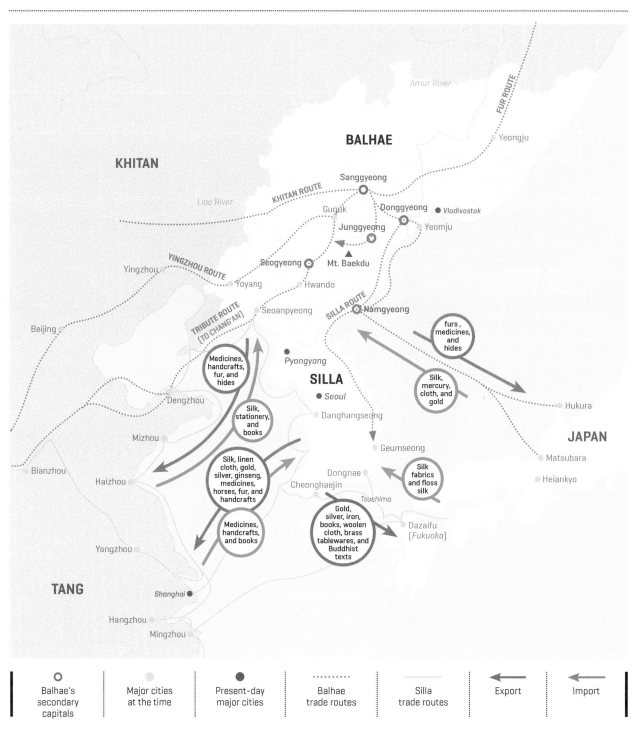

○ Balhae's secondary capitals	● Major cities at the time	● Present-day major cities	·········· Balhae trade routes	──── Silla trade routes	← Export	← Import

MONARCHS OF LATER SILLA

661–681	King Munmu	[文武王 문무왕]
681–692	King Sinmun	[神文王 신문왕]
692–702	King Hyoso	[孝昭王 효소왕]
702–737	King Seongdeok	[聖德王 성덕왕]
737–742	King Hyoseong	[孝成王 효성왕]
742–765	King Gyeongdeok	[景德王 경덕왕]
765–780	King Hyegong	[惠恭王 혜공왕]
780–785	King Seondeok	[宣德王 선덕왕]
785–798	King Wonseong	[元聖王 원성왕]
798–800	King Soseong	[昭聖王 소성왕]
800–809	King Aejang	[哀莊王 애장왕]
809–826	King Heondeok	[憲德王 헌덕왕]
826–836	King Heungdeok	[興德王 흥덕왕]
836–838	King Huigang	[僖康王 희강왕]
838–839	King Minae	[閔哀王 민애왕]
839	King Sinmu	[神武王 신무왕]
839–857	King Munseong	[文聖王 문성왕]
857–861	King Heonan	[憲安王 헌안왕]
861–875	King Gyeongmun	[景文王 경문왕]
875–886	King Heongang	[憲康王 헌강왕]
886–887	King Jeonggang	[定康王 정강왕]
887–897	Queen Jinseong	[眞聖女王 진성여왕]
897–912	King Hyogong	[孝恭王 효공왕]
912–917	King Sindeok	[神德王 신덕왕]
917–924	King Gyeongmyeong	[景明王 경명왕]
924–927	King Gyeongae	[景哀王 경애왕]
927–935	King Gyeongsun	[敬順王 경순왕]

CHRONOLOGY OF LATER SILLA [UNIFIED SILLA]

7TH CENTURY

660, FIFTH MONTH: Silla sends troops to attack Baekje.
SEVENTH MONTH: Baekje surrenders to the combined armies of Silla and Tang. Fall of Baekje.

661, The monk Uisang [625–702] goes to study in Tang.

668, NINTH MONTH: Goguryeo surrenders to the combined armies of Silla and Tang; fall of Goguryeo.

674, NINTH MONTH: Anseung, a member of the Goguryeo royal family, is given the title of King of Bodeok.

675, FIRST MONTH: Government seals made of copper are distributed to offices in the capital and the provinces.

676, SECOND MONTH: Uisang founds Buseok Temple.
ELEVENTH MONTH: Silla defeats the Tang army at Gibeolpo and drives it out of the country, completing the unification of the Three Kingdoms.

680, THIRD MONTH: Anseung marries the niece of King Munmu.

681, EIGHTH MONTH: Rebellion of Gim Heumdol, King Sinmun's father-in-law.

682, SECOND MONTH: A government academy called the Gukhak is established.
: Gameun Temple is founded; the "Flute to Calm Ten Thousand Waves" is made.

683, TENTH MONTH: Two new divisions are formed in the central army – the Hwanggeum seodang consisting of former Goguryeo subjects and the Heukgeum seodang consisting of Mohe tribesmen.

685, FIFTH MONTH: A system of regional administration is established consisting of nine provinces and five secondary capitals.

687, FIFTH MONTH: A new division is formed in the central army, the Chonggeum seodang.
FIFTH MONTH: "Office Land" is distributed to government officials.

689, FIRST MONTH: The stipend village system is abolished.

692, SEVENTH MONTH: Appointment of the first medical official.
The Confucianist Gang Su dies.

695, TENTH MONTH: The Western and Southern Markets are established in the capital Gyeongju.
: The monk Woncheuk [613–696] translates the *Flower Garland Sutra* while staying in Tang.

8TH CENTURY

702, MONTH UNKNOWN: Gim Daemun writes the *Annals of the Hwarang* and the *Lives of Eminent Monks*.

717, THIRD MONTH: Construction of a new palace.

718, SIXTH MONTH: An office called the Nugakjeon is established to operate a water clock.

722, FOURTH MONTH: A type of land called *jeongjeon* is granted to the commoner population.

723: The monk Hyecho [704–787] makes a pilgrimage to India.
: Ssanggye Temple is founded in Hadong.

731, FOURTH MONTH: 300 Japanese warships attacking Silla's east coast are destroyed.

735, SECOND MONTH: Tang recognizes Silla's sovereignty over areas south of the Daedong River.

737: Sinchung composes the *hyangga* poem "Wonga."

738, FOURTH MONTH: A copy of Laozi's *Dao De Jing* is sent from Tang.

749, THIRD MONTH: Appointments are made to the positions of official astronomer and keeper of the clepsydra.

751: Gim Daeseong [700–774] begins the renovation of Bulguk Temple, adding the Seokga and Dabo Pagodas.
: Gim Daeseong begins the construction of the Seokguram Buddhist grotto.
: The *Great Dharani Sutra of Immaculate and Pure Light* is printed using woodblocks around this time.

CHINA

618–907: Tang
  626–649: Emperor Taizong
  690–705: Wu Zetian (Empress Wu)
  712–756: Emperor Xuanzong
  755: An Lushan Rebellion
  805–820: Emperor Xianzong

JAPAN

710–794: Nara period
  724–749: Emperor Shōmu
794–1185: Heian period
  781–806: Emperor Kanmu
  858–876: Emperor Seiwa

9TH CENTURY

10TH CENTURY

754, EIGHTH MONTH: The bell of Hwangnyong Temple is cast.

755, MONTH UNKNOWN: An official commendation is given to a man named Hyangdeok for his filial piety.

757, THIRD MONTH: The monthly salaries of government officials are abolished, and they are once again granted stipend villages.

758, FOURTH MONTH: Two officials of law are appointed.

759, FIRST MONTH: The Gukhak (State Academy) is renamed Taehakgam, and central government offices are renamed according to Chinese conventions.

760, FOURTH MONTH: The monk Weolmyeongsa composes the *hyangga* poem "Dosolga."

774, MONTH UNKNOWN: The construction of the Seokguram grotto may have been completed in this year.

771, TWELFTH MONTH: The casting of the sacred bell of King Seongdeok the Great is completed (also known as the Emille Bell).

783, MONTH UNKNOWN: Construction of Sajik Altar, where state ceremonies were conducted for the deities of the earth and of the five grains.

788: The *dokseo sampum* system for selecting government officials is established.

790, FIRST MONTH: The Byeokgolje reservoir in Gimje is enlarged.

802, EIGHTH MONTH: Haein Temple is established.

809: The Silla-style zither (*Sillageum*) is introduced to Japan by Silla master musicians.

815, EIGHTH MONTH: Famine is widespread, and bands of thieves become common.

819, THIRD MONTH: Peasant armies called *chojeok* rise up all over the country.

821: The monk Doui finishes his studies in Tang and returns to Silla, introducing the Southern School of Chan to the country.

822, THIRD MONTH: Rebellion of Gim Heonchang.

828, FOURTH MONTH: Jang Bogo (787–846) sets up the Cheonghaejin garrison on the Wan Island and is appointed to the position of lord. **TWELFTH MONTH:** Gim Daeryeom is sent as an ambassador to Tang and returns with the seeds of the tea plant.

846: Death of Jang Bogo, according to the *History of the Three Kingdoms*.

854: Ssanggye Temple is established.

858, SEVENTH MONTH: The seated Vairocana Buddha statue of Borim Temple is created.

885, THIRD MONTH: Choe Chiwon (857–?) returns from Tang and becomes a government official.

888: Wihong and Daeguhwasang compile a collection of *hyangga* poetry called *Samdaemok* on the king's orders.

892: Gyeon Hwon starts a rebellion in Wansan province (today's Jeonju) and declares himself king in Mujin province (today's Gwangju).

900: Gyeon Hwon names his state Later Baekje and becomes its king.

901: Gungye (?–918) establishes the state of Later Goguryeo and becomes its king.

904: Later Goguryeo changes its name to Majin.

927, FIRST MONTH: The kingdom of Majin changes its name to Taebong.

927, ELEVENTH MONTH: The Later Baekje army takes the Silla capital and forces King Gyeongae to commit suicide, putting King Gyeongsun on the throne in his place.

935, SIXTH MONTH: Gyeon Hwon of Later Baekje surrenders to Goryeo.

935, ELEVENTH MONTH: King Gyeongsun surrenders to Goryeo. Fall of Silla.

Balhae

Yeonggwang Pagoda.
Built in the Balhae era.
Located in Jilin province,
China. (Song Kiho)

The territory of the Balhae kingdom covered northern Korea, part of south and east Manchuria, and part of what is now the Russian Maritime Province (Primorsky Krai) between 698 and 926 CE. It was founded by refugees from Goguryeo and occupied Goguryeo's former territory. Balhae and Silla, which occupied the southern part of the peninsula, constitute the two kingdoms of the Northern and Southern States period. The kingdom was first called Jin, but it changed its name when Tang China invested Dae Joyeong (?–719), the founder of the country, with the title Lord of Balhae.

KHITAN

HOEWON

YEONGJU

CHEOLLI

DONGPYEONG

ANWON

Songhua River

BUYEO

YONGCHEON

Sanggyeong

SOLBIN

ANBYEON

SOKJU

DONGJU

Xiliao River

Dongliao River

Guguk

JEONGNI

MAKHIL

JANGNYEONG

HYEONDEOK

Junggyeong

Donggyeong

TANG

Duman (Tumen) River

Liao River

▲ Mt. Baekdu

Tumen River

BALHAE

Seogyeong

YONGWON

Amnok (Yalu) River

AMNOK

Cheongcheon River

NAMHAE

Namgyeong

Daedong River

Pyongyang ●

Imjin River

Han River

Ulleung

● Seoul

Dok

SILLA

Nakdong River

Geum River

◉ Geumseong
(Gyeongju)

JAPAN

Tsushima

Jeju

● Fukuoka

◉ Capitals

◉ Secondary
capitals of Balhae

◄---- Movement of
capital city

● Present-day
major cities

Excavation of a **Balhae house** at a site in Kraskino in Primorsky Krai (Maritime Province) in Russia. The house had an *ondol*–style heating system similar to houses in Goguryeo. (Song Kiho)

Politics

Goguryeo refugees, who had been taken to Tang after Goguryeo's fall, drove out the Tang army and established a new kingdom in Goguryeo's former territory. They viewed themselves as the successors of Goguryeo and even used the name Goryeo (a shortened form of Goguryeo) for their country on diplomatic documents. Relations between Balhae and Tang remained hostile despite the fact that the two countries made peace and began diplomatic relations in 705 and that Tang bestowed the title of Lord of Balhae on Dae Joyeong. During the reign of the second king, when the Heishui Mohe tribe of the Amur River valley attempted to form an alliance with Tang, Balhae sent out forces to subdue the Mohe. Jang Munhyu then took an army to attack Dengzhou on the Shandong peninsula in Tang territory, killing its governor. Balhae also generally had strained relations with Silla, but it had friendly relations with Japan

and with the Göktürk state to the northwest. During the reign of the third king, it restored friendly relations with Silla and Tang in an attempt to achieve greater political and economic stability and prosperity.

Balhae's political system adopted the Tang system of Three Chancelleries and Six Ministries of Personnel, Revenue, Rites, Military, Justice, and Public Works. In the provinces, there were five regional capitals, and the government adopted a three-tiered administrative structure of *bu*, *ju*, and *hyeon*. The country was first divided into fifteen *bu*, and then each *bu* was further divided into *ju* with each *ju* divided into *hyeon*, the lowest administrative unit. Balhae civilization reached its peak during the ninth century, and the country was called Haedong Seongguk or "Prosperous Country in the East." At the beginning of the tenth century, it came under attack from the newly united Khitan tribes and met its downfall in 926.

Culture

Balhae represented a continuation of Goguryeo culture and also absorbed the culture of Tang China. Of the surviving Balhae tombs, the principal ones are the tombs at Liuding Mountain, and they faithfully follow the form of late Goguryeo era tombs – mounds of earth lined with stones. The tomb of Princess Jeonghye is a representative example of this style. However, from the mid-Balhae period, much of Tang culture was introduced to the country, and brick tombs appeared that showed the influence of the Tang style. The tomb of Princess Jeonghyo at Longtou represents a compromise between the two styles – a brick tomb with a stone-covered roof. A government academy devoted to Confucian education called the Jujagam was established in order to teach the Confucian classics to the sons of the aristocracy. Students were also sent to Tang to study, and several of them were able to pass the special state examinations for foreigners. Buddhism, which had been introduced to the region in the Goguryeo period, was popular among the royal family and aristocracy, and King Mun even styled himself as a Buddhist sage king.

Two sitting stone Buddhas excavated at Hunchun, Jilin province, China. The two Buddhas represent Sakyamuni and Prabhutaratna. (Song Kiho)

Society

The ruling class of Balhae mainly came from Goguryeo since the kingdom was founded by Goguryeo refugees. The Mohe people, who had been subject to Goguryeo's rule, constituted the subject population except for a small minority who moved into the elite. There was conflict between those of Goguryeo background and those of Mohe background, and this was an important factor behind the downfall of Balhae. After the fall of the kingdom, the people separated into Goguryeo people and Mohe (Jurchen) people. Many of the Goguryeo people, including the Balhae royal family, emigrated to Goryeo.

Decorative roof-end tile (*chimi*) excavated in a temple site in Ning'an, Heilongjiang province, China. 36 inches (92 cm) in height. (Oh Youngchan)

Economy

Although the cold climate of Balhae was not favorable for agriculture, agricultural production was high since it had vast plains near the Hailan River and the lower reaches of the Duman River. The Noseong region was famous for its rice, but dry-field farming was the predominant form of rice cultivation. The country was also actively engaged in livestock farming and hunting. Famous for its horses and pigs, the country exported horses to Tang. Its people also hunted rabbits and deer and exported animal hides to Japan and other countries. Weaving was developed in Balhae, and it sent cloth to Tang as tribute and traded it with the Khitan, Mohe, and other tribes and countries. Wiseong was well-known as an iron-producing region and used Goguryeo iron-making technology to produce high-quality tools.

CHRONOLOGY OF BALHAE

CHINA	JAPAN
618–907: Tang	**794–1185:** Heian period
626–649: Emperor Taizong	**781–806:** Emperor Kanmu
712–756: Emperor Xuanzong	**858–876:** Emperor Seiwa

696: Under the leadership of Geolgeol Jungsang and Dae Joyeong [?–719], the remnants of the Goguryeo population escape to the northeast of Mount Baekdu.

698: Dae Joyeong defeats the Tang army at the battle of Cheonmunnyeong and then founds the state of Jin at Dongmou Mountain in Jilin.

713: Dae Joyeong is given the official title of "Lord of Balhae" by Tang and changes the name of the country to Balhae.

726: Internal strife emerges over the issue of attacking the Heishui Mohe tribe.

727: Balhae sends an envoy to Japan for the first time.

732: Balhae General Jang Munhyu attacks Dengzhou in the Shandong Peninsula in Tang territory, killing its governor Wei Jun.

BEFORE 732: The capital is moved to Hyeonju.

756: The capital is moved to Sanggyeong yongcheonbu.

762: The status of the Balhae monarch is elevated to that of *gukwang*.

780: Construction of the tomb of Princess Jeonghye [738–777].

LATE 780s: The capital is moved to Donggyeong yongwonbu.

792: Completion of the construction of the tomb of Princess Jeonghyo [757–792].

793?: The capital is moved back to Sanggyeong yongcheonbu.

818–820: Balhae invades Silla and the Liaodong peninsula.

828: Japan prohibits private trade with Balhae envoys.

832: A Tang envoy reports on the establishment of a new government system in Balhae.

872: O Sodo passes the Tang civil service examination for foreigners.

873: Choe Jongjwa and his party travel to Tang but encounter a storm and are cast adrift, landing in Japan.

924: Balhae attacks the Khitan, killing the governor of Liaozhou.

925: General Sindeok surrenders to Goryeo.

926: The Balhae capital at Sanggyeong yongcheonbu surrenders when besieged by the Khitan.
: The Khitan establish the state of Dongdan in the territory of Balhae.
: Balhae falls.

934: Balhae crown prince Dae Gwanghyeon surrenders to Goryeo together with tens of thousands of Balhae people.

979: Tens of thousands of Balhae people escape to Goryeo.

MONARCHS OF BALHAE

698–719	King Go	[高王 고왕]	794–809	King Gang	[康王 강왕]	831–857	King Ijin	[彝震 이진]
719–737	King Mu	[武王 무왕]	809–812	King Jeong	[定王 정왕]	858–871	King Geonhwang	[虔晃王 건황]
737–793	King Mun	[文王 문왕]	813–817?	King Hui	[僖王 희왕]	872—894?	King Hyeonseok	[玄錫王 현석왕]
793–793?	King Wonui	[元義 원의]	817?–818	King Gan	[簡王 간왕]	894?—906?	King Wihae	[瑋瑎 위해]
793?–794	King Seong	[成王 성왕]	818–830	King Seon	[宣王 선왕]	907?—926	King Inseon	[諲譔王 인선왕]

When the ruling order of Silla began to break down in the ninth century, rebellions broke out in various parts of the country. Two rebel leaders emerged who founded new kingdoms, Gyeon Hwon of Later Baekje and Gungye of Later Goguryeo, which later changed its name to Majin and then Taebong. The peninsula was once again divided into three countries that battled each other for political dominance.

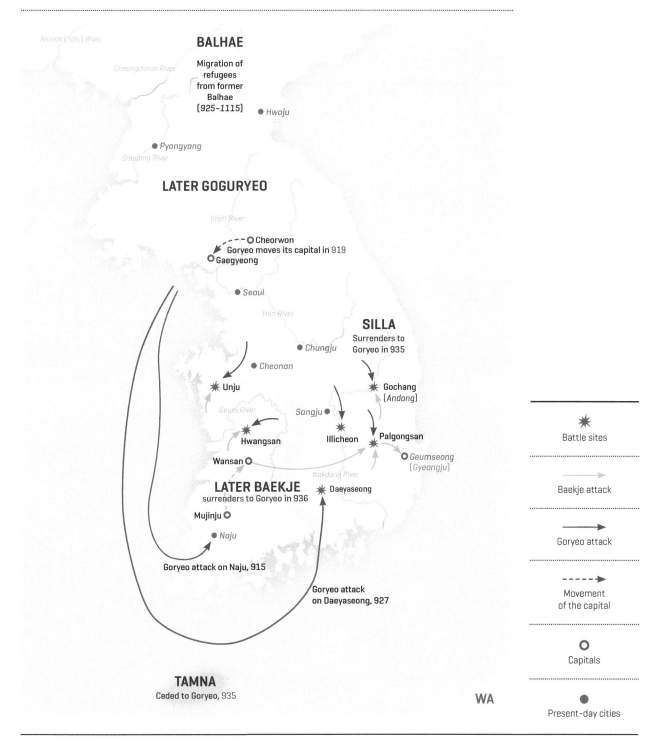

BALHAE

Migration of refugees from former Balhae (925–1115)

● *Hwaju*

● *Pyongyang*
Daedong River

Amnok (Yalu) River

Cheongcheon River

LATER GOGURYEO

Imjin River

⊙ Cheorwon
Goryeo moves its capital in 919
⊙ Gaegyeong

● *Seoul*
Han River

SILLA
Surrenders to Goryeo in 935

● *Chungju*

● *Cheonan*

✸ Unju

✸ Gochang
[*Andong*]

Geum River

Sangju ●

✸ Illicheon

Palgongsan ✸

✸ Hwangsan

Wansan ⊙

● *Geumseong*
[*Gyeongju*]

Nakdong River

LATER BAEKJE
surrenders to Goryeo in 936

✸ Daeyaseong

Mujinju ⊙

● *Naju*

Goryeo attack on Naju, 915

Goryeo attack on Daeyaseong, 927

TAMNA
Ceded to Goryeo, 935

WA

Legend:
- ✸ Battle sites
- → Baekje attack
- → Goryeo attack
- --→ Movement of the capital
- ⊙ Capitals
- ● Present-day cities

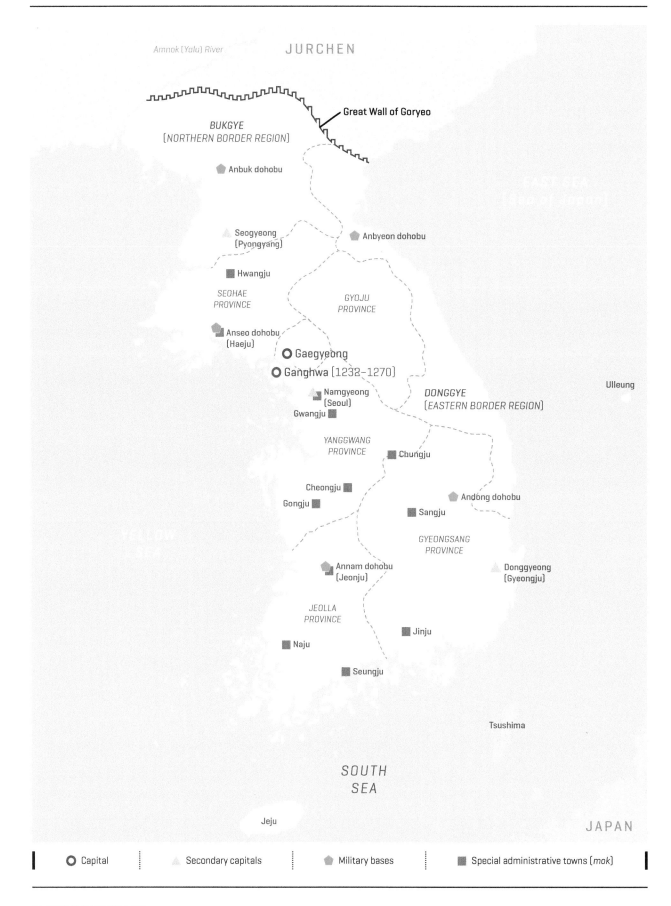

Amnok (Yalu) River

JURCHEN

Great Wall of Goryeo

BUKGYE
(NORTHERN BORDER REGION)

Anbuk dohobu

EAST SEA
(Sea of Japan)

Seogyeong
(Pyongyang)

Anbyeon dohobu

Hwangju

GYOJU
PROVINCE

SEOHAE
PROVINCE

Anseo dohobu
(Haeju)

Gaegyeong

Ganghwa (1232–1270)

Ulleung

Namgyeong
(Seoul)

Gwangju

DONGGYE
(EASTERN BORDER REGION)

YANGGWANG
PROVINCE

Chungju

Cheongju

Andong dohobu

Gongju

Sangju

GYEONGSANG
PROVINCE

Annam dohobu
(Jeonju)

Donggyeong
(Gyeongju)

JEOLLA
PROVINCE

Jinju

Naju

Seungju

Tsushima

SOUTH
SEA

Jeju

JAPAN

| ○ Capital | ▲ Secondary capitals | ⬠ Military bases | ■ Special administrative towns (mok) |

5

GORYEO

Bronze statue of Wang Geon, founder of the Goryeo Dynasty. Eleventh century. The statue was discovered during the restoration of Wang Geon's tomb at Haeseon-ri, near Gaeseong in 1992. (National Museum of Korea)

The contemporary of the Song Dynasty in China, the kingdom of Goryeo was founded by Wang Geon (877–943), whose power base was located in the city of Gaeseong. He conquered Silla and Later Baekje to create a unified state and named his kingdom Goryeo to indicate that it was the successor to the former kingdom of Goguryeo. After the fall of Balhae in 926, Goryeo took in its people and pursued a northern expansion policy in order to recover Goguryeo's former territory. It was at this time that the name Goryeo became known in the western world and gave rise to today's term for the country "Korea." Its downfall was hastened by the rise of the Mongols in the thirteenth century.

Tomb of King Gongmin and Queen Noguk
near Gaeseong, the former Goryeo capital. National Treasure no. 123. Construction began in 1365 and was completed in 1372. [Eckart Dege]

Culture

Buddhism, Daoism, and shamanism were dominant in the everyday lives and beliefs of the people. An edition of the Tripitaka, carved on woodblocks, was printed during this period, helping to deepen understanding of Buddhist thought. The geomantic theories of feng shui also were popular in Goryeo. Confucian culture coexisted and developed together with Buddhist and traditional culture. Confucianism was emphasized in politics, and the Goryeo government made efforts to propagate Confucian laws and social customs. To promote Confucian education, the State Academy (Gukjagam) was established in 992, and academies were also established in the provincial areas. In the mid-Goryeo period, twelve private Confucian academies flourished. The compilation of the Veritable Records (Sillok) of the dynasty and the writing of *History of the Three Kingdoms (Samguk sagi)* were both done according to the conventions of Confucian historiography. Neo-Confucianism was introduced to the country in the late Goryeo period and became very influential. Woodblock printing underwent development, and metal movable type was invented in the thirteenth century. The growth of aristocratic culture led to the development of luxury goods; in particular, Goryeo ceramics of Goryeo were of high aesthetic quality. In the twelfth century, Goryeo invented an original kind of inlaid celadon porcelain. Despite the disorder of the late Goryeo period, many great works of art continued to be created.

Society

The population of Goryeo is estimated to have ranged from three to five million people, comparable in size to England in the same period. The social status system in Goryeo divided the population into the aristocracy, middle class, commoners, and low-born. The aristocracy monopolized government positions through the civil service examination system and the protected appointment system (*eumseo*). They not only owned large amounts of land but also received *sujoji* from the state. After the establishment of a military regime, the military took power, and in the late Goryeo period, a new group of powerful families became the privileged class. The middle class consisted of lower-level administrators and those who made up the de facto ruling group in the countryside. Some local clerks (*hyangni*) were able to rise into the central aristocracy through the civil service examination. The new literati who emerged in the late Goryeo period also emerged from the local clerks. The majority of commoners were farmers, and they were expected to perform a variety of duties for the state, including military service. However, commoners received different treatment depending on the region. The majority of the low-born were unfree. Men married around the age of twenty and women around the age of eighteen with the practice of monogamy being prevalent. In comparison to the Joseon period, the status of women was relatively high, with great importance placed on the maternal line and the wife's family background. A woman was relatively free to remarry.

Economy

Agriculture was the foundation of the economy in Goryeo. The practice of fallow farming continued to the end of the Goryeo period. Land ownership rights were guaranteed to all regardless of social status, but in reality, the largest and most fertile lands were owned by the aristocracy and Buddhist monasteries. Large landowners generally owned parcels of land in different parts of the country, and they used their unfree people to cultivate it or rented it to tenant farmers. The rent for tenants was usually half of the harvest. Many commoners and people of low-born status worked as tenant farmers since they did not have enough land of their own or were entirely landless. Landowners had to pay one tenth of the harvest as taxes to the government. In addition, commoner men between the ages of sixteen and sixty were also obliged to provide labor to the state, including military service, while each region had to offer local products as tribute.

The Goryeo state granted the rights to collect taxes over a parcel of land to government offices and Buddhist monasteries and to those who performed duties for the state such as government officials, local government clerks, and full-time soldiers. The tax income was then used to provide for the recipient's livelihood or the operating costs of the institution. This system was called *jeonsigwa*, and the land parcelled out in this way was called *sujoji*. There were many instances when the right to collect taxes prevailed over ownership rights. Though in principle rights to collect taxes could not be passed on to one's descendants, there were many cases in which powerful figures used their position to enable later generations to inherit those rights. In the late Goryeo period, *sujoji* came to be inherited, causing severe social problems. Handicraft production was carried out by trained artisans or in special districts called *so*. Commerce was mainly conducted by Buddhist monasteries and took the form of barter exchanges. Goryeo was also active in international trade, dealing not only with Chinese, Japanese, and Jurchen merchants but also with ones from as far as Arabia.

Portrait of Confucianist An Hyang (1243–1306). National Treasure no. 111. One of the oldest surviving Korean paintings. Kept at Sosu Seowon in North Gyeongsang province. (PD–South Korea)

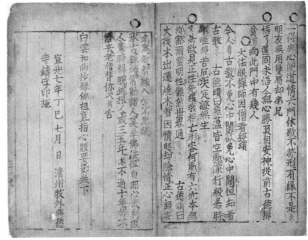

Pages from the *Jikji* [Baegun's Anthology of the Great Priests' Teachings on Identification of the Buddha's Spirit by the Practice of Seon]. This anthology of Buddhist writings, published in 1377, is believed to be the oldest extant book in the world printed with movable metal type. (Bibliothèque Nationale de France)

Politics

The central power group in Goryeo was the local gentry who had emerged in the late Silla period. After the founding of the new dynasty, they took up positions in the central government and created a lineage-based aristocratic society together with former Silla nobility. The governing ideology was based on Confucian political thought, and the state implemented a Chinese-style civil service examination. The structure of government was based on the Tang system of the Three Chancelleries and Six Ministries of Personnel, Revenue, Rites, Military, Justice, and Public Works. But in actuality, the government operated in a way suited to Goryeo's particular needs. It had organs such as the Jungchuwon, which processed royal commands and handled military secrets, and the Eosadae, which investigated charges of corruption and illegal activities by officials. Other unique government organs were the Sikmokdogam, where high-ranking officials deliberated and made decisions on legislative matters, and the Dobyeongmasa, where military matters were discussed. Administratively, the government divided the country into five provinces (*do*), two border regions (*gye*), and the capital region. There were three secondary capitals, and in 983, Goryeo designated twelve special administrative towns (*mok*) and appointed magistrates to them in an effort to increase direct control over the provinces. In the late twelfth century, a military regime was established after a coup in which military officials and soldiers rose up against the discrimination that they suffered. After battling the invading Mongols for about sixty years, Goryeo became a subject state of the Mongol Empire in 1270.

The Goryeo–Khitan War | *10th–11th Centuries*

In the late tenth and early eleventh centuries, Goryeo faced a series of invasions by the expansionist Khitan-Liao Dynasty, which had been formed in the early tenth century by a nomadic people from Manchuria. The Khitan first attacked Goryeo in 993 with subsequent invasions following in 1010 and 1018, all ending in defeat. One of the major battle sites was Heunghwajin. The Khitan laid siege to the fortress there three times because of its strategic importance but failed each time. Gwiju was another site of important battles. In both 1011 and 1018, Goryeo forces achieved decisive victories over retreating Khitan forces.

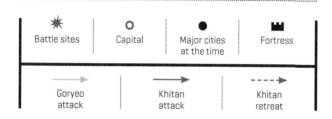

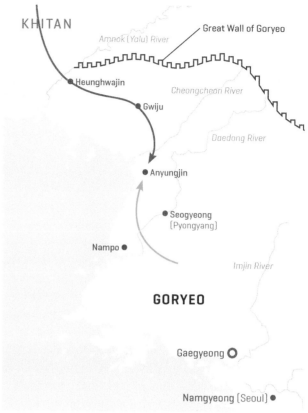

FIRST KHITAN INVASION | 993

The Goryeo–Mongol War | *1231–1239*

The Mongols invaded Goryeo in 1231, about two decades after invading the Jurchen kingdom of Jin. The invasion began a series of campaigns lasting almost thirty years that led Goryeo to move its capital to the island of Ganghwa. One of the first battles was at Gwiju; Goryeo forces successfully defended three sieges of the fortress in the first few months of the war. The Mongol army took the capital and then reached the southern part of the peninsula; near Chungju, though an army of Goryeo elites fled, an army of those of unfree status successfully defended the fortress. The Mongols retreated after defeats such as the Battle of Cheoin Fortress and the failure to capture Ganghwa Island. The Mongols also invaded Goryeo in 1235, 1238, 1247, 1253, and 1257.

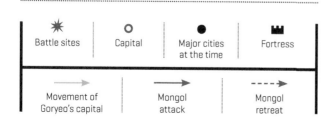

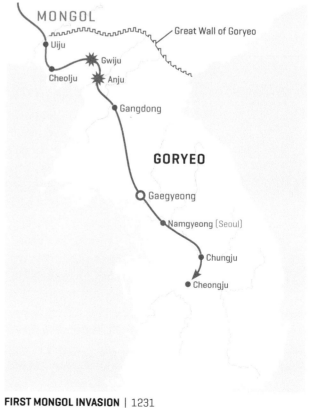

FIRST MONGOL INVASION | 1231

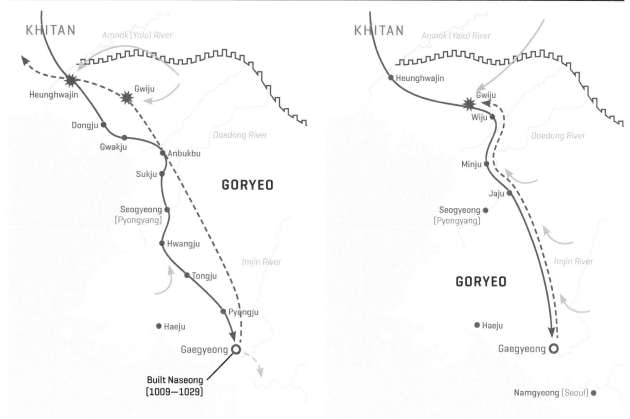

SECOND KHITAN INVASION | 1010

THIRD KHITAN INVASION | 1018

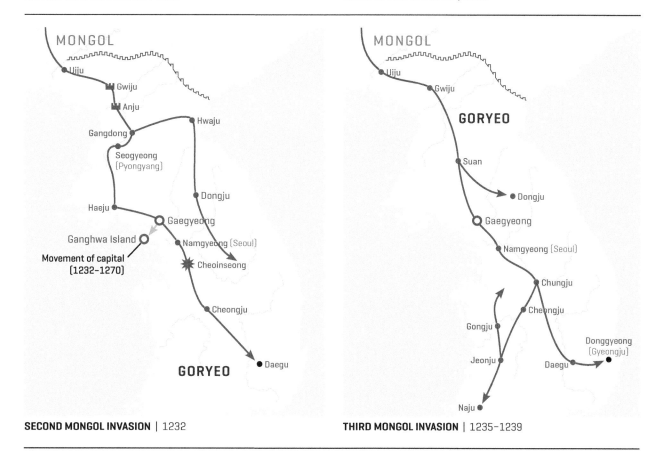

SECOND MONGOL INVASION | 1232

THIRD MONGOL INVASION | 1235–1239

Gaegyeong (Gaeseong) | *The capital of Goryeo*

Wang Geon made Gaegyeong the capital of his newly-founded state of Goryeo in 919, and it was an important center of national and international trade as well as administration. The city lost its political significance when Yi Seonggye moved the capital south in 1394, but it continued to be a major commercial center during the Joseon dynasty.

Map of Gaeseong from a mid-18th-century atlas, Haedong jido. (Kyujanggak Archives)

MAP OF GAESEONG

Main gates

Residence of prominent individual

Streams

Main streets

Former city wall

Railway line

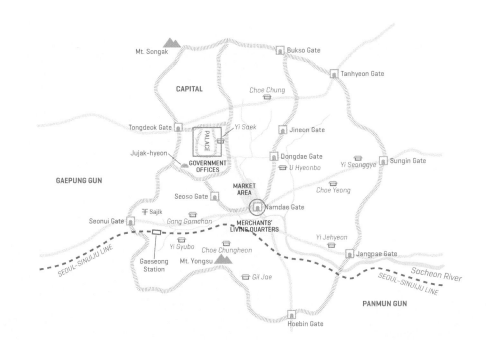

Commerce and trade played an important part in the Goryeo economy – not surprising for a kingdom founded by a scion of a merchant family. While traveling merchants sold goods in the provinces, merchant houses were founded in the capital Gaeseong as demand for luxury goods increased. Handicraft industries flourished, and special administrative districts were organized for the production of certain products. Gaeseong was also a major regional trade hub linked by both land and sea routes to the rest of East Asia as well as the Middle East and India. Its principal trade partners were China, Japan. and the northern tribes, but Arab traders were also known to reach the country.

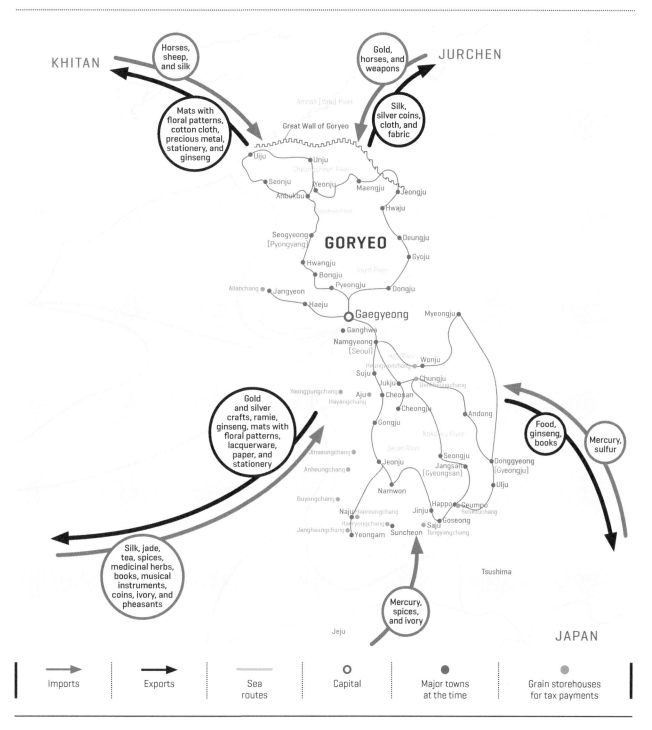

Celadon Pottery | *10th–15th Century*

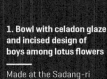

Celadon porcelain represents one of the highest artistic achievements of the Goryeo period. Originally developed in southern China, celadon techniques were introduced to Goryeo in the tenth century. The porcelain was first produced along the western and southern coasts of Goryeo, from today's Hwanghae province to Jeolla province. To produce celadon, clay containing some iron was first fired in a kiln at 700–800°C (~1,290–1,470°F). To create its distinctive grayish green color, a glaze containing 1–3 percent iron was then applied, and the porcelain would be fired again at a temperature of 1,150–1,200°C (~2,100–2,190°F). In the early Goryeo period, the main types of celadon were tea sets and implements and ritual utensils. Around the late eleventh and early twelfth centuries, production increased as it came into more widespread use. At this time, Goryeo developed its own distinctive style of celadon as a result of innovations in glazing and kiln structure, and it is considered to have reached its aesthetic peak in the early twelfth century, as a type of inlaid celadon was developed that was rare in China. The quality of celadon began to decline in the thirteenth century, and production appears to have stopped by the fifteenth.

1. Bowl with celadon glaze and incised design of boys among lotus flowers

Made at the Sadang-ri kilns in the first half of the 12th century.
(Fitzwilliam Museum)

2. Incense burner

12th century. National Treasure no. 95.
(National Museum of Korea)

3. Melon-shaped bottle

Mid-12th century. National Treasure no. 94. Thought to be from the tomb of King Injong. (National Museum of Korea)

1.

2.

3.

918–943	Taejo	[太祖 태조]
943–945	Hyejong	[惠宗 혜종]
945–949	Jeongjong	[定宗 정종]
949–975	Gwangjong	[光宗 광종]
975–981	Gyeongjong	[景宗 경종]
981–997	Seongjong	[成宗 성종]
997–1009	Mokjong	[穆宗 목종]
1009–1031	Hyeonjong	[顯宗 현종]
1031–1034	Deokjong	[德宗 덕종]
1034–1046	Jeongjong	[靖宗 정종]
1046–1083	Munjong	[文宗 문종]
1083	Sunjong	[順宗 순종]
1083–1094	Seonjong	[宣宗 선종]
1094–1095	Heonjong	[獻宗 헌종]
1095–1105	Sukjong	[肅宗 숙종]
1105–1122	Yejong	[睿宗 예종]
1122–1146	Injong	[仁宗 인종]
1146–1170	Uijong	[毅宗 의종]
1170–1197	Myeongjong	[明宗 명종]
1197–1204	Sinjong	[神宗 신종]
1204–1211	Huijong	[熙宗 희종]
1211–1213	Gangjong	[康宗 강종]
1213–1259	Gojong	[高宗 고종]
1259–1274	Wonjong	[元宗 원종]
1274–1308	King Chungnyeol	[忠烈王 충렬왕]
1308–1313	King Chungseon	[忠宣王 충선왕]
1313–1330	King Chungsuk	[忠肅王 충숙왕]
1330–1332	King Chunghye	[忠惠王 충혜왕]
1332–1339	King Chungsuk	[Second reign]
1339–1344	King Chunghye	[Second reign]
1344–1348	King Chungmok	[忠穆王 충목왕]
1348–1351	King Chungjeong	[忠定王 충정왕]
1351–1374	King Gongmin	[恭愍王 공민왕]
1374–1388	King U	[禑王 우왕]
1388–1389	King Chang	[昌王 창왕]
1389–1392	King Gongyang	[恭讓王 공양왕]

CHRONOLOGY OF GORYEO

918, SIXTH MONTH: Wang Geon revolts and establishes the state of Goryeo. Gungye is killed.
ELEVENTH MONTH: The Palgwanhoe festival is held.

919, FIRST MONTH: The capital is moved to Songak (Gaeseong).

922, MONTH UNKNOWN: People are moved to the Western Capital (Pyongyang); government offices are established there.

935, ELEVENTH MONTH: King Gyeongsun surrenders to Goryeo. Fall of Silla.

936, NINTH MONTH: Singeom of Later Baekje surrenders to Goryeo. Fall of Later Baekje. Goryeo unifies the Later Three Kingdoms.

938, TWELFTH MONTH: The crown prince of Tamna comes to Gaegyeong to present tribute to Goryeo.

940, MONTH UNKNOWN: Land is given to favored subjects under the *yeokbunjeon* system.

942, TENTH MONTH: An envoy is sent from Khitan. Goryeo cuts off diplomatic relations with the Khitan state for conquering Balhae and banishes the envoy.

956, MONTH UNKNOWN: Enactment of the Slave Review Law.

958, FIFTH MONTH: A civil service examination system is implemented for the first time.

960, ELEVENTH MONTH: The capital Gaegyeong is renamed Hwangdo, indicating the Goryeo king's elevation to the status of emperor. The western capital is renamed Seodo.

963, SEVENTH MONTH: Establishment of the Jewibo, an office that handled funds for poverty relief.

976, ELEVENTH MONTH: The *jeonsigwa* land system is enacted.

981, TWELFTH MONTH: Adoption of the practice of allowing officials to take leave on the day of their parents' memorial rites.

983, SECOND MONTH: The country is divided into twelve administrative units called *mok*. Local officials are dispatched for the first time.
FIFTH MONTH: The central government system is reorganized on the Tang model. The management of regional clerks is reorganized.
TENTH MONTH: Six licensed inns are established for the first time to sell alcohol.

987, EIGHTH MONTH: One Confucian scholar and one medical teacher are sent to each of the twelve mok in the country.

990, TWELFTH MONTH: Establishment of the Suseowon, a kind of national library, in Seogyeong.

991, SECOND MONTH: Construction of the Sajik Altar.

992, TWELFTH MONTH: The central academy in Gaeseong is reorganized and named the Gukjagam.

993, SECOND MONTH: The Sangpyeongchang (Ever Normal Granaries) are established in Gaeseong, the Western Capital, and the twelve provinces in order to regulate prices.
TENTH MONTH: The first Khitan invasion.

996, FOURTH MONTH: A coin called the *Geonwon jungbo* is minted.

1010, ELEVENTH MONTH: The second Khitan invasion.
MONTH UNKNOWN: The first Tripitaka Koreana is printed.

1013, NINTH MONTH: Choe Hang (?-1024) and others are ordered to start compiling the history of Goryeo.

1018, TWELFTH MONTH: The third Khitan invasion.

1019, SECOND MONTH: Gang Gamchan (948-1031) routs the Khitan force at Gwiju.
SEVENTH MONTH: People from Usan fleeing the Jurchens settle in Goryeo.

1020, NINTH MONTH: The bell and seven-story pagoda of Hyeonhwa Temple are created.

1024, NINTH MONTH: A group of around 100 Arabian merchants come to trade with Goryeo.

1032, THIRD MONTH: The *Veritable Records of Seven Generations* is compiled.

1033, EIGHTH MONTH: Beginning of the construction of the Great Wall of Goryeo.

1039, MONTH UNKNOWN: A law is enacted under which low-born status is determined according to the mother's status.

1055, SEVENTH MONTH: Choe Chung (984-1068) establishes a private academy called the Munheon gongdo.

1067: TWELFTH MONTH: Yangju is designated a secondary capital and is renamed Namgyeong.

1086, SIXTH MONTH: The monk Uicheon (1055-1101) compiles the *Supplement to the Tripitaka.*

1101, SECOND MONTH: A printing bureau called the Seojeokpo is established in the Gukjagam (State Academy).
SIXTH MONTH: The Goryeo vase-shaped silver coin is minted for the first time.

CHINA

960–1279: Song
    1100–1126: Emperor Huizong
1271–1368: Yuan
    1260–1294: Khubilai Khan

JAPAN

794–1185: Heian period
    781–806: Emperor Kanmu
    858–876: Emperor Seiwa
1185–1333: Kamakura period
    1192–1199: Minamoto no Yoritomo

1105: Tamna becomes a county of Goryeo.

1112, SECOND MONTH: A medical institution called the Hyeminguk is set up to treat disease among the commoners.

1135, FIRST MONTH: Myocheong's Rebellion erupts at the Western Capital. The rebels' new state is named Daewi with the reign name of Cheongae.

1145, TWELFTH MONTH: Gim Busik (1075–1151) compiles the *History of the Three Kingdoms.*

1151, FIFTH MONTH: Jeong Seo is exiled to Dongnae and composes the *hyangga*-style poem *Jeonggwajeong-gok.*

1170, EIGHTH MONTH: After a coup by military officials, a military government is established.

1173, EIGHTH MONTH: Rebellion of Gim Bodang.

1190, MONTH UNKNOWN: The Buddhist monk Jinul (1158–1210) presents his *Compact of the Samadhi and Prajña Community* and forms the Suseonsa, a meditation group.

1196: Choe Chungheon (1149–1219) takes power and establishes the sixty-one-year military dictatorship of the Choe house.

1198, FIFTH MONTH: A slave named Manjeok plans a rebellion aimed at abolishing slavery. His plan is discovered, and he is executed.

1200, MONTH UNKNOWN: Jinul moves to Songgwang Temple and establishes the Jogye Order.

1215, MONTH UNKNOWN: The monk Gakhun writes the *Lives of Eminent Korean Monks.*

1218, TWELFTH MONTH: Goryeo has its first encounter with the Mongols.

1231, EIGHTH MONTH: First invasion of the Mongol armies.

1232, SIXTH MONTH: The capital is moved to Ganghwa Island.

1234, MONTH UNKNOWN: Fifty copies of Choe Yunui's (1102–1162) *Prescribed Rites from the Past and Present* are printed using metal type.

1238, FOURTH MONTH: The Mongol army burns down the nine-story pagoda of Hwangnyong Temple.

1251, NINTH MONTH: The carving of the woodblocks for the second Tripitaka Koreana is completed.

1270, FIFTH MONTH: Goryeo surrenders to the Mongol army.
SIXTH MONTH: The troops of the Sambyeolcho (Three Elite Patrols) continue their resistance against the Mongols, crowning Wang On (?–1271) as their king.

1273, FOURTH MONTH: The Sambyeolcho are subdued with an attack by a combined Goryeo and Mongol force.

1285, MONTH UNKNOWN: The monk Iryeon (1206–1289) compiles the *Memorabilia of the Three Kingdoms.*

1287, MONTH UNKNOWN: Yi Seunghyu (1224–1300) composes the *Song of Emperors and Kings.*

1290, THIRD MONTH: An Hyang (1242–1306) introduces Zhu Xi's Neo-Confucian thought to Goryeo.

1295, MONTH UNKNOWN: The name of Tamna is changed to Jeju.

1310, MONTH UNKNOWN: Gim Umun and others create the "Yangnyu Gwaneumdo," a painting of the Bodhisattva Avalokitesvara (now kept at the Kagami Shrine in Japan).

1356, FIFTH MONTH: King Gongmin initiates an anti-Yuan policy, executing the pro-Yuan faction at court.
SEVENTH MONTH: Goryeo recovers areas occupied by Yuan including Ssangseong.

1359, TWELFTH MONTH: First invasion of the Red Turbans.

1361, TENTH MONTH: Second invasion of the Red Turbans.

1363, MONTH UNKNOWN: Mun Ikjeom (1329–1398) returns from Yuan with cotton seeds. The cultivation of cotton begins.

1368, ELEVENTH MONTH: Goryeo sends an envoy to Ming.

1377, TENTH MONTH: General Choe Museon (?–1395) manufactures gunpowder and canons.
MONTH UNKNOWN: The Buddhist text *Essentials of the Sutra of Direct Pointing to Mind and Body* (aka *Jikji*) is printed using metal type.

1388, FOURTH MONTH: An expedition is sent to attack Ming.
FIFTH MONTH: The general of the expeditionary army, Yi Seonggye, turns his forces around at Wihwa Island in the Amnok (Yalu) River and returns to the capital to seize power.

1391, FIFTH MONTH: The Rank Land Law is enacted, giving government officials the right to collect taxes from certain lands.

1392, SEVENTH MONTH: Yi Seonggye establishes the state of Joseon. Fall of Goryeo.

Songhua River

Liao River

MING/QING

Shenyang ● Sarhū (Fushun)

Hun River

Duman (Tumen) River

▲ Mt. Baekdu ● Gyeongseong

Liaoyang ●

Anshan ○

Taizi River

HAMGYEONG

Fenghuangcheng ○

Amnok (Yalu) River

Wihwa Island ● ▲ Uiju

PYEONGAN

Cheongcheon River

Anju ●

Hamheung ■

Daedong River

Pyongyang ■

Hwangju ●

HWANGHAE

Imjin River

Han River

Haeju ■

GYEONGGI

GANGWON

Gangneung ●

◎ Hanyang (Seoul)

Gwangju ■

Wonju ■

Ulleung

Dok

Han River

Chungju ●

Punggi ●

Cheongju ■

CHUNGCHEONG

Andong ●

Boryeong ⚓

Geum River

Sangju ■

Gyeongju ●

Jeonju ■

GYEONGSANG

Namwon ●

Nakdong River

JEOLLA

Dongnae ⚓

Naju ●

Yeosu ⚓

▲ ⚓ Geoje Island

Haenam ⚓

▲

Tsushima

JAPAN

Jeju

◎ Capital	● Major towns and cities	■ Provincial governors' offices	● Ming/Qing cities	⋯ Tribute mission routes	▲ Beacons	⚓ Naval bases	–––– Border of Joseon from 1434 · · · · Border of Joseon in 1392

6
JOSEON

Portraits of **King Taejo** (left), founder of the Joseon Dynasty and **King Yeongjo** (right). The painting of King Taejo is National Treasure no. 317. (National Museum of Korea and the National Palace Museum)

Sent to invade Ming China, General Yi Seonggye turned back at Wihwa Island and overthrew the Goryeo government. He established a new dynasty called Joseon in 1392, moving the capital to a new city along the Han River two years later. The name of the new kingdom harked back to the ancient state with the same name. Yi was supported by Neo-Confucian scholar-officials such as Jeong Dojeon who sought to remove the influence of Buddhism and establish a state based more thoroughly on Confucian principles. The end of the Imjin Wars of 1592–1598 is generally seen as the beginning of the late Joseon period. After a difficult period of recovery, Joseon underwent a relatively prosperous eighteenth century under the reigns of two powerful kings – Yeongjo and Jeongjo. The nineteenth century, however, saw a decline that left the country ill-equipped to face the sudden encroachment by the capitalist powers at the end of the century.

**Painting of a yangban
riding a donkey**
by Gim Deuksin
(1754–1822).

Politics

At the apex of the centralized Neo-Confucian monarchy was the State Council (Uijeongbu) led by three High State Councillors. Under this were the Six Ministries that dealt with the more detailed affairs of state, covering Taxation, Personnel, Military Affairs, Punishments, Public Works, and Rites. A system of administrative checks and balances was also introduced under three government organs: the Office of Special Advisors (Hongmungwan), the Office of the Inspector–General (Saheonbu), and the Office of the Censor–General (Saganwon). For local administration, the country was divided into eight provinces which were further divided into counties (*gun*) and districts (*hyeon*). The provinces were administered by centrally appointed governors, while each of the counties below them was overseen by a magistrate. Appointment to official position required passage of a civil service examination that tested knowledge of the Confucian classics. Tensions between the "merit subjects," the dominant force in government, and the *sarim* literati erupted into open political conflict in the four literati purges of the late fifteenth and early sixteenth centuries during which many literati were killed or banished.

Culture

The adoption of Neo-Confucianism brought about changes not only to thought and philosophy but also to literature, art, and everyday life. The promotion of study and research into Confucianism led to the emergence of two prominent thinkers, Yi Hwang (Toegye, 1501–1570) and Yi I (Yulgok, 1536–1584). Taking opposing positions on whether *ri* (*li*) or *gi* (*qi*) had primacy, they represented the two major schools of Neo-Confucian thought in Joseon. At the same time, there was development of native culture, most notably with the invention of a phonetic script for the native language in the early 1440s, later called Hangeul. Native forms of poetry, such as *gasa* and *sijo*, were popular among the yangban class, though there was also much production of literature in classical Chinese. Portraits and paintings of landscapes and scenes of yangban at leisure were popular. Instead of the celadon of the Goryeo period, grayish stoneware with a greenish glaze called *buncheong* was popular, though porcelain was also produced. In an effort to weaken the hold of Buddhism, the government encouraged the commoners to conduct ancestral rites and other Confucian rituals.

Society

Joseon's code of laws divided the population into *yangin* (freeborn) and *cheonmin* (low-born). The freeborn had to pay taxes, but they also had rights and privileges denied to the low-born. The civil service examination was theoretically open to all men of freeborn status; those who passed the exams and became civil or military officials were called yangban ("the two orders"). The social status system developed into more of a rigid class structure with four main classes. At the top were the yangban, who were often called *sajok*. Next came the *jungin*, who worked as clerks called *ajeon* or *hyangni* and in technical professions such as accounting, astronomy, law, medicine, and translating. The commoners were mainly peasants who tilled the land, but some also worked as merchants or artisans. At the bottom were the low-born, who worked at professions considered lowly such as butchers and executioners as well as wicker makers, tanners, musicians, and female entertainer-courtesans (*gisaeng*). Most of the low-born were unfree people (*nobi*) who were owned by the yangban class. At the beginning of the period, yangban probably constituted less than 5 percent of the population, while unfree people totaled about 30 percent. The educational system was divided into three levels, beginning at village schools (*seodang*), continuing at county-level secondary schools (*hyanggyo*), and then concluding at one of the Four State Schools or the State Confucian Academy (Seonggyungwan). The country underwent a Neo-Confucian transformation. Society became much more patriarchal with patrilineal descent and inheritance becoming the norm and with elite women experiencing a decline of status compared to the Goryeo period.

Economy

Agriculture underwent improvements in productivity, contributing to an increase in population. Farmers no longer left fields to lie fallow and engaged in continuous cultivation. Peasants were expected to provide labor services, land taxes, and tribute goods to the state and often paid rents to their yangban landlords. They had to pay up to half of their harvest in such dues and lived largely in a self-sufficient economy. Commerce was generally limited to the trade in luxury goods for the consumption of the yangban class and small-scale periodic markets around which itinerant peddlers circulated. In the sixteenth century, the number of these periodic markets, usually held every five days, began to increase markedly. During the fifteenth century, attempts to introduce both paper and metallic money generally failed, and commodity currencies such as rice, hemp, and cotton cloth continued to be used throughout this period. International trade was highly circumscribed as trade with Japan was limited to the island of Tsushima and the three open ports, and trade with China was conducted over land generally through the regular tribute missions to the Ming court. The production of manufactured goods such as textiles was dominated by self-sufficient households. But the state closely controlled craft production and the manufacture of luxury goods such as court clothing, brass cutlery, and porcelain.

THE CIVIL SERVICE EXAMINATION

The civil service examination (*mungwa*) was supposed to be held every three years. It consisted of two separate parts; candidates had to pass the *sogwa* in order to take the *daegwa*. In the *sogwa*, the *saengwonsi* tested knowledge of the Confucian classics, and the *jinsasi* tested ability in composition. The passers of the *sogwa* were allowed to enter the Seonggyungwan. The *daegwa* consisted of three stages. The first two, the *chosi* and the *boksi*, had three examinations: the *chojang* on the Confucian classics, the *jungjang* on composition, and the *jongjang* on policy and current affairs. The thirty-three passers of the *boksi* took the *jeonsi* in the presence of the king to determine their final rankings.

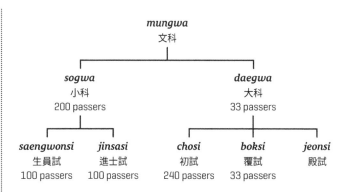

Hanyang (Seoul) | *The capital of Joseon*

The Joseon capital, officially named Hanseong but more generally known as Hanyang, was founded in 1394 when King Taejo moved the capital from Gaeseong. Hanyang was a fortified city located to the north of the Han River, surrounded by a high wall and bounded to the north by Bukhan Mountain. The city's location and layout were based on the principles of *feng shui* and East Asian conventions. The palace complex was situated in the north with residential and market districts to the south. While its primary function was administrative, the capital increasingly became an important commercial center in the country.

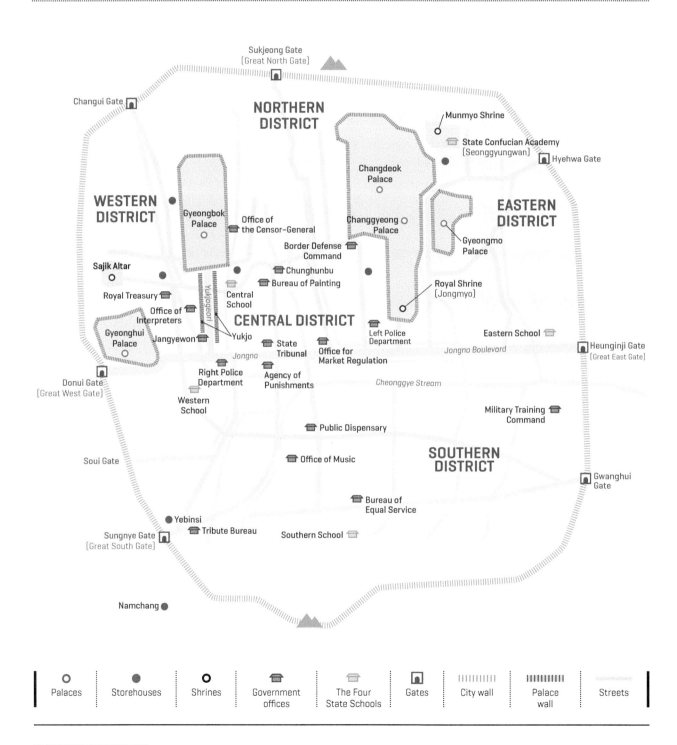

○	●	◎	🏛	🏛	🔲	‖‖‖‖‖	‖‖‖‖‖	
Palaces	Storehouses	Shrines	Government offices	The Four State Schools	Gates	City wall	Palace wall	Streets

Government Offices | *The Six Ministries*

1. Ministry of Rites (Yejo, 禮曹)
2. Office of Ministers-without-portfolio (Jungchubu)
3. Office of the Inspector-General (Saheonbu)
4. Ministry of Military Affairs (Byeongjo, 兵曹)
5. Ministry of Punishment (Hyeongjo, 刑曹)
6. Ministry of Public Works (Gongjo, 工曹)
7. State Council (Uijeongbu)
8. Ministry of Personnel (Ijo, 吏曹)
9. Hanseong City Administration (Hanseongbu)
10. Ministry of Taxation (Hojo, 戶曹)

Yukjo Street, the government district of Joseon Seoul. Early 20th century photograph.

Merchant Houses

1. Bosingak Bell Tower
2. Chinese silk
3. Cotton cloth
4. Domestic silk
5. Paper
6. Ramie cloth
7. Hemp cloth
8. Dried fish
9. Felt and cloth
10. General goods
11. Rice
12. Cotton
13. Jewellers
14. Brassware
15. Straw hat
16. Black hat
17. Haberdashers
18. Furriers
19. Fruit
20. Pipes
21. Silver merchants
22. Jade merchants
23. Honey
24. Butchers
25. Brewer's yeast

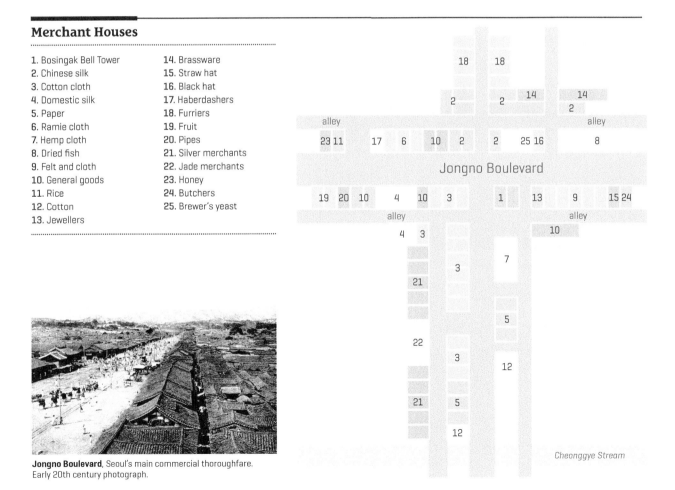

Jongno Boulevard, Seoul's main commercial thoroughfare. Early 20th century photograph.

Gyeongbok Palace, whose construction was completed in 1395, was the main palace of the Joseon kingdom. It was burned down in 1592 during the Imjin War and was not rebuilt until the mid 1860s. It was located in the northern part of the capital, with Mt. Baegak to its rear, and its main gate faced south, following Chinese convention. Along its central axis were the main gate and two compounds. The outer compound was where the king met officials, and it contained buildings for official functions and ceremonies. The inner compound had the living quarters of the king and queen. Some government offices were located in the southwestern corner of the palace, and the crown prince's residence was in the southeast. At the rear were gardens and leisure areas for the royal family. In 1963, the South Korean government designated the palace as Historic Site no. 117.

Gwanghae Gate. The main gate of the palace. Photograph from 1904. (PD–Library of Congress)

Gyeonghoeru. National Treasure no. 224. Photograph from 1904. (PD–Library of Congress)

PRINCIPLES OF PALACE CONSTRUCTION

Many aspects of Gyeongbok Palace were based on principles that were taken, with some alteration, from Chinese classics such as the *Rites of Zhou*, a text from the second century BCE.

左廟右社 (Jwamyo Usa)

Looking southward from the main gate of the palace, the royal shrine (Jongmyo) should be located to the left, and the altar for grain ceremonies (Sajikdan) should be located to the right.

前朝後市 (Jeonjo Husi)

Government offices should be located in front of the palace, and markets should be in the rear. This was because the king was supposed to look to the south in order to rule the people. However, since Mt. Baegak was adjacent to the rear of the palace, the markets were placed in front of the street with the Six Ministries.

三門三朝 (Sammun Samjo)

The palace should have three main gates and three main compounds: one for government offices, one where the king and officials conducted official government business, and one for the living quarters of the king and the royal family. This differed from the Chinese principle of 五門三朝 (Omun Samjo) which called for a palace to have five main gates.

Based on the Buggwol dohyeong — a map of Gyeongbok Palace that is estimated to have been made some time in the late nineteenth or early twentieth century. The size of the original is 280cm by 432cm.

Having unified Japan under his rule, Toyotomi Hideyoshi undertook a grandiose plan to conquer Joseon and China. The first Japanese invasion of Korea began with a landing at Busan in May 1592, and though the court was forced to flee north, the Joseon and Ming forces fought Japan to a standstill, leading to a halt in hostilities in 1593. With the failure of negotiations, Hideyoshi launched another invasion in early 1597 whose objective was not to conquer China but to take control of southern Joseon. The second invasion was less successful and ended soon after his death in 1598.

THE FIRST INVASION

Japanese First Division
Konishi Yukinaga

Japanese Second Division
Katō Kiyomasa

Japanese Third Division
Kuroda Nagamasa

Japanese Fourth Division
Shimazu Yoshihiro

THE SECOND INVASION

Japanese invasion

Japanese retreat

THE FIRST INVASION 1592–1593

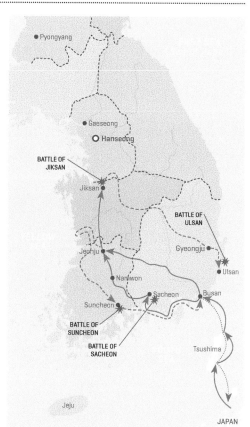

THE SECOND INVASION 1597–1598

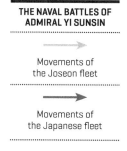

THE NAVAL BATTLES OF ADMIRAL YI SUNSIN

Movements of
the Joseon fleet

Movements of
the Japanese fleet

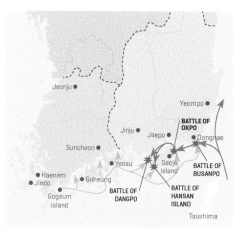

THE NAVAL BATTLES OF ADMIRAL YI SUNSIN 1592

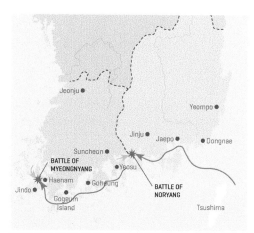

THE NAVAL BATTLES OF ADMIRAL YI SUNSIN 1597–1598

CHRONOLOGY OF THE IMJIN WARS

FIRST INVASION

1592, FOURTH MONTH: [13th day] Toyotomi Hideyoshi lands a force of around 210,000 troops at Busan, intending to invade Ming China.
[14th day] Fall of Busan.
[30th day] King Seonjo flees the capital.
A rebellion breaks out in Seoul; the royal palaces are burned down.

FIFTH MONTH: [2nd day] Japanese troops occupy the Joseon capital.
[7th day] Battle of Okpo, Joseon's first naval victory in the war.
[17th day] Battle of the Imjin River. Joseon's defeat removed the last major line of defense protecting Pyongyang.
[29th day] Battle of Sacheon; first use of the turtle ship in battle.

SIXTH MONTH: [2nd day] Battle of Dangpo, a victory for the Joseon navy with minimal losses.
[11th day] King Seonjo flees to Uiju.
[15th day] Fall of Pyongyang.

SEVENTH MONTH: [8th day] Admiral Yi Sunsin defeats the Japanese navy in the Battle of Hansan Island.
[15th day] A Ming relief force of 3,000 attacks Japanese forces in Pyongyang but is defeated.

NINTH MONTH: [1st day] Admiral Yi Sunsin attacks the Japanese navy, sinking 100 of 470 enemy ships but failing to retake the port.

TENTH MONTH: [5th day] Siege of Jinju; Japan fails to take the fortress.

1593, FIRST MONTH: A Ming Chinese force of 40,000 troops enters the war.
[9th day] Joint Joseon-Ming forces retake Pyongyang.
[27th day] Battle of Byeokjegwan; Ming forces fail to drive Japanese forces out of Seoul.

SECOND MONTH: [12th day] Battle of Haengju; Japan's siege of the town fails.

FOURTH MONTH: [19th day] Seoul is retaken.

SIXTH MONTH: [22nd–29th day] Second siege of Jinju; Japan takes the fortress. According to legend, a *gisaeng* named Nongae sacrificed her life after the battle by embracing a Japanese commander and plunging off a cliff.

EIGHTH MONTH: The Japanese armies begin to leave Joseon. Ming proposes truce talks.

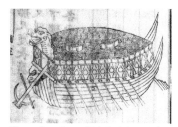

Illustration of one of Admiral Yi Sunsin's turtle ships (geobukseon). Dating from 1795. [PHGCOM–Wikipedia]

SECOND INVASION

1597, FIRST MONTH: Hideyoshi's forces begin a second invasion of Joseon with around 150,000 troops.

SECOND MONTH: [6th day] Admiral Yi Sunsin is relieved of duty and jailed on the basis of false accusations from his rival Won Gyun.

FIFTH MONTH: Ming forces arrive again in Joseon.

SEVENTH MONTH: [15th day] The Joseon navy, under the command of Admiral Won Gyun, suffers a crushing defeat at the Battle of Chilcheollyang. Yi Sunsin is reinstated as admiral.

EIGHTH MONTH: [15th day] Fall of Namwon.

NINTH MONTH: [7th day] Battle of Jiksan; Ming's defeat of Japanese forces halts their northward advance.
[16th day] Battle of Myeongnyang Straits; Yi Sunsin defeats a much larger Japanese force.

TWELFTH MONTH: Battle of Ulsan; siege by Joseon and Ming forces fails.

1598, EIGHTH MONTH: Toyotomi Hideyoshi dies.

NINTH MONTH: Battle of Sacheon; Joseon–Ming siege fails. Japanese forces begin to withdraw from the peninsula.

ELEVENTH MONTH: [18th day] Battle of Noryang, the last major battle of the Imjin Wars. Yi Sunsin dies in battle.

CHRONOLOGY OF THE EARLY JOSEON PERIOD

14TH CENTURY

1392, FOURTH MONTH: Confucian scholar Jeong Mongju is murdered by Yi Seonggye's son Yi Bangwon on the Seonjuk Bridge in Gaeseong.
SEVENTH MONTH: Yi Seonggye ascends the throne.

1393, SECOND MONTH: The name of the kingdom is changed to Joseon at the suggestion of Ming Emperor Hongwu.

1394, EIGHTH MONTH: Hanyang is chosen as the site for the new capital city (today's Seoul).

1395, NINTH MONTH: Completion of the construction of Gyeongbok Palace, the main royal palace.

1396, NINTH MONTH: The construction of the new capital's city walls is completed with the mobilization of some 118,000 peasant laborers from around the country.

1398, SIXTH MONTH: Price of an unfree person is set.
SEVENTH MONTH: Beginning of a countrywide land survey.
EIGHTH MONTH: Yi Seonggye's son Yi Bangwon engages in a bloody struggle for succession, killing his brother and designated heir, Yi Bangseok, as well as the powerful Confucian scholar Jeong Dojeon.

15TH CENTURY

1402, EIGHTH MONTH: Introduction of a system of identification tags called *hopae*.

1405, TENTH MONTH: Completion of the construction of Changdeok Palace.

1407: Introduction of the *nokbong* system under which officials are paid salaries in grain or cloth as well as being granted land.

1414: Construction work is completed on Hanyang's market buildings on Jongno Boulevard.

1420, THIRD MONTH: Sejong establishes the Hall of Worthies (Jiphyeonjeon).

1423: Three southern ports are reopened to trade with Japanese merchants from Tsushima.

1429: An agricultural manual called *Straight Talk on Farming* (*Nongsa jikseol*) is published.

1433, SECOND MONTH: The *Conduct of the Three Bonds* (*Samgang haengsildo*), a primer of Confucian morals, is published for the first time.
SIXTH MONTH: The *Compilation of Native Korean Prescriptions* (*Hyangyak jipseongbang*), a collection of medical remedies based on locally available plants and materials, is published.

1443: Creation of a new script for writing the Korean language (*Hangeul*).

1444: Promulgation of the Tribute Tax Law (Gongbeop).
: SECOND MONTH: Choe Malli opposes the new script, calling it "vulgar letters" (*eonmun*).

1445, FOURTH MONTH: *Songs of Flying Dragons* (*Yongbieocheonga*), a collection of poems in *Hangeul*, is compiled.

1446, TWELFTH MONTH: The new script is promulgated with the publication of *Correct Sounds to Instruct the People* (*Hunmin jeongeum*).

1451, EIGHTH MONTH: The official history of the Goryeo dynasty (*Goryeosa*) is completed.

1455, SIXTH INTERCALARY MONTH: Sejo deposes King Danjong and places himself on the throne and then purges high officials.

1466, EIGHTH MONTH: The Rank Land Law established at the end of the Goryeo period is replaced by the Office Land Law (Jikjeonbeop) under which former officials were no longer given land.

1471, NINTH MONTH: A new legal code called the *Gyeongguk daejeon* is promulgated under King Seongjong.

1476: Completion of the compilation of the first genealogy of the Andong Gwon family.

1480, ELEVENTH MONTH: Execution of Eoudong, a yangban woman who became a *gisaeng*.

1482, EIGHTH MONTH: Execution of Lady Yun, deposed queen and mother of Prince Yeonsan.

1485, FIFTH MONTH: Completion of renovations to Sugang Palace, which is renamed Changgyeong Palace.

1494, THIRD MONTH: Riots break out around the country due to rising rice prices.

1498, SEVENTH MONTH: First literati purge. Fifty-one officials received punishments, including six who were sentenced to death (Muo sahwa).

CHINA
1271–1368: Yuan
  1260–1294: Khubilai Khan
1368–1644: Ming
  1368–1398: Hongwu Emperor (Taizu)
  1402–1424: Yongle Emperor (Chengzu)
  1572–1620: Wanli Emperor (Shenzong)

JAPAN
1336–1573: Muromachi period
  1467–1573: Sengoku period
  1467–1477: Ōnin War
  1543: Arrival of the Portuguese
1582–1598: Toyotomi Hideyoshi

16TH CENTURY

1503: Buddhist monks are banned from entering the capital.

1504: Discovery of leaflets in the vernacular criticizing the king leads Yeonsangun to forbid the use and study of Korean (*eonmun*).
: Second literati purge. 239 officials received punishments (Gapja sahwa).

1506, NINTH MONTH: King Yeonsangun is deposed by a group of literati led by Seong Huian and Bak Wonjong who place Prince Jinseong on the throne as King Jungjong.

1510, FOURTH MONTH: Japanese residents at the three open ports riot, causing the ports to be closed.

1512: ELEVENTH MONTH: All land and unfree people owned by Buddhist monasteries revert to state ownership.
: Treaty with the Lord of Tsushima resuming trade between Joseon and Japan.

1517, SIXTH MONTH: Establishment of the Border Defence Command (Bibyeonsa).

1519, ELEVENTH MONTH: Third literati purge. Execution of Jo Gwangjo (b. 1482) (Gimyo sahwa).

1521: A plot to eliminate officials who rose to power after the literati purge of 1519 is revealed, leading to the execution of An Dang and over ten other officials (Sinsa muok).

1524, FOURTH MONTH: The Ever Normal Granary system is introduced as a way of regulating prices.

1527: Publication of *Hunmong jahoe*, a textbook for children compiled by Choe Sejin.

1543, FIRST MONTH: Ju Sebung founds the first *seowon* in Punggi, North Gyeongsang province.

1544, FOURTH MONTH: About twenty Japanese ships pillage Saryangjin in Tongyeong, South Gyeongsang province.

1545, EIGHTH MONTH: Fourth literati purge (Eulsa sahwa).

1547, SECOND MONTH: Treaty of Jeongmi signed with the Lord of Tsushima.

1555, FIFTH MONTH: Japanese pirates begin to launch attacks on ports and villages in Jeolla province.

1556: The Office Land Law is abolished and replaced by a system under which officials are paid salaries rather than being granted land.

1558: Yulgok Yi I (1536–1584) passes the higher civil service examination in first place.

1559, FIRST MONTH: Toegye Yi Hwang begins his famous Four-Seven debate with Gi Daeseung (1527–1572) on the principles of Neo-Confucian philosophy.
THIRD MONTH: The Im Ggeokjeong Rebellion breaks out, lasting until 1562.

1561, SEVENTH MONTH: Rebellion in Naju, South Jeolla province.

1565: Joseon's most famous woman poet, Hwang Jini, writes the *sijo* poem *Cheongsanri byeokgyesu-ya*.

1568: Yi Hwang compiles the *Ten Diagrams on Sage Learning* (*Seonghak sipdo*).

1575: Conflict between Sim Uigyeom and Gim Hyowon marks the beginning of the factional strife in politics.

1582: First record of European sailors coming ashore in Joseon.

1588: Jeong Cheol pens the *gasa* songs *Mindful of My Seemly Lord* (Samiingok) and *Again Mindful of My Seemly Lord* (Sokmiingok).

1589, TENTH MONTH: Jeong Yeorip's plot for a rebellion is revealed, leading to the execution of many members of the Easterner faction (Gichuk oksa).

1592, FOURTH MONTH: Toyotomi Hideyoshi sends a force of some 210,000 Japanese troops to invade Joseon, beginning a regional war known as the Imjin waeran (Imjin War).
: King Seonjo flees the capital. A rebellion of unfree people breaks out in Seoul, and the royal palaces are burned down.

1593, FIRST MONTH: Ming China sends a force of 50,000 troops to Joseon.

1596, SEVENTH MONTH: Rebellion of Yi Monghak in Chungcheong province.

1597, FIRST MONTH: Hideyoshi's forces begin a second invasion of Joseon with some 200,000 troops.
NINTH MONTH: Admiral Yi Sunsin's greatest naval victory at Myeongnyang Strait.

1598, EIGHTH MONTH: Toyotomi Hideyoshi dies.
ELEVENTH MONTH: Yi Sunsin is killed in one of the final battles of the Imjin War.

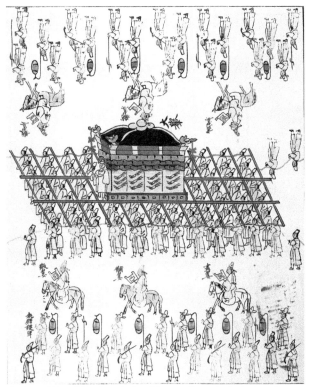

The funeral bier of King Jeongjo. Detail from an illustration in the *Jeongjo gukjang dogam uigwe* [Record of the State Funeral of King Jeongjo]. [Kyujanggak Archives]

Society

The invasions of the late sixteenth and early seventeenth centuries brought about major social upheaval with large-scale population movements and significant depopulation. Despite these upheavals, the basic status system of the early Joseon period stayed intact but underwent a gradual loosening in the late Joseon period. One major change was the emergence of wealthy peasants who were able to accumulate land, grow cash crops, and hire agricultural laborers. The distinction between commoner and yangban status became undermined as rich peasants bought titles and attained yangban status, while so-called "fallen yangban," whose families had lost both landholdings and access to official positions, lived in poverty. At the same time, the unfree population was dropping; in 1801, the Joseon state freed thousands of its unfree people, mainly those belonging to government offices. However, private ownership of unfree people was not abolished until 1894. The *jungin* class of specialists rose to greater cultural prominence. A

layer of merchants also emerged who grew rich through various avenues, including the lucrative tribute trade with the state, the patronage of powerful individuals, and their domination of the wholesale distribution of particular goods. In the countryside, village life underwent significant change. As the authority of the *sajok* declined, they attmepted to protect their status. They built shrines to ancestors and established their own private schools (*seowon*), leading to the decline of *hyanggyo*. Peasants gained a greater voice in village affairs. Rather than joining organizations led by local yangban, they began to form their own; most notably, the *dure*. In the nineteenth century, Joseon experienced unprecedented levels of social unrest. There were numerous smaller incidents throughout the century, including riots in the capital itself, but the two biggest rebellions were the Hong Gyeongnae Rebellion of 1811–1812 and the Jinju Uprising of 1862. Although these uprisings were all quelled by the government, they marked a significant decrease in the stability and legitimacy of the regime.

Economy

To help revive the agricultural economy that had been devastated by the invasions, the government implemented a major reform of the tax system called the Uniform Tax Law (Daedongbeop) under which the tribute tax was replaced with a land tax paid in rice, cloth, or cash. In the short term, this reduced the tax burden on peasants, and in the longer term, it stimulated the development of commerce and a cash economy.

Another major development in this period was the rise of markets. As a result of the Uniform Tax Law, a new group of wealthy "tribute merchants" emerged who provided the state with the goods it had previously collected directly from peasants. Other factors included the introduction or development of new cash crops such as tobacco, cotton, and ginseng; the further spread of local markets and development of transportation networks; and the widespread introduction of copper coinage. In the capital, the merchant houses expanded considerably, and an elite group of six or seven merchant houses called the Yuguijeon emerged that sold profitable commodities such as silk, cotton, paper, and dried fish.

The relative economic prosperity of eighteenth-century Joseon was also a result of the widespread dissemination of the technique of rice transplantation which, although risky, allowed double cropping and thus higher yields. Productivity also increased as a result of government-backed improvements in irrigation facilities. As a safety net, the government established a system of grain loans (*hwangok*) to enable peasants to survive the period when grain stores were low. However, in the nineteenth century Joseon experienced a general economic and demographic decline, attributable in part to a period of particularly severe droughts and floods, resulting in famines and major epidemics.

Culture

One major development in this period was an increasingly critical attitude toward Neo-Confucianism. A group of scholars, later called the "Silhak school," focused their work on more practical issues, also undertaking a reexamination of the Confucian classics. Silhak scholars such as Yu Hyeongwon and Jeong Yagyong proposed comprehensive proposals for the fundamental reform of Joseon state and society. Some took an interest in Catholicism and Jesuit science, signaling a weakening of the China-centered worldview.

A **white porcelain** (baekja) "moon jar." 18th century. [National Museum of Korea]

Another major development was the rise of commoner culture. Literature employed more realistic depictions of the world, including portrayals of commoner life. Novels written in the vernacular emerged, such as Heo Gyun's *Hong Gildong* and Gim Manjung's *Nine-Cloud Dream*; some contained sharp satires of yangban elites. Writers from outside the yangban class became important figures in the literary world, as exemplified by the so-called *wihang* poetry by *jungin* writers. The rise of markets helped to stimulate the rise of popular entertainments, such as *pansori* (one-person opera) and the mask dance. As these entertainers traveled around the country to perform, there emerged a set of popular stories, including the "Tale of Chunhyang" and the "Tale of Sim Cheong," that gave voice to the experience of commoners. Similarly, painters turned to more subjects within Joseon and depicted the life of the commoners at both work and play; their work led to the rise of a new type of painting called "genre painting" (*pungsokhwa*), reaching its height in the work of Gim Hongdo and Sin Yunbok. The production of *buncheong* pottery stopped after the Imjin War, and white porcelain (*baekja*) became popular.

Commoners eating lunch. Genre painting by Gim Hongdo. Late 18th century. [National Museum of Korea]

Politics

While the basic governmental structure remained the same after the two invasions, new organs were created that led to a reorganization of the state. The Border Defense Council, which had been established in the sixteenth century, became increasingly important and began to eclipse the administrative role of the State Council and the Six Ministries. The late Joseon state continued to develop its legal system, publishing three revised legal codes between 1744 and 1865. A new system of public appeals also emerged in the capital city during the late Joseon period called *gyeokjaeng*. Under this system, members of the commoner population would make their grievances known directly to the king by banging on gongs or drums in front of the royal palace or close to the king during a royal procession.

One of the hallmarks of late Joseon politics was the intense factionalism of the ruling elite. The first major factions – the Easterners and the Westerners – formed in the mid-sixteenth century. After further splits, there emerged four major factions: the Northerners, the Southerners, the Soron (Young Doctrine), and the Noron (Old Doctrine). From the early eighteenth century onward, the Noron was the strongest faction at court. Intra-elite conflict was finally tamed during the reigns of Yeongjo and Jeongjo, who adopted a policy of impartiality (*tangpyeongchaek*) under which they actively tried to create equilibrium among the various factions through official appointments. The death of Jeongjo in 1800 ushered in a new period in which powerful royal in-law families controlled the throne. These families dominated politics in the early to mid-nineteenth century and helped to exacerbate the breakdown of Joseon.

The politics of Joseon entered a new phase when factions emerged in the late sixteenth century. Factionalism began in 1575 with a split among *Sarim* officials into Easterner and Westerner factions during a dispute over whom to appoint to an important post that had authority over personnel matters. In the early 1590s, the Easterners split into Northerner and Southerner factions over how harshly to punish the Westerners, who caused a controversy by proposing that King Seonjo, who had no legitimate son, designate his heir. Factions remained major political actors until the mid eighteenth century when King Yeongjo implemented a policy of drawing officials equally from all the major factions.

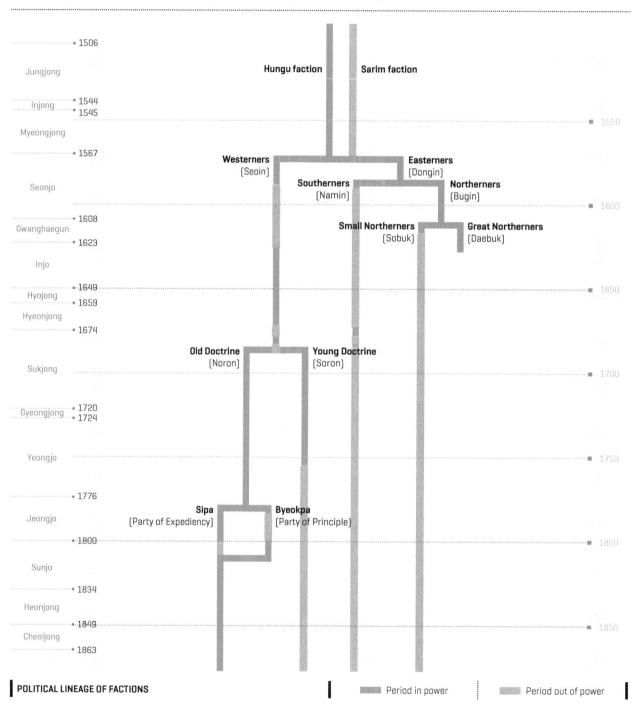

POLITICAL LINEAGE OF FACTIONS

Period in power | Period out of power

The Manchu Invasions | *1627, 1636–1637*

The Manchu overthrow of the Ming Dynasty had profound implications for Joseon, and the kingdom could not remain untouched by the violent transition. Joseon's support for the Ming led to the first invasion of Joseon in 1627. The second Manchu invasion began in 1636 when Joseon refused to assume appropriate diplomatic relations with the newly declared Qing Dynasty. With Qing's victory, King Injo was forced to surrender and break ties with Ming, with Joseon becoming a tributary of Qing.

During the late Joseon period, Korea remained part of the East Asian tributary system centered on China, even after the establishment of the Manchu Qing dynasty. Joseon sent tribute missions to Qing every year that had to travel on an overland route. It also sent regular diplomatic envoys to Tokugawa Japan, with whom it had "neighborly" relations. Because of the opportunities for trade on these missions, a three-way trade developed among the countries, involving ginseng from Korea, precious metals from Japan, and silk from China. From the early fifteenth century, trade with Japan was permitted at the three ports of Dongnae, Jepo, and Yeompo. In the late Joseon period, it was conducted at Japan House (Waegwan) in the port of Dongnae, with the Sō Clan of Tsushima Island acting as an intermediary.

Legend:
- ○ Capital
- ● Major towns and cities
- ● International trade center
- ● Major commercial center
- → Export
- → Import
- Main trade routes
- Official border trade
- Private border trade

The Rise of Markets

In the seventeenth century, as Joseon began to recover from the wars of that era, the number of markets in the country grew. By the early eighteenth century, a countrywide network of local markets was well established, with most opening every five days. Alongside government-licensed merchants, large private merchants began to appear who were able to circumvent regulations and amass considerable capital.

A one-*mun* coin.
Minted by the Gaeseong Township Military Office in 1882. [Fitzwilliam Museum]

A two-*mun* coin.
Minted by the Gangwon Provincial Office between 1742 and 1752. [Fitzwilliam Museum]

A five-*mun* coin.
Minted by the Ministry of Finance [Hojo] in 1883. [Fitzwilliam Museum]

A one hundred-*mun* coin.
Minted by the Ministry of Finance in 1866. [Fitzwilliam Museum]

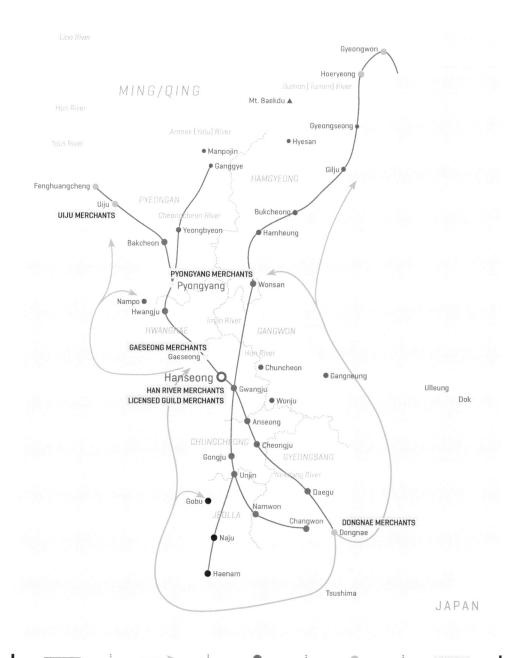

Land transport routes

Sea transport routes

Major trade and transport centers

International trade city

Important merchant groups

THE BREAKDOWN OF JOSEON

● Sites related to the **1862 Rebellion**

● Sites related to **Silhak**

● Sites related to **Donghak**

● Sites related to the **Hong Gyeongnae** Rebellion [1811-1812]

● Places where **Jang Gilsan** was active. [late 17th Century]

○ Capital

✳ Sites of other rebellions

The Breakdown of Joseon | *Late 17th–19th century*

In the nineteenth century, a series of uprisings and rebellions marked the breakdown of Joseon state and society. The first large-scale movement was the Hong Gyeongnae Rebellion of 1811–1812 in Pyeongan province; it was followed by uprisings in the southern provinces during the early 1860s.

Statistics of the Joseon Period | *1392-1910*

Population growth

Year	Joseon	Seoul
1392	5,549,000	—
1400	5730000	—
1425	6,332,000	—
1450	7,112,000	—
1475	8,181,000	—
1500	9,412,000	—
1525	10,772,000	—
1550	11,963,000	—
1575	13,222,000	—
1600	11,722,000	—
1625	11,151,000	—
1650	10,889,000	95,569
1675	13,145,000	167,406
1700	14,359,000	—
1725	16,966,000	188,597
1750	18,657,000	180,090
1775	17,965,000	197,558
1800	18,497,000	193,783
1825	16,297,000	—
1850	16,476,000	204,053
1875	16,876,000	200,951
1900	17,082,000	—
1910	17,427,000	—

Sources: Kwon Taehwan and Sin Yongha. "Joseon wangjo sidae in'gu chujeong e gwanhan ilsingnon." *Donga munhwa* 14, (1977); Ko Donghwan. *Joseon hugi Seoul sangeop baldalsa* (Seoul: Jisik saneopsa, 1998), p28.

Changes in social structure: Class composition in Daegu, Danseong County, and Jirye County (Gyeongsang province)

(units = %)

Year	Region	Social class			
		Yangban	*Jungin*	Commoners	Unfree
1678	Danseong	13.6	4.2	35.5	46.7
1690	Daegu	9.2	—	53.7	37.1
1717	Danseong	19.1	8.7	46.3	25.9
1729	Daegu	18.7	—	54.6	26.7
1759	Danseong	24.4	10.6	47.4·	17.6
1783	Daegu	37.5	—	57.5	5
1786	Danseong	31.4	16.4	44.6	7.7
1842	Jirye	15.6	43	33.8	7.6
1858	Daegu	70.3	—	28.2	1.5

Sources: Daegu: Shikata Hiroshi. "Richō jinkō ni kansuru ichi kenkyū" in *Chōsen shakai hōseishi kenkyū* (1937); Danseong: Yi Jungu, "Joseon hugi yangban sinbun idong e gwanhan yeon'gu – ha." *Yeoksa hakbo* 97 (1988), p.2; Jirye: Yi Jungu. "19 segi Gyeongsangdo Jiryehyeon eupchi jiyeok ui sahoe guseong gwa ijok gamun." *Joseon sidaesa hakbo* 2 (1997), p.93.

Rural markets

	Number of rural markets			
Year	Gyeongsang province	Jeolla province	Chungcheong province	entire country
1593	71	53	53	334
1726	286	219	160	1,076
1770	276	215	156	1,064
1808	276	211	157	1,061
1830	268	186	155	1,052
1832	272	—	—	—
1872	—	169	105	—
1876	237	—	—	—
1909	201	148	125	849

Source: Jun Seong Ho, James B. Lewis, and Kang Han-Rog, "Korean Expansion and Decline from the Seventeenth to the Nineteenth Century: A View Suggested by Adam Smith," *The Journal of Economic History*, Vol. 68, No. 1 (Mar. 2008); Han Sanggwon, "18segimal–19segicho ui jangsi baldal e daehan gicho yeongu," *Hanguk saron* 7 (1981).

Quantity of copper cash in circulation
Sangpyeong tongbo

year	Quantity minted (in *nyang*)	Copper cash (in circulation)
1680	600,000	600,000
	1,700,000	1,760,000
1690	1,000,000	2,760,000
	1,200,000	3,960,000
1700	—	3,960,000
1710	—	3,960,000
1720	—	3,960,000
1730	250,000	4,210,000
1740	30,000	4,240,000
	400,000	4,640,000
1750	400,000	5,040,000
	607,000	5,647,000
	200,000	5,847,000
1760	400,000	6,247,000
1770	1,000,000	7,247,000
	500,000	7,747,000
1780	900,000	8,647,000
1790	100,000	8,747,000
	150,000	8,897,000
	140,000	9,037,000
	100,000	9,137,000
1800	300,000	9,437,000
1810	391,400	9,828,400
	80,000	9,908,400
	500,000	10,408,400
1820	367,500	10,775,900
1830	733,600	11,509,500
	784,300	12,293,800
1840	500,000	12,793,800
1850	1,571,500	14,365,300
	916,000	15,281,300

Source: Yi Heonchang. "1678—1865 Nyeon'gan hwapyeryang gwa hwapye gachi ui chui," *Gyeongje sahak* 27 (1999).

Land ownership

(units = %)

Units	1634		1720	
	landlords	land ownership	landlords	land ownership
Jinju (Nadong-ri)				
over 10 *gyeol*	0.4	9.2	0.3	30.1
5–10 *gyeol*	0.9	9.2	—	—
1–5 *gyeol*	14.0	46.4	8.8	26.8
50 *bu*–1 *gyeol*	13.5	14.6	10.7	15.6
25–50 *bu*	21.0	11.5	18.5	13.6
under 25 *bu*	50.2	9.1	61.7	13.9
Jinju (Geumdongeo-ri)				
over 10 *gyeol*	—	—	0.5	16.9
5–10 *gyeol*	0.8	11.7	0.5	8.2
1–5 *gyeol*	14.8	52.1	6.6	30.9
50 *bu*–1 *gyeol*	13.7	16.5	9.0	15.1
25–50 *bu*	13.7	8.6	13.8	11.6
under 25 *bu*	57.0	11.1	69.6	17.4
Sangju (Dandong-myeon)				
over 10 *gyeol*	—	—	—	—
5–10 *gyeol*	0.2	2.2	0.1	1.8
1–5 *gyeol*	20.3	55.2	9.3	35.7
50 *bu*–1 *gyeol*	18.8	21.4	15.4	27.5
25–50 *bu*	22.9	13.5	21.9	19.2
under 25 *bu*	37.7	7.7	53.5	15.8

Source: Gim Geontae, *Joseon sidae yangbanga ui nongeop gyeongyeong* (Seoul: Yeoksa piyeongsa, 2004); Yi Yeonghun, "Hanguksa e isseoseo geundaero ui ihaeng gwa teukjil," *Gyeongje sahak* 21 (1996).

Grain loans

(rice in *seok*)

Year	Grain loan quantity	Year	Grain loan quantity
Early 18th century	5,000,000	1797	9,380,000
1760	9,300,000	1807	9,995,599
1769	10,100,000	1828	8,000,000
1788	9,900,000	1862	8,000,000
1788	9,900,000		

Source: Jun Seongho, *Joseon hugi migasa yeongu* (Seoul: Han'guk haksul jeongbo, 2007), p. 194.

Units of measurement in Joseon

Unit	in Korean	in Chinese	Measurement
Units of length			
ri	리	釐	1 ri
bun	분	分	1 bun = 10 ri
chon	촌	寸	1 chon = 10 bun
cheok	척	尺	1 cheok = 10 chon
jang	장	丈	1 jang = 10 cheok
Units of distance			
jucheok	주척	周尺	1 jucheok = 10 chon
jang	장	丈	1 jang = 10 cheok
bo	보	步	1 bo = 5 or 6 cheok
ri	리	里	1 ri = 1,800 cheok
sik	식	息	1 sik = 30 ri
Units of volume			
jak	작	勺	1 jak
hop	홉	合	1 hop = 10 jak
doe	되	升	1 doe = 10 hop
mal	말	斗	1 mal = 10 doe
seok or seom	석 or 섬	石	1 seok/seom = 10 mal
sogok pyeongseok	소곡평석	小斛平石	1 sogok pyeongseok = 15 mal
daegok jeonseok	대곡전석	大斛全石	1 daegok jeonseok = 20 mal
Units of weight			
ri	리	釐	1 ri
bun	분	分	1 bun = 10 ri
jeon	전	錢	1 jeon = 10 bun
yang	양	兩	1 yang = 10 jeon
geun	근	斤	1 geun = 16 yang
Units of currency			
mun or pun	문/푼	文	1 mun/pun
jeon	전	錢	1 jeon = 10 mun/pun
nyang	냥	兩	1 nyang = 10 jeon
gwan	관	貫	1 gwan = 10 nyang

Source: *Hanguk ui doryanghyeong* (Seoul: National Folk Museum, 1997).

MONARCHS OF JOSEON

1392–1398	Taejo	[太祖 태조]
1398–1400	Jeongjong	[定宗 정종]
1400–1418	Taejong	[太宗 태종]
1418–1450	Sejong	[世宗 세종]
1450–1452	Munjong	[文宗 문종]
1452–1455	Danjong	[端宗 단종]
1455–1468	Sejo	[世祖 세조]
1468–1469	Yejong	[睿宗 예종]
1469–1494	Seongjong	[成宗 성종]
1494–1506	Yeonsangun	[燕山君 연산군]
1506–1544	Jungjong	[中宗 중종]
1544–1545	Injong	[仁宗 인종]
1545–1567	Myeongjong	[明宗 명종]
1567–1608	Seonjo	[宣祖 선조]
1608–1623	Gwanghaegun	[光海君 광해군]
1623–1649	Injo	[仁祖 인조]
1649–1659	Hyojong	[孝宗 효종]
1659–1674	Hyeonjong	[顯宗 현종]
1674–1720	Sukjong	[肅宗 숙종]
1720–1724	Gyeongjong	[景宗 경종]
1724–1776	Yeongjo	[英祖 영조]
1776–1800	Jeongjo	[正祖 정조]
1800–1834	Sunjo	[純祖 순조]
1834–1849	Heonjong	[憲宗 헌종]
1849–1863	Cheoljong	[哲宗 철종]
1863–1907	Gojong	[高宗 고종]
1907–1910	Sunjong	[純宗 순종]

CHRONOLOGY OF THE LATE JOSEON PERIOD

17TH CENTURY

1608, FIFTH MONTH: The Uniform Tax Law (Daedongbeop) is first introduced in Gyeonggi province.
: The Northerner faction comes to power after the coronation of Prince Gwanghae.

1609, SIXTH MONTH: Reestablishment of relations between Tokugawa Japan and Joseon.

1610: The physician Heo Jun (1539–1615) completes his *Exemplar of Korean Medicine* (*Dongeui Bogam*).

1611, TENTH MONTH: A palace without a name is renamed Gyeongun Palace (today's Deoksu Palace).

1612: Heo Gyun (1569–1618) writes the novel *The Tale of Hong Gildong*.

1613: Supporters of Prince Yeongchang are accused of treason, leading to the prince's exile and the rise of the Great Northerner faction (Gyechuk oksa).

1615: The chili pepper is introduced from Japan.

1616: Tobacco is introduced from Japan.

1619, THIRD MONTH: A combined Ming-Joseon force is defeated by the Manchus in the Battle of Sarhū; General Gang Hongnip surrenders to Nurhaci.

1623, THIRD MONTH: Gwanghaegun is forced to abdicate the throne by the pro-Ming Westerner faction.

1624, FIRST-SECOND MONTHS: Rebellion of Yi Gwal.

1627, FIRST MONTH: First Manchu invasion.
DATE UNKNOWN: The Dutch sailor Jan Janse Weltevree (1595–?) arrives on Jeju Island.

1636, TWELFTH MONTH: Second Manchu invasion.

1637, FIRST MONTH: King Injo surrenders to Qing. Joseon becomes a tributary of the Qing state.

1646, NINTH MONTH: A biannual market is opened for trade between Joseon and Qing on an island in the Amnok (Yalu) River.

1653: Hendrick Hamel (1630–1692) is shipwrecked on Jeju Island.

1659: A major factional conflict begins between the Southerner faction and the Westerner faction over mourning rites for King Hyojong.

1670: Yu Hyeongwon completes his multi-volume plan for government reform, *Bangye surok*.

1671: Joseon is struck by a great famine.

1674: The Southerner faction comes to power with the coronation of King Sukjong.

1678, FIRST MONTH: The *sangpyeong tongbo* copper coin is minted in large quantities for the first time.

1680, FOURTH MONTH: Fall of the Southerners from power.

1683, FOURTH MONTH: The Westerner faction splits into the Noron and Soron factions.

1689: Gim Manjung (1637–1692) writes the novel *The Dream of Nine Clouds* (*Guunmong*).
FIRST MONTH: Fall of the Noron faction from power (Gisa hwanguk).

1694, THIRD MONTH: The Noron faction regains power.

1697, FIRST MONTH: Rebellion of Jang Gilsan in the northern provinces.

18TH CENTURY

1706: The monopoly of Seoul's merchant houses is established in law.

1708, TWELFTH MONTH: The Uniform Tax Law system is introduced in Hwanghae province.

1721, FIRST MONTH: Yi Imyeong travels to Qing as an ambassador and returns with books on Catholicism, astronomy, and mathematics.
: Beginning of a series of events in which the Noron faction is charged with disloyalty and treason, leading to the execution of some Noron officials and the rise of the Soron faction to power (Sinim sahwa).

1725, FIRST MONTH: King Yeongjo attempts to overcome factional conflict in politics through a new policy of impartiality (*tangpyeongchaek*).

1727: King Yeongjo expels Noron hardliners and brings Soron officials into the government (Jeongmi hwanguk).

1728, THIRD MONTH: The Musin Rebellion begins in Chungcheong province.

1732, SEVENTH MONTH: An attempt is made to ban the cultivation of tobacco in the three southern provinces due to fears that it is threatening food supplies.

1734: Jeong Seon paints his famous work *Geumgang Mountains*.

1750, SEVENTH MONTH: The military cloth tax is reformed to reduce the burden on commoners (Gyunyeokbeop).

1762: Crown Prince Sado is killed by being locked in a rice chest.

1763: A diplomatic mission to Japan returns with sweet potatoes.

CHINA
1368–1644: Ming
1644–1911: Qing
   1661–1722: Kangxi Emperor
   1735–1796: Qianlong Emperor
   1839–1842: First Opium War
   1856–1860: Second Opium War

JAPAN
1603–1867: Tokugawa period
   1602–1605: Tokugawa Ieyasu
   1623–1651: Tokugawa Iemitsu
   1716–1745: Tokugawa Yoshimune
   1853: Arrival of Commodore Perry

19TH CENTURY [TO 1863]

1768, FIRST MONTH: The "Three Prohibitions" – against catching cattle, felling pines, and brewing alcohol - are enforced in order to promote agricultural productivity.

1776, NINTH MONTH: A royal library called the Gyujanggak is established.

1778, SEVENTH MONTH: Bak Jega (1750–1805) publishes *Discourse on Northern Learning*.

1780, TWELFTH MONTH: Bak Jiwon writes *Jehol Diary*.

1784, THIRD MONTH: Yi Seunghun (1756–1801) returns from Beijing with Catholic books.
TWELFTH MONTH: Gim Hongdo (1745–1809) completes a series of genre paintings depicting everyday life in Joseon (Danwon pungsokdo cheop).

1785: Yi Seunghun establishes the first Catholic church in Joseon.

1787: A French ship surveys the coast of Jeju Island and approaches Ulleung Island.

1791, SECOND MONTH: The Commercial Equalization Act abolishes the privileges of many of the city merchant houses, but leaves those of the seven elite merchant houses intact.
ELEVENTH MONTH: Martyrdom of yangban Yun Jichung, a convert to Catholicism.

1796, NINTH MONTH: Construction work on a new fortified city at Suwon is completed.

1797, NINTH MONTH: The British ship *Providence* enters the harbor at Dongnae.

1800, SEVENTH MONTH: King Sunjo comes to the throne at the age of ten and the Queen Dowager Jeongsun becomes regent.

1801, FIRST MONTH: The central government decides to free some of its unfree people and the registers of unfree people are burned.
SECOND MONTH: First persecution of Catholics.

1805, FIRST MONTH: Sunjo's father-in-law Gim Josun seizes power, marking the start of a period in which Joseon monarchs are dominated by royal in-law families (sedo jeongchi).

1808, EIGHTH MONTH: A comprehensive manual of governance entitled *Ten Thousand Techniques of Government* is completed.

1811, SECOND MONTH: The last major diplomatic mission to Japan is dispatched.
TWELFTH MONTH: Rebellion of Hong Gyeongnae begins in Pyeongan Province.

1812, FOURTH MONTH: Hong Gyeongnae is killed and his rebellion is defeated.

1813, TWELFTH MONTH: An uprising breaks out on Jeju Island.

1818, EIGHTH MONTH: Jeong Yagyong completes *Admonitions on Governing the People* (*Mongmin simseo*).

1821, EIGHTH MONTH: A cholera epidemic spreads through Pyongyang and Hwanghae.

1823: Publication of Han Chiyun's *History of Korea* (*Haedong yeoksa*) covering the period from Dangun to Goryeo.

1832, SIXTH MONTH: The British East India Company trading ship *Lord Amherst* sails up Joseon's west coast stopping at various islands and requesting the opening of trade.

1833, SECOND MONTH: Severe rioting breaks out in Seoul in response to soaring rice prices.

1834, ELEVENTH MONTH: Heonjong comes to throne at the age of seven, and the Queen Dowager Sunwon becomes regent.

1839, THIRD MONTH: Second persecution of Catholics.

1846, NINTH MONTH: Third persecution of Catholics.

1851, SECOND MONTH: Uprising in Ddukseom in Seoul.

1859, FOURTH MONTH: The establishment of new Confucian academies (seowon) is prohibited.

1860, FOURTH MONTH: Choe Jeu (1824–1864) founds the Donghak (Eastern Learning) religion.

1861, NINTH MONTH: A Russian ship arrives at Wonsan requesting the opening of trade.
DATE UNKNOWN: Gim Jeongho creates the *Daedong yeojido*, a map of the Korean peninsula.

1862, SECOND MONTH: A peasant uprising in Jinju and the surrounding area begins a year of peasant revolt all over the country.

1863, TWELFTH MONTH: King Gojong ascends the throne at the age of eleven and his father becomes regent.

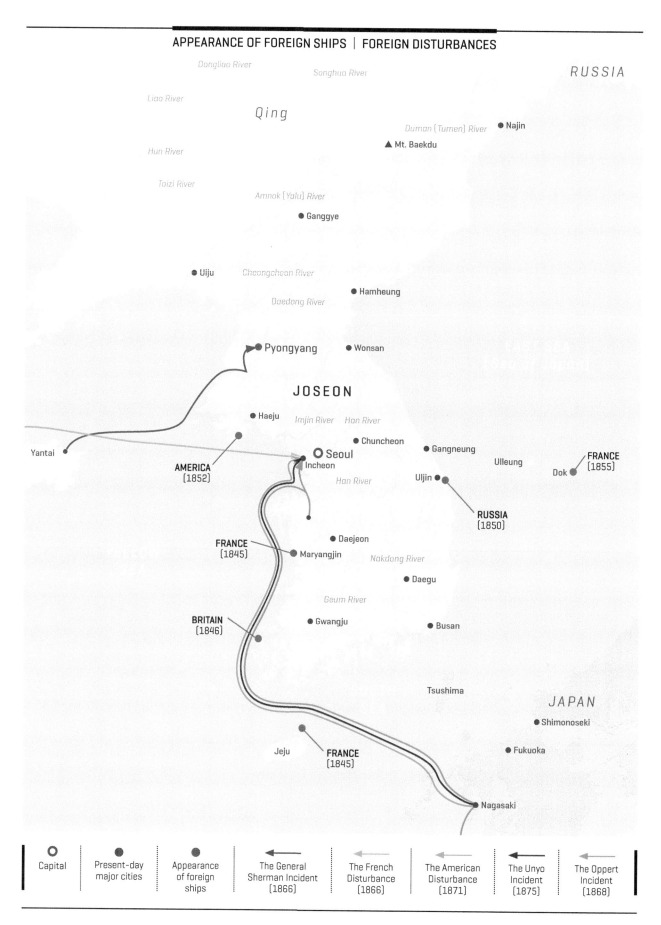

Dongliao River

Songhua River

RUSSIA

Liao River

Qing

Duman (Tumen) River ● Najin

▲ Mt. Baekdu

Hun River

Taizi River

Amnok (Yalu) River

● Ganggye

● Uiju *Cheongcheon River*

● Hamheung

Daedong River

➤ ● Pyongyang ● Wonsan

JOSEON

● Haeju *Imjin River* *Han River*

● Chuncheon ● Gangneung

Yantai ◯ Seoul Ulleung **FRANCE**
  Incheon Dok ● **[1855]**

AMERICA
[1852] *Han River* Uljin ●

RUSSIA
[1850]

FRANCE ● Daejeon
[1845] ● Maryangjin *Nakdong River*

● Daegu

Geum River

BRITAIN ● Gwangju
[1846] ● Busan

Tsushima *JAPAN*

● Shimonoseki

Jeju **FRANCE** ● Fukuoka
[1845]

● Nagasaki

| ◯ Capital | ● Present-day major cities | ● Appearance of foreign ships | ← The General Sherman Incident [1866] | ← The French Disturbance [1866] | ← The American Disturbance [1871] | ← The Unyo Incident [1875] | ← The Oppert Incident [1868] |

7

THE LATE NINETEENTH CENTURY

Gojong (r. 1863–1907) and **Sunjong** (r. 1907–1910), the second-to-last and last monarchs of the Joseon period. [Cornell University Library–Willard Straight Papers]

China's defeat by the Western powers in the Opium Wars shocked the East Asian states, auguring the end of the Chinese world order. Foreign imperialism both exacerbated political instability in Joseon and led to the rise of new political actors. In Seoul, a new group emerged called the Enlightenment Faction, and they engaged in a struggle for power with the Daewongun, who was the father of the monarch, and Queen Min and her faction. In the countryside, decades of growing peasant unrest intensified into a countrywide rebellion with the Gabo Peasants' War of 1894. At the same time, China, Japan, and Russia contended with each other for dominance on the peninsula, leading to the outbreak of two major wars. With Japan's victory in the Sino-Japanese War, the Treaty of Shimonoseki officially ended China's suzerain status over Joseon.

The Open Ports

Under the Ganghwa Treaty of 1876, Joseon agreed with Japan that it would open the three ports of Busan, Incheon, and Wonsan to Japanese trade. From 1882, Joseon concluded a number of unequal treaties with the Western powers, leading to the further opening of the ports of Jinnampo, Mokpo, and Gunsan to foreign trade. The opening enabled foreign powers to acquire concessions from the Joseon government.

Wonsan harbor in 1895.
[PD–Library of Congress]

Incheon harbor in 1903.
[PD–Library of Congress]

O
Capital

●
Major cities

⚓
Open ports

O
Bay

CONCESSIONS

Ⓛ
Logging rights

Ⓜ
Mining rights

Ⓖ
Gold mining rights

Mt. Baekdu ▲

CHEONGJIN
[1908]

HAMGYEONG

SINUIJU
[1909]

PYEONGAN

Ⓖ Unsan

Cheongcheon River

YEONGHEUNG BAY

WONSAN
[1880]

JINNAMPO
[1897]

● Pyongyang

Ⓖ Suan

HWANGHAE

● Haeju

● Gaeseong

Imjin River

Han River

GANGWON

INCHEON
[1883]

O Hanyang

Han River

NAMYANG BAY

GYEONGGI

Jiksan

CHUNGCHEONG

Nakdong River

YEONGIL BAY

GUNSAN
[1899]

● Daejeon

Geum River

● Daegu

JEOLLA

GYEONGSANG

BUSAN
[1899]

● Gwangju

MOKPO
[1897]

Seoul in the Late Nineteenth Century | *1880s–1910*

Foreign imperialism brought significant changes to Seoul from the mid-nineteenth century. Foreign powers established a presence in the southwestern part of the capital as well as in the area between Seoul and the Han River. The city also became the scene of violent political incidents between old and new political forces. From the 1890s, Seoul began to transform into a modern city, helping to lay the foundation for its tremendous growth in the twentieth century.

Mt. Inwang

House of Gim Okgyun

Gyeongbok Palace

House of Bak Gyusu

House of Seo Gwangbeom

Changdeok Palace

Unhyeon Palace

Japanese Consulate

Daehan Maeil Sinbo

Jongmyo

Ujeongguk

Seobuk Hakhoe

House of Bak Yeonghyo

Independence Gate

Gyeonghui Palace

Wongaksa

House of Min Yeonghwan

Danseongsa

Independence Hall

JONGNO

Russian Consulate

Hwangseong sinmun

Deoksu Palace

Great West Gate

House of Choe Namseon

American Legation

Underwood Academy

Jejungwon

Ewha Academy

Jeongdong First Church

Baejae Academy

Office of the *Independent*

Great South Gate

●	○	○	○	○	▟	⫿⫿⫿⫿⫿	⫿⫿⫿⫿⫿
Palace	Important sites	Newspaper offices	House	Sites related to the Gapsin Coup [1884]	Gate	Old city wall	Palace wall

The Year 1894 | *Gabo Peasants' War, Sino-Japanese War*

The tensions caused by internal breakdown and external threat climaxed in the year 1894. When the Joseon government was unable to suppress the Gabo Peasants' War, it requested help from China. Japan used the dispatch of Chinese troops to launch the Sino-Japanese War, which led to the end of Joseon's tributary relations with the Qing. Joseon also attempted large-scale reforms known as the Gabo Reforms, the first effort to create a modern nation-state.

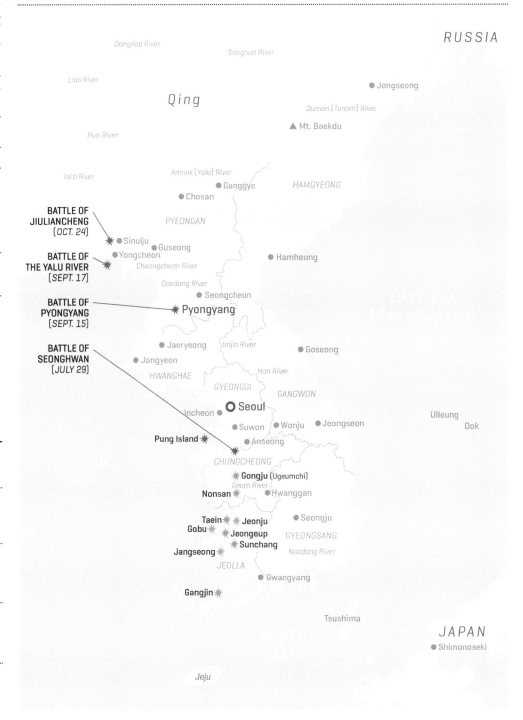

○
Capital

●
Sites of earlier
peasant uprisings

✳
First uprising
(Gabo Peasants' War)

✴
Second uprising
(Gabo Peasants' War)

✳
Battles of the
Sino-Japanese War

CHRONOLOGY OF THE YEAR 1894

JANUARY 10: The Gabo Peasants' War begins with an uprising in Gobu led by Jeon Bongjun (1854–1895).

FEBRUARY 22: Gim Okgyun is assassinated in Shanghai.

APRIL: Peasant uprisings spread to Chungcheong, Gangwon, and Gyeongsang provinces. **27:** The peasant army occupies Jeonju.

MAY 5: The Qing army lands at Asan in Chungcheong province. **6:** The Japanese navy arrives in Incheon. **7:** After a negotiated agreement, the peasant army withdraws from Jeonju. Japanese troops occupy Seoul.

JUNE 21: Japanese troops occupy Gyeongbok Palace and return the Daewongun to power.

JULY 15: Gim Hongjip (1842–1896) becomes prime minister and the Gabo Reform program begins. **25:** The Japanese launch a surprise attack on Chinese warships near Pung Island (Feng Island). **28:** The Battle of Seonghwan (Battle of Asan), the first major land battle of the Sino-Japanese War.

AUGUST 1: War officially declared between China and Japan.

SEPTEMBER 3: Beginning of the second peasant uprising. **15:** The Qing army is defeated by Japan in the Battle of Pyongyang. **17:** The Japanese navy defeats the Chinese Beiyang Fleet in the Battle of the Yalu River.

OCTOBER 8: The united peasant armies are defeated by Japanese and Joseon government forces in the Battle of Ugeumchi (South Chungcheong province). **21:** Plans for a coup by the Daewongun come to light. **24:** Battle of Jiuliancheng.

NOVEMBER 21: Formation of the second Gim Hongjip cabinet; Battle of Lüshunkou in Manchuria. **25:** The peasant army fights its last battle in Taein (North Jeolla province).

DECEMBER 2: Peasant leader Jeon Bongjun is captured in Sunchang (Jeolla province).

Attack on Daedong Gate, Pyongyang. Woodblock print by Watanabe Nobukazu, 1894. (Museum of Fine Arts, Boston)

1863, TWELFTH MONTH [1864 SOLAR]: Gojong comes to the throne at the age of twelve with his father serving as regent.

1864, FOURTH MONTH: Execution of Choe Jeu, the founder of the Donghak religion.

1865, FOURTH MONTH: The reconstruction of Gyeongbok Palace begins.

1866, FIRST MONTH: Third persecution of Catholics.
SEVENTH MONTH: The General Sherman incident.
EIGHTH MONTH: A French naval force is sent to Ganghwa Island to demand reparations for the killing of French priests.

1868, FOURTH MONTH: A German merchant, Ernst Oppert, attempts to steal the remains of the Daewongun's father and hold them for ransom.
FOURTH MONTH: Attack by an American naval force on Ganghwa Island.

1871, THIRD MONTH: Outbreak of the Yi Pilje Rebellion in North Gyeongsang province.

1873, ELEVENTH MONTH: The end of the regency of the Daewongun.

1875, EIGHTH MONTH: The *Unyo* incident.

1876, SECOND MONTH: Signing of the Ganghwa Treaty between Japan and Joseon. Opening of the port of Busan.

1878, SIXTH MONTH: Japan's Dai-Ichi Bank opens a branch in Busan.

1880, THIRD MONTH: Opening of Wonsan port.
TWELFTH MONTH: Establishment of the Tongni gimu amun.

1881, FOURTH MONTH: A delegation (Sinsa yuramdan) is sent to Japan.

1882, FOURTH MONTH: Conclusion of a treaty with the United States. Signing of a treaty with Great Britain.
FIFTH MONTH: Signing of a treaty with Germany.
SIXTH MONTH: The Imo Soldiers' Riot breaks out in Seoul.
SEVENTH MONTH: The Daewongun is taken into forced exile in Tianjin.

1883, FIRST MONTH: The Taegeukgi is adopted as the national flag.
TENTH MONTH: The first newspaper, *Hanseong sunbo*, begins publication.

1884, FIFTH INTERCALARY MONTH: Joseon concludes treaties with Russia and Italy.
SEPTEMBER: Arrival of Protestant missionary Horace Allen.
TENTH MONTH: The Gapsin Coup.
MONTH UNKNOWN: Laying of the first submarine telegraph cable across the Korea Strait.

1885, THIRD MONTH: Great Britain seizes the Geomun Islands off the south coast of Joseon.
TENTH MONTH: Yuan Shikai is appointed Qing Imperial Resident in Seoul.
MONTH UNKNOWN: China builds a telegraph line from Uiju to Seoul.

1886, MAY 3: Joseon signs a treaty with France.

1888, JUNE: The Seoul–Busan telegraph line is completed.

1889, MAY: Yu Giljun completes his *Seoyu gyeonmun*.

1894, JANUARY 10: Beginning of the Gabo Peasants' War with an uprising in Gobu led by Jeon Bongjun.
JULY: Beginning of the Sino-Japanese War. Beginning of the Gabo Reforms.

SEPTEMBER: Outbreak of the second peasant uprising.
OCTOBER: The united peasant armies are defeated in the Battle of Ugeumchi.
DECEMBER 2: Donghak leader Jeon Bongjun is captured at Sunchang in Jeolla Province.

1895, APRIL 17: The Treaty of Shimonoseki brings a formal end to the tributary relationship between Joseon and Qing.
OCTOBER 8: Assassination of Queen Min.

1896, JANUARY: Joseon uses its own era name (Geonyang).
FEBRUARY: Gojong takes refuge in the Russian Legation (Agwan pacheon).
APRIL: Founding of the newspaper *The Independent* (*Dongnip sinmun*).
JULY: Founding of the Independence Club.

1897, FEBRUARY: Gojong leaves the Russian legation and returns to the Deoksu Palace.
OCTOBER: The country's name is changed to the Great Han Empire (DaeHan jeguk).

1898, MARCH: The Independence Club holds the first public rally (Manmin gongdonghoe).
DECEMBER: The Independence Club is forcibly disbanded.

1899, MAY: The first tram line is opened in Seoul.
SEPTEMBER: The first railway line is opened between Seoul and Incheon.

1900, MARCH: The dockworkers of Mokpo hold the first strike in Korean history.
JULY: The first bridge across the Han River in Seoul is completed.

1901, FIFTH MONTH: Outbreak of the Yi Jaesu rebellion in Jeju Island.

QING (1644–1911)	JAPAN
1861–1875: Tongzhi Emperor (Zaichun)	**1868–1912:** Meiji Period
1861: Establishment of the Zongli Yamen	**1877:** Satsuma Rebellion
1871: Li Hongzhang becomes Viceroy of Zhili	**1885:** Signing of the Convention of Tientsin (Li-Itō Convention)
1875–1908: Guangxu Emperor (Zaitian)	**1905:** Taft-Katsura Agreement; Treaty of Portsmouth
1908–1911: Xuantong Emperor (Puyi)	

1902, DECEMBER: The first Koreans emigrate to Hawaii.

1904, JULY: Founding of the newspaper *Daehan maeil sinbo*.
AUGUST: Founding of the pro-Japanese organization Iljinhoe.

1905, JANUARY: Opening of the Seoul–Busan railway.
NOVEMBER: Signing of the Protectorate Treaty (Eulsa joyak).
DECEMBER: Itō Hirobumi is appointed as Resident-General of Korea.

1906, MARCH–JUNE: New uprisings of the Righteous Armies break out in various provinces.
JULY: Publication of the first new-style novel, *Tears of Blood* (*Hyeol ui nu*) by Yi Injik.

1907, JANUARY: Beginning of the Movement to Repay the Government Debt.
APRIL: Gojong secretly sends emissaries to the Hague Peace Conference.
JULY: Emperor Gojong is forced to abdicate in favour of his son Sunjong.
AUGUST: Disbandment of the Joseon army.

1908, JULY: Korea's first purpose-built theatre, Wongaksa, is established.
AUGUST: The serialization of Sin Chaeho's "A New Way of Reading Korean History" (Doksa sillon).
NOVEMBER: Choe Namseon founds the journal *Sonyeon* (Youth).
DECEMBER: Founding of the Oriental Development Company.

1909, OCTOBER: An Junggeun assassinates Itō Hirobumi at Harbin train station. The founding of the Bank of Korea.

1910, AUGUST 22: Signing of the annexation treaty.

National flag of Korea, c. 1890. Once owned by Owen N. Denny. Oldest surviving flag with the *taegeuk* symbol. (National Museum of Korea)

Independence Gate in 1904. (PD–Library of Congress)

RUSSIA

CHINA

Duman [Tumen] River

Seishin [Cheongjin]
Ranan [Nanam]
Kyōjō [Gyeongseong]

KANKYŌ
[HAMGYEONG]

Amnok [Yalu] River

Shingishū● ◉Gishū [Uiju]
[Sinuiju]

HEIAN
[PYEONGAN]

◉Kankō
[Hamheung]

◉Heijō
[Pyongyang]

●Genzan
[Wonsan]

KŌKAI
[HWANGHAE]

KŌGEN
[GANGWON]

Kaishū◉
[Haeju]

KEIKI
[GYEONGGI]

◉Shunsen
[Chuncheon]

O Keijō
[Seoul]

Jinsen●
[Incheon]

CHŪSEI
[CHUNGCHEONG]

◉Seishū
[Cheongju]

Kōshū◉
[Gongju]

●Taiden
[Daejeon]

KEISHŌ
[GYEONGSANG]

◉Zenshū
[Jeonju]

◉Taikyū
[Daegu]

ZENRA
[JEOLLA]

◉Koshū
[Gwangju]

◉Shinshū
[Jinju]

●Fusan
[Busan]

●Moppo
[Mokpo]

Tsushima

JAPAN

Saishū
[Jeju]

●Fukuoka

◉ Provincial government offices   ● City spelled in Japanese [name of city in Korean]

8

THE JAPANESE OCCUPATION PERIOD

Terauchi Masatake. Governor-General of Korea, 1910–1916. [PD–Library of Congress]

Ugaki Kazushige. Governor-General of Korea, 1927 and 1931–1936. [PD–Japan]

On August 22, 1910, Prime Minister Yi Wanyong signed the treaty that turned over control of the country to the Japanese. The takeover of Korea was the first step in Japan's expansion into mainland Asia that later targeted Manchuria and led to all-out war with China. Historians generally divide the history of the occupation into three periods: the heavy repression of the years 1910–1919; the years of the so-called "Cultural Policy," 1919–1931; and the period of wartime mobilization, 1931–1945. Lasting for over three decades, the occupation ended on August 15, 1945 after Japan's surrender to the Allied forces in World War II.

The Government General of Chosen, Keijo.

府督總鮮朝（所名城京）

Postcard of the **Government-General building**. [Kernbeisser]

Society

During the occupation period, Korea underwent some of the social changes associated with the transition to modernity. The population began to increase rapidly, and people were increasingly living in cities. Modern education also spread rapidly with primary school attendance reaching 50 percent in the early 1940s. However, the only university in the country was Keijo Imperial University which was founded in 1923. By the end of the period, the percentage of peasants decreased from 80 percent to about 70 percent. At the same time, the differentiation of the peasant class accelerated as large numbers of them became landless tenants. From the early 1920s, peasants began to organize peasant unions, and tenant farmers engaged in protests against landlords. A women's movement emerged, and their presence was increasing in modern schools. However, the "comfort woman" issue demonstrated how precarious their status was. Many Koreans went into exile or went abroad to make a living. Tens of thousands of landless peasants went to Manchuria to find land to farm, and large numbers of laborers worked in factories and mines in Japan.

Culture

The introduction of modern ideologies continued in this period as Western forms of knowledge became more widespread. Both Christianity and the Cheondogyo religion grew rapidly and played important roles in education, the press, and social movements. Within Christianity, Protestants were more numerous than Catholics, and the largest Protestant sects were the Methodists and the Presbyterians. Though it came under criticism in this period, Confucianism remained strong; in fact, the Confucian family system became strengthened in some ways. The intellectual world was centered in Seoul; with the relaxation of publication laws in 1919, vernacular newspapers began publishing again, and there was a boom in the publication of journals. Modern literature fully emerged in this period; the first silent films were produced in the 1920s; and radio broadcasts began in 1927. A modern leisure culture developed in cities such as Seoul and Pyongyang, and new cultural figures emerged such as the so-called "modern girl." Some important archaeological discoveries were made in this period, such as the Seokguram grotto, but many important heritage sites were damaged or destroyed as well, such as the royal palaces.

Economy

The main focus of colonial economic policy was to turn Korea into Japan's main supplier of rice. From 1910 to 1918, the colonial government conducted a cadastral survey throughout the country that established a modern land registration system and a revision of the tax system. It became the largest landowner in the country, much of it owned by the Oriental Development Company. In 1920, Japan implemented the Program to Increase Rice Production that introduced Japanese varieties of rice and required farmers to undertake land improvements and adopt scientific methods of cultivation. It achieved a modest increase in production and accelerated the trends of the late Joseon period. By the mid-1930s, half of the harvest was being exported, supplying about 10 percent of Japan's domestic consumption. Since the increase of production lagged behind the increase of exports, per capita consumption of rice declined. Tenancy increased significantly, and tenant farmers often had to pay up to 70–80 percent of their crop to landlords. Agriculture became increasingly commercialized with farmers focusing on a few cash crops; it became more subject to market forces and the intervention of the colonial government. The Japanese established a centralized financial system, headed by the Bank of Chosen and the Industrial Bank of Chosen, that enhanced its control over the colonial economy. Korean industrialists began to emerge after 1919, and industrialization was promoted from the early 1930s in order to support the war effort. The emphasis was on light industry, such as textiles, in the south, and heavy industry was concentrated in the northern part of the peninsula. Korean-owned businesses tended to be more numerous and smaller in scale than Japanese ones, but a few later became major conglomerates, such as Samsung.

Postcard of **Hwasin Department Store** in Jongno Boulevard. [Kernbeisser]

Advanced mathematics class at **Ewha Girl's School**. [USC–Taylor Collection]

Politics

The head of the colonial government was the Governor-General (Sōtoku), and in contrast to Taiwan, all of the appointees were from the military. He reported directly to the emperor and was thus not under the authority of any Japanese government office; he had virtually complete authority over the country, including over the Japanese army and navy units in its territory. The Government-General originally consisted of four departments (Home Affairs, Finance, Judicial, and Agriculture, Commerce, and Industry) and a secretariat. There were also "Affiliated Offices" that reported directly to the Governor-General such as the Railway Bureau and the Land Survey Bureau. The territory continued to be divided into thirteen provinces, with Pyeongan, Hamgyeong, Chungcheong, Jeolla, and Gyeongsang further divided into northern and southern provinces. Provincial government offices in Gishū, Kyōjō, and Shinshū were later moved to Shingishū, Ranan, and Fusan, respectively. Japan reorganized the provincial administration system, undermining the existing *gun* (county) system and introducing the *myeon* system of Japan.

Koreans engaged in resistance against the Japanese both within and outside of the country. Armed resistance movements were particularly active in the Manchuria region, and a domestic nationalist movement emerged with the March First Movement of 1919. However, the movement soon underwent an ideological split into nationalist and socialist camps; there were efforts to create a united front, but they ended in failure. At the grassroots level, the peasant movement became more modern in nature with a central organization in Seoul; more radical elements organized Red Peasant Unions which were strong in the northern regions. A labor movement also emerged in the 1920s; despite the small number of industrial workers, they were able to engage in collective action, including organizing general strikes.

Seoul under Japanese Rule

When the occupation began in 1910, Japan changed the name of the former capital to Keijō (Gyeongseong) and undertook a reorganization of its administrative structure. Though many Japanese began to move to the city, the population decreased in the 1910s but increased steadily from the early 1920s. The Japanese primarily lived in the southern part of the city, where the Government–General building originally stood, and Koreans lived in the northern part – more specifically, north of Cheonggye Stream. Seoul began to look more and more like a modern city with the renovation of existing roads, the construction of new buildings, new roads, and cultural facilities, and the expansion of electricity, trolleys, and modern lighting. In the process, many palace buildings and much of the city walls were torn down, and many place names were officially changed to Japanese ones. The city was also a site of political struggle where some of the most important incidents of those years occurred.

On March 1, 1919, twenty-nine leaders gathered at a Chinese restaurant in Seoul and read aloud a Declaration of Independence. Peaceful demonstrations occurred on the streets of Seoul and other cities, organized in secret during the previous few months. When the colonial government, taken by surprise, began to suppress the protests violently, uprisings broke out throughout the country, lasting into the summer.

THE LOCATION OF UPRISINGS

○
Regions with
multiple large-scale
demonstrations

●
Sites of
demonstrations with
more than 10,000
participants

·
Sites of
small-scale
demonstrations

1911, JUNE: Establishment of the Sinheung Military Academy in Liuhe.

1919, MARCH 17: Establishment of the Korean National Council (Dae Han gungmin uihoe) in Vladivostok.

1920, JUNE: Battle of Fengwudong (Bongodong).

1920, OCTOBER: Battle of Qingshanli (Cheongsan-ri).

1921, JUNE: The Free City (Alekseyevsk) Incident.

1929, APRIL: Establishment of the Gungminbu in Jilin.

1929, DECEMBER 20: Formation of the Joseon Revolutionary Party (Joseon Hyeongmyeongdang).

1932, SEPTEMBER: Battle of Shuangchengbao (Ssangseongbo) near Harbin.

1933, APRIL: Battle of Sidaohezi (Sadohaja).

1937, JUNE 4: Battle of Bocheonbo in Gapsan county.

SHANGHAI / SOUTH CHINA

1919, APRIL: Establishment of the Korean Provisional Government (KPG).

1919, NOVEMBER: Formation of the anarchist organization Uiyeoldan.

1922, MARCH 28: Attempted assassination of General Tanaka Giichi.

1925, MARCH 23: Impeachment of Syngman Rhee by the KPG.

1930, JANUARY: Formation of the Korean Independence Party (Gim Gu).

1932, APRIL 29: Yun Bonggil sets off a bomb at a ceremony in Hongkou Park.

1935, JULY: Five parties combine to form the Joseon National Revolutionary Party (Joseon minjok hyeongmyeongdang) in Nanjing.

1940, SEPTEMBER: Formation of the Korea Restoration Army (Hanguk gwangbokgun) in Chongqing.

JAPAN

1932, JANUARY 8: Yi Bongchang attempts to assassinate Emperor Hirohito in Tokyo (Sakuradamon Incident).

The Independence Movement

Armed resistance against the Japanese begean in the years before the occupation began in 1910. Most of the armed groups were located in Manchuria, where a sizable Korean settler community developed. Though a provisional government was established in Shanghai in 1919, the resistance movement was not unified. There were instances in which regional organizations banded together in an effort to create a more unified exile government. With the outbreak of the Sino-Japanese War, Korean resistance groups became active in other areas of China.

△	●	→		▬▬	✳
Location of Korean Independence Armies	Korean Provisional Goverment	Movement of the Korean Provisional Goverment	Areas of activity of Independence Armies	Areas under Japanese occupation 1941	Battle sites

Comfort Stations | *1932–1945*

During its wars of expansion in Asia, the Japanese army had teenage girls and young women serve as sex slaves, euphemistically called "comfort women." The first "comfort station" was established in 1932, and they became widespread after the Nanjing Massacre in 1937. Credible estimates of the total number of sex slaves range from 50,000 to 200,000 women. The largest proportion were Korean, but there were also Chinese, Taiwanese, Filipina, Indonesian, Vietnamese, Burmese, Australian, and Dutch women, as well as Japanese. The locations of comfort stations have been taken from research on testimonies by former sex slaves, soldiers, and other witnesses.

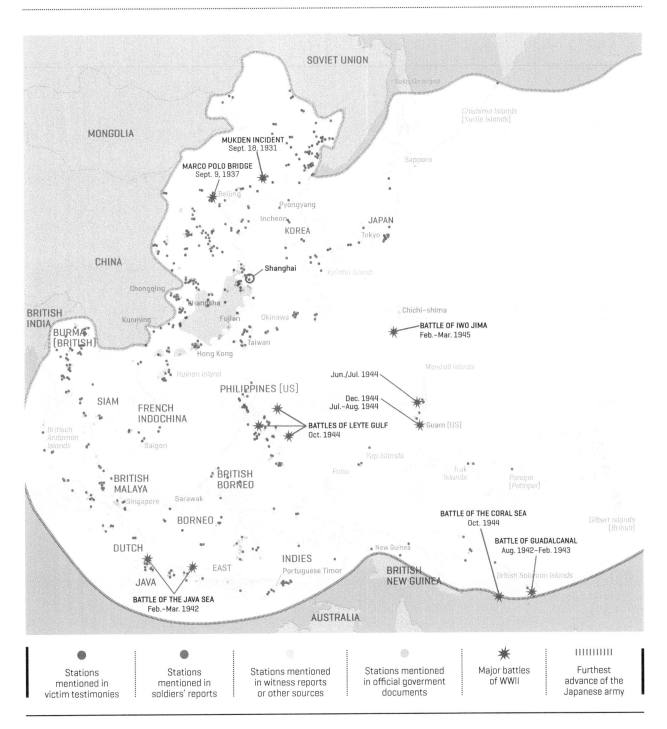

❶ Seoul–Busan
1899–1905
580 km

❷ Seoul–Uiju
1904–1906
706km

❸ Honam
1910–1914
286km

❹ Seoul–Wonsan
1910–1914
226km

❺ Hamgyeong
1914–1928
792km

❻ Domun
1927–1933
162km

❼ Jeolla
1929–1936
199km

❽ Hyesan
1931–1937
142km

❾ Manpo
1931–1939
342km

❿ Pyongyang–Wonsan
1936–1941
213km

⓫ Jungang
1936–1942
383km

**RAILROADS
AND INDUSTRIAL SITES**

Station

Railroad

Main industrial area

Hydroelectric dam

Industrial
sites

Economic Changes under Japanese Rule

Japanese rule brought about significant economic changes in Korea. The main goals of its economic polices were to turn Korea into its main foreign supplier of rice and, later, to allow a certain degree of industrialization to facilitate its continental expansion.

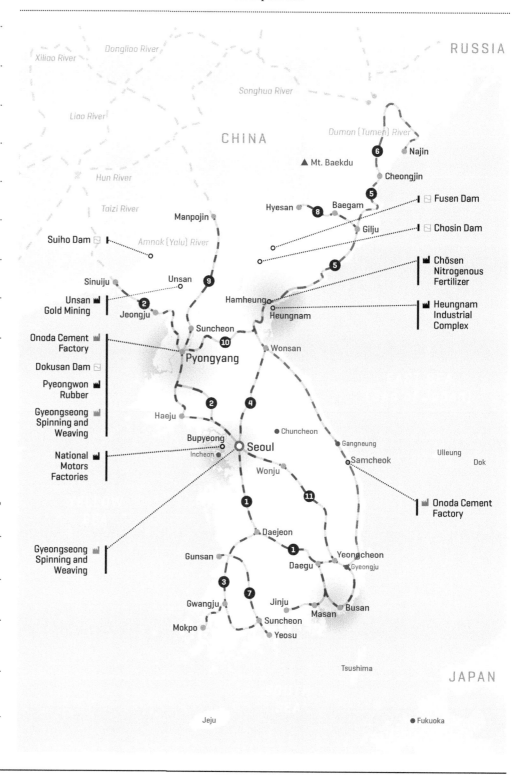

Statistics of the Japanese Occupation Period | 1910–1945

Population and birth rate
1910–1945

Year	Population			Estimated birth rate (per 1,000 people)
	Government-General	Bak Gyeongsuk	Nakseongdae Institute	
1911	14,055,869	16,689,683	16,614,967	20.1
1912	14,827,101	16,839,685	16,895,760	28.9
1913	15,458,863	16,992,223	17,181,298	29.8
1914	15,929,962	17,159,002	17,471,662	28.1
1915	16,278,389	17,326,883	17,767,782	27.4
1916	16,648,129	17,456,221	17,934,799	33.9
1917	16,968,997	17,568,550	18,103,386	33.9
1918	17,057,032	17,654,546	18,273,558	34.1
1919	17,149,909	17,731,977	18,445,329	27.8
1920	17,288,989	17,854,109	18,619,205	27.7
1921	17,452,918	18,092,988	18,796,087	29.9
1922	17,626,761	18,321,291	18,974,650	34.0
1923	17,884,963	18,556,171	19,154,909	40.7
1924	18,068,116	18,767,307	19,336,881	38.6
1925	19,015,528	19,020,000	19,522,945	38.4
1926	19,103,900	19,327,123	19,821,646	35.8
1927	19,137,638	19,603,184	20,124,917	36.9
1928	19,189,699	19,844,562	20,432,828	38.1
1929	19,331,061	20,130,887	20,745,451	38.3
1930	20,256,563	20,438,000	21,058,305	38.6
1931	20,262,958	20,860,111	21,414,190	35.6
1932	20,599,876	21,210,382	21,776,090	30.2
1933	20,791,321	21,571,412	22,144,106	29.2
1934	21,125,827	21,893,217	22,518,341	30.0
1935	21,891,180	22,208,000	22,899,038	29.5
1936	22,047,836	22,572,981	23,173,826	28.8
1937	22,355,485	22,913,494	23,451,912	29.0
1938	22,633,751	23,241,991	23,733,335	36.1
1939	22,800,647	23,435,448	24,018,135	36.9
1940	23,709,057	23,547,000	24,301,959	32.0
1941	24,703,897	23,828,080	—	33.3
1942	26,361,401	24,234,052	—	39.7
1943	26,662,150	24,576,032	—	32.9
1944	—	25,120,000	—	—
1945	—	25,266,258	—	—

Sources: Government-General of Chosen; Bak Gyeongsuk,"Singminji sigi (1910–1945) Joseon ui ingu dongtae wa gujo," *Hanguk inguhak*, vol.32, no.3 (Aug. 2009).

GDP and economic growth rate
1911–1940

Year	Nominal GDP (1,000s of yen)	Real GDP (1,000s of yen)	GDP growth rate	Per capita GDP (yen)
1911	518,896	950,054	—	56.9
1912	633,696	986,311	3.8	58.6
1913	703,084	1,065,840	8.1	62.7
1914	634,134	1,133,886	6.4	66.1
1915	573,344	1,179,016	4.0	68.0
1916	667,929	1,255,385	6.5	71.9
1917	903,209	1,312,833	4.6	74.7
1918	1,423,867	1,409,220	7.3	79.8
1919	1,842,653	1,275,348	-9.5	71.9
1920	1,971,127	1,447,700	13.5	81.1
1921	1,584,484	1,466,110	1.3	81.0
1922	1,729,024	1,494,259	1.9	81.6
1923	1,710,395	1,522,864	1.9	82.1
1924	1,815,465	1,456,543	-4.4	77.6
1925	1,892,638	1,518,822	4.3	79.9
1926	1,833,087	1,592,585	4.9	82.4
1927	1,860,761	1,724,715	8.3	88.0
1928	1,766,924	1,653,947	-4.1	83.3
1929	1,706,745	1,684,236	1.8	83.7
1930	1,412,807	1,856,664	10.2	90.8
1931	1,359,491	1,909,863	2.9	91.6
1932	1,512,262	1,955,450	2.4	92.2
1933	1,649,279	2,046,849	4.7	94.9
1934	1,846,707	2,051,735	0.2	93.7
1935	2,232,545	2,232,545	8.8	100.5
1936	2,363,386	2,258,921	1.2	100.1
1937	3,017,793	2,685,191	18.9	117.2
1938	3,274,545	2,708,098	0.9	116.5
1939	3,717,161	2,447,843	-9.6	104.5
1940	4,588,729	2,859,065	16.8	121.4

Source: Gim Naknyeon, ed., *Hanguk ui gyeongje seongjang* (Seoul: Seoul National University Press, 2006), pp.353, 372.

Economic production by industry
1912–1940

Year	Agriculture	Forestry	Fishing	Mining	Manufacturing	Utilities	Construction	Total
1912	374,115	51,461	5,854	3,714	26,339	529	11,569	605,313
1914	356,000	55,135	8,362	4,611	33,168	1,282	11,422	605,837
1916	366,351	45,451	11,059	8,277	40,647	3,100	10,790	634,977
1918	834,494	92,809	22,781	9,452	87,189	12,792	20,669	1,381,978
1920	1,094,837	159,169	27,436	10,853	115,291	9,034	39,222	1,905,161
1922	870,488	131,272	33,294	7,074	122,655	8,940	47,800	1,644,844
1924	946,307	107,811	37,106	9,501	138,520	8,643	37,939	1,728,787
1926	926,159	102,447	38,851	11,457	147,247	11,242	39,985	1,735,403
1928	780,980	114,837	47,985	12,581	155,077	14,484	52,380	1,673,084
1930	522,581	109,184	36,277	12,109	124,564	44,592	49,233	1,320,530
1932	639,738	81,313	33,660	18,479	126,373	65,001	42,544	1,424,074
1934	784,373	90,045	41,891	31,946	180,182	55,822	53,419	1,747,628
1936	895,130	99,042	58,477	58,350	280,558	99,401	98,699	2,256,064
1938	1,196,215	130,543	64,268	110,367	443,459	187,410	130,276	3,129,530
1940	1,576,613	191,680	131,959	168,835	721,838	173,667	216,806	4,408,030

Source: Gim Naknyeon, ed., *Hanguk ui gyeongje seongjang*, pp.365–366.

Relative size of industrial sectors
1912–1940

[units = %]

Year	Primary industries	Secondary industries	Tertiary industries	Total
1912	71.3	7.0	21.8	100
1914	69.2	8.3	22.4	100
1916	66.6	9.9	23.5	100
1918	68.7	9.4	21.8	100
1920	67.3	9.2	23.6	100
1922	62.9	11.3	25.7	100
1924	63.1	11.3	25.6	100
1926	61.5	12.1	26.4	100
1928	56.4	14.0	29.6	100
1930	50.6	17.5	32.0	100
1932	53.0	17.7	29.3	100
1934	52.4	18.4	29.2	100
1936	46.7	23.8	29.5	100
1938	44.4	27.8	27.7	100
1940	43.1	29.1	27.8	100

Source: Gim Naknyeon, ed., *Hanguk ui gyeongje seongjang*, p.368.

Number of factories and workers
1932–1943

Year	Factories	Workers
1932	4,643	110,650
1935	5,635	168,771
1939	6,953	270,439
1940	7,142	294,971
1941	10,889	301,752
1942	12,669	331,181
1943	13,293	362,953

Sources: Government-General of Korea, *Chōsen Sōtokufu tōkei yōran*; Tonggyecheong, *Tonggyero dasiboneun gwangbok ijeon ui gyeongje-sahoesang* [Seoul: National Statistical Office, 1995), p.50; Heo Suyeol, *Gaebal eopneun gaebal* (Seoul: Unhaeng namu, 2005), p.50.

Agricultural land under cultivation and Japanese-owned land
1910–1942

Year	Land under cultivation (jeongbo)			Japanese-owned land [%]		
	Paddy field	Dry field	Total	Paddy field	Dry field	Total
1910	1,506,101	2,772,267	4,278,368	2.8	1.0	1.6
1911	1,510,080	2,773,542	4,283,622	3.8	1.3	2.2
1912	1,514,064	2,774,813	4,288,877	4.5	1.4	2.5
1913	1,518,053	2,776,078	4,294,131	5.9	2.2	3.5
1914	1,522,047	2,777,338	4,299,385	6.3	2.3	3.7
1915	1,526,046	2,778,593	4,304,639	7.1	2.2	3.9
1916	1,530,051	2,779,843	4,309,894	7.7	2.4	4.3
1917	1,534,061	2,781,087	4,315,148	8.0	2.5	4.5
1918	1,544,430	2,797,661	4,342,091	8.3	2.6	4.6
1919	1,543,090	2,781,590	4,324,680	8.5	2.7	4.8
1920	1,543,702	2,778,333	4,322,035	8.7	2.7	4.9
1921	1,543,664	2,778,826	4,322,490	8.8	2.8	4.9
1922	1,545,123	2,772,195	4,317,318	8.9	2.8	5.0
1923	1,549,461	2,771,403	4,320,864	8.9	2.8	5.0
1924	1,553,998	2,768,207	4,322,205	9.0	2.8	5.0
1925	1,563,736	2,784,619	4,348,355	9.0	2.8	5.0
1926	1,574,157	2,804,800	4,378,957	9.0	2.7	5.0
1927	1,587,053	2,800,674	4,387,727	9.0	2.8	5.0
1928	1,598,224	2,793,171	4,391,395	9.1	2.8	5.1
1929	1,608,888	2,783,228	4,392,116	9.7	3.0	5.4
1930	1,617,696	2,770,968	4,388,664	11.3	3.4	6.3
1931	1,628,984	2,755,526	4,384,510	14.6	4.4	8.1
1932	1,647,009	2,743,434	4,390,443	16.1	4.8	9.0
1933	1,660,255	2,751,549	4,411,804	16.6	5.0	9.3
1934	1,671,389	2,760,094	4,431,483	16.9	5.0	9.5
1935	1,681,340	2,750,939	4,432,279	18.3	5.2	10.2
1936	1,689,786	2,736,983	4,426,769	16.7	4.7	9.3
1937	1,703,835	2,723,334	4,427,169	17.1	4.8	9.5
1938	1,717,232	2,719,593	4,436,825	17.5	4.9	9.8
1939	1,729,539	2,718,834	4,448,373	16.7	4.6	9.3
1940	1,737,632	2,699,547	4,437,179	16.8	4.6	9.4
1941	1,734,760	2,669,847	4,404,607	16.9	4.6	9.5
1942	1,735,898	2,660,105	4,396,003	16.9	4.6	9.5

Source: Heo Suyeol, *Gaebal eopneun gaebal* [Seoul: Unhaeng namu, 2005], p.343.

Rice production
1910–1944

Year	Government-General statistics	Revised estimates
1910	11,568,362	13,772,171
1911	11,568,362	13,834,592
1912	10,865,051	13,897,014
1913	12,109,840	13,959,436
1914	14,130,578	14,021,858
1915	12,846,085	14,084,280
1916	13,933,009	14,146,701
1917	13,687,895	14,209,123
1918	15,294,109	14,531,124
1919	12,708,208	12,067,093
1920	14,882,352	14,409,370
1921	14,342,352	14,117,774
1922	15,014,292	15,071,950
1923	15,174,645	15,497,750
1924	13,219,322	13,727,202
1925	14,773,102	15,593,777
1926	15,300,707	16,416,900
1927	17,298,887	18,848,512
1928	13,511,725	14,936,727
1929	13,701,746	15,384,211
1930	19,180,677	21,834,021
1931	15,872,999	18,326,968
1932	16,345,825	19,137,000
1933	18,192,720	21,352,068
1934	16,717,238	20,095,485
1935	17,884,669	21,752,988
1936	19,410,763	19,410,763
1937	26,796,950	26,796,950
1938	24,138,874	24,138,874
1939	14,355,793	14,355,793
1940	21,527,393	21,527,393
1941	24,886,000	24,886,000
1942	15,687,000	15,687,000
1943	18,719,000	18,719,000
1944	16,052,000	16,052,000

Source: Heo Suyeol, *Gaebal eopneun gaebal*, p.344.

CHRONOLOGY OF THE JAPANESE OCCUPATION PERIOD

1910, AUGUST: Beginning of Japanese occupation.
SEPTEMBER: Suicide of Hwang Hyeon (1855-1910).
DECEMBER: Passage of the Company Law.

1911, JANUARY: Beginning of the Incident of the 105.
MARCH: Establishment of the Bank of Chosen.
: Changgyeong Palace reopened as a park and museum site called Changgyeongwon.
MAY: Closure of the journal *Sonyeon*.
JULY: Discovery of Seokguram Grotto.
AUGUST: Passage of the Joseon Education Ordinance.

1912, AUGUST: Start of cadastral survey.

1913, MAY: Formation of the Heungsadan in San Francisco.

1914, JANUARY: Opening of the Honam Railway Line.
: Construction of the theater Danseongsa.
MARCH: Reorganization of administrative structure of Joseon.
AUGUST: Opening of the Seoul-Wonsan Railway Line.
SEPTEMBER: founding of the journal *Cheongchun*.

1915: Publication of Bak Eunsik's *Hanguk tongsa* in Shanghai.
SEPTEMBER: Joseon Industrial Exhibition.

1916, JUNE: Beginning of construction of the Government-General building on the grounds of Gyeongbok Palace.

1917, JANUARY: Beginning of serialization of Yi Gwangsu's *Mujeong* (The Heartless).

1918: A Korean branch of the Russian Communist Party is formed in Irkutsk, Siberia.
JUNE: Completion of cadastral survey.
OCTOBER: Establishment of the Joseon Industrial Bank.

1919, FEBRUARY: Publication of the literary magazine *Changjo*.
MARCH: March First Movement.
APRIL: Formation of the Korean Provisional Government in Shanghai.
MAY: Establishment of the Sinheung Military Academy.
SEPTEMBER 2: Gang Ugyu attempts to assassinate the new Governor-General Saitō Makoto.
OCTOBER: Founding of Gyeongseong Spinning and Weaving Company.
NOVEMBER: Formation of the anarchist group Uiyeoldan.

1920, MARCH: Beginning of publication of the *Joseon ilbo*.
APRIL: Beginning of publication of the *Donga ilbo*.
: Revision of the Company Law.
: Formation of the Joseon Workers Mutual Aid Association (Joseon nodong gongjehoe).
: Founding of the Joseon Women's Educational Association.
MAY: Founding of the Sinheung Military Academy in Manchuria.
AUGUST: Formation of the Joseon Native Products Promotion Society.
JUNE: Publication of the first issue of *Gaebyeok*.
NOVEMBER: Formation of the DaeHan Independence Army.
DECEMBER: Beginning of the Program to Increase Rice Production.

1921, JUNE: The Free City (Alekseyevsk) incident.
SEPTEMBER: General strike in Busan.

1922, JANUARY: Over fifty Koreans attend the First Congress of the Toilers of the Far East in Moscow.
FEBRUARY: Promulgation of the second Education Ordinance.
MARCH: Establishment of the YWCA in Seoul.
JUNE: First Joseon Arts Exhibition.
DECEMBER: The Government-General established the Committee for the Compilation of Joseon History.

1923, APRIL: Formation of Hyeongpyeongsa.
: Sin Chaeho drafts the anarchist-influenced *Manifesto of the Korean Revolution*.
JULY: Hunger strike by female workers in rubber factories.

1924, APRIL: Tenancy dispute on Amtae Island.
MAY: Opening of the preparatory course of Keijō Imperial University.

1925, JANUARY: Publication of Gim Dongin's short story "Potatoes."
APRIL: Formation of the Korean Communist Party.
: Enactment of the Peace Preservation Law.
MAY: Promulgation of the Peace Preservation Law.
: Formation of the Koreana Artista Proletaria Federatio (KAPF).
SEPTEMBER: Completion of construction of the Joseon Shrine (Chosen Jinja).
NOVEMBER: First Communist Party Incident.

1926, MAY: Han Yongun (1879-1944) publishes his poetry collection *Nim ui chimmuk* (*Silence of the Lover*).
JUNE: Second Communist Party Incident.
: (10th) Funeral of Sunjong; demonstrations against Japanese rule.
OCTOBER: Opening of the film *Arirang* by Na Ungyu (1902-1937).

1927, JANUARY: Formation of the Singanhoe.
MAY: Formation of the Geunuhoe.
: Founding of Chosen Nitrogenous Fertilizer Company (Chosen Chisso Hiryo).

1928, JANUARY: Third Community Party Incident.
JULY: Fourth Communist Party Incident.
NOVEMBER: Beginning of the serialization of Hong Myeonghui's novel *Im Ggeokjeong*.
DECEMBER: Comintern's "December Theses."

1929, JANUARY: General strike in Wonsan.
APRIL: Opening of an airport on Yeoui Island.
JULY: Establishment of the Chosen Savings Bank.
: The *Joseon ilbo* newspaper begins a literacy campaign.
NOVEMBER: The Gwangju Student Movement.

1930, AUGUST: Strike of rubber workers in Pyongyang.
OCTOBER: Opening of Mitsukoshi Department Store.

1931, MAY: Dissolution of the Singanhoe; end of the United Front movement.
JULY: The Manbosan (C. Wanbaoshan) Incident.
SEPTEMBER: The Manchurian Incident.
: Establishment of Hwasin General Store (Hwasin sanghoe).

1932, JANUARY: Opening of Donga Department Store.
APRIL: Kim Il Sung begins guerrilla activity in Manchuria.
JULY: Beginning of the Rural Revitalization Movement.
DECEMBER: Promulgation of the Tenant Arbitration Ordinance.

1933, MARCH: Establishment of the first confirmed military comfort station.
OCTOBER: Strike of rubber workers in Busan.

1934, APRIL: Promulgation of the Agricultural Lands Ordinance.

1935, OCTOBER: Opening of *The Story of Chunhyang*, the first sound film.

1936, AUGUST 9: Son Gijeong (Sohn Kee-Chung) wins the gold medal in the marathon in the Olympics in Berlin.
SEPTEMBER: Publication of Yi Sang's short story "Wings."

1937, JUNE: The Suyang Donguhoe Incident.

1938, FEBRUARY: The Heungeop Gurakbu Incident.
MARCH: Founding of Samsung in Deagu.
APRIL: Promulgation of the State Mobilization Law.
JULY: Establishment of the Joseon League for Total Spiritual Mobilization (Kokumin seisin sōdōin Chōsen renmei).

1939, DECEMBER: Promulgation of the Tenancy Fee Control Ordinance.

1940, FEBRUARY: Implementation of the Name Order.
MAY: Three parties join to form the Korean Independence Party.
AUGUST: Closure of the *Donga ilbo* and the *Joseon ilbo*.
SEPTEMBER: Formation of the Korean Liberation Army.
OCTOBER: Reorganization of the Joseon League for Total Spiritual Mobilization into the Joseon League for Total Mobilization (Kokumin sōryoku Chōsen renmei).

1941, AUGUST: The Suiho Dam on the Amnok (Yalu) River begins operation.

1942, OCTOBER: Joseon Language Society Incident.

1943, AUGUST: Koreans begin to be drafted into the Japanese army.

1945, AUGUST 15: Liberation from Japanese rule.

GOVERNORS-GENERAL OF CHŌSEN
1910–1945

1910–1916	Terauchi Masatake	寺内正毅
1916–1919	Hasegawa Yoshimichi	長谷川好道
1919–1927	Saitō Makoto	齋藤實
1927	Ugaki Kazushige	宇垣一成
1927–1929	Yamanashi Hanzō	山梨半造
1929–1931	Saitō Makoto	齋藤實
1931–1936	Ugaki Kazushige	宇垣一成
1936–1942	Minami Jirō	南次郎
1942–1944	Koiso Kuniaki	小磯國昭
1944–1945	Abe Nobuyuki	阿部信行

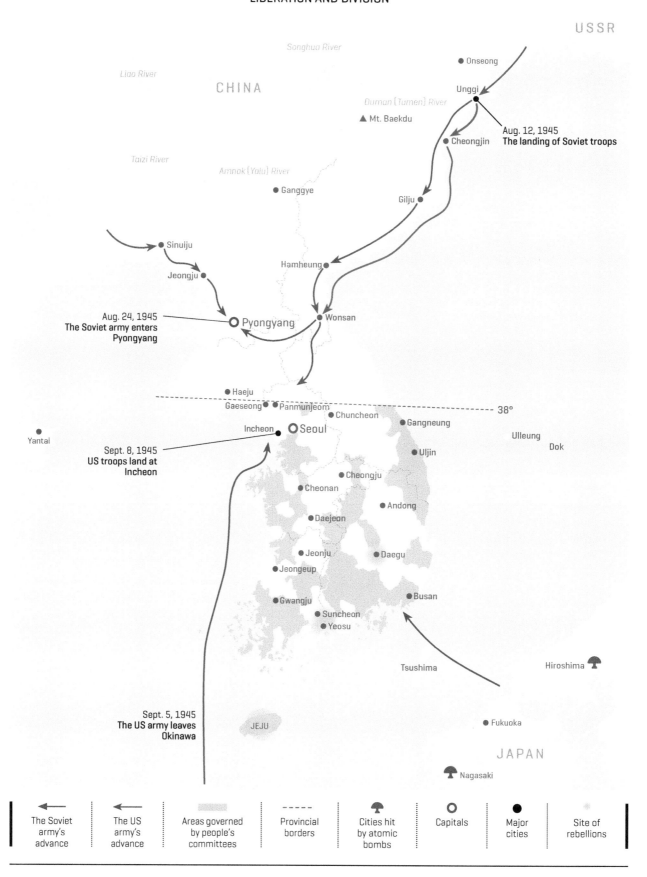

USSR

● Onseong

Songhua River

Liao River

CHINA

Duman (Tumen) River

▲ Mt. Baekdu

Unggi

Aug. 12, 1945
The landing of Soviet troops

● Cheongjin

Taizi River

Amnok (Yalu) River

● Ganggye

Gilju ●

Sinuiju ●

Jeongju ●

Hamheung ●

Aug. 24, 1945
**The Soviet army enters
Pyongyang**

○ Pyongyang

● Wonsan

● Haeju

Gaeseong ● ● Panmunjeom

Chuncheon ●

● Gangneung

38°

Ulleung

Dok

● Yantai

Incheon ● ○ Seoul

Sept. 8, 1945
**US troops land at
Incheon**

● Uljin

● Cheongju

● Cheonan

● Andong

● Daejeon

● Jeonju

● Daegu

● Jeongeup

● Gwangju

● Busan

● Suncheon
● Yeosu

Tsushima

Hiroshima 🍄

Sept. 5, 1945
**The US army leaves
Okinawa**

JEJU

● Fukuoka

JAPAN

🍄 Nagasaki

| ← The Soviet army's advance | ← The US army's advance | Areas governed by people's committees | - - - - Provincial borders | 🍄 Cities hit by atomic bombs | ○ Capitals | ● Major cities | Site of rebellions |

9

THE LIBERATION PERIOD AND THE KOREAN WAR

Citizens in
Seoul celebrating
the liberation of
their country.
(PD–South Korea)

When Korea was liberated from Japanese rule on August 15, 1945, few people suspected that the country would soon be divided or that, in fact, the process was already under way. At a late night meeting of the State–War–Navy Coordinating Committee in Washington, DC on August 10, Dean Rusk and Charles Bonesteel drafted a proposal to divide Korea into two occupation zones at the thirty-eighth parallel. Three years later, separate governments were formed in the north and the south. In June 1950, a civil war broke out between the two sides that killed millions of people and achieved no resolution. Since the fighting ended with an armistice and not a peace treaty, the two Koreas remain technically at war today.

The Cold War created a new world order that divided most countries into two ideologically opposed blocs centered on the United States and the Soviet Union. The United States formed the North Atlantic Treaty Organization (NATO) in Europe and reached a number of bilateral agreements with countries in Asia. The Soviet Union headed the Warsaw Pact and was allied with the People's Republic of China, the major communist power in Asia. The Korean peninsula became one of the hotspots of the Cold War. Like Germany, it emerged from World War II a divided country; like Vietnam, it experienced a civil war that developed into a proxy superpower conflict.

Belgium
Canada
Denmark (including Greenland)
France
Iceland
Italy
Luxembourg
Netherlands
Norway
Portugal
United Kingdom
United States

WARSAW PACT	1955	NON-ALIGNED MOVEMENT	1961		ASSOCIATION OF SOUTHEAST ASIAN NATIONS	1967

Greece (1952)
Turkey (1952)
West Germany (1955)
Spain (1982)

WARSAW PACT | 1955

Albania (withdrew 1968)
Bulgaria
Czechoslovakia
East Germany
Hungary
Poland
Romania
Soviet Union

NON-ALIGNED MOVEMENT | 1961

Afghanistan
Algeria
Burma (Myanmar)
Cambodia
Congo (DR)
Cuba
Cyprus
Egypt
Ethiopia
Ghana
Guinea
India

Indonesia
Iraq
Lebanon
Mali
Morocco
Nepal
Saudi Arabia
Somalia
Sudan
Tunisia
United Arab Emirates
Yemen

Yugoslavia
Sri Lanka (1961)
Laos (1964)
Malaysia (1970)
Singapore (1970)
North Korea (1976)

ASSOCIATION OF SOUTHEAST ASIAN NATIONS | 1967

Indonesia*
Malaysia*
The Philippines
Singapore*
Thailand
Brunei (1984)

(*Also a member of the Non-Aligned Movement)

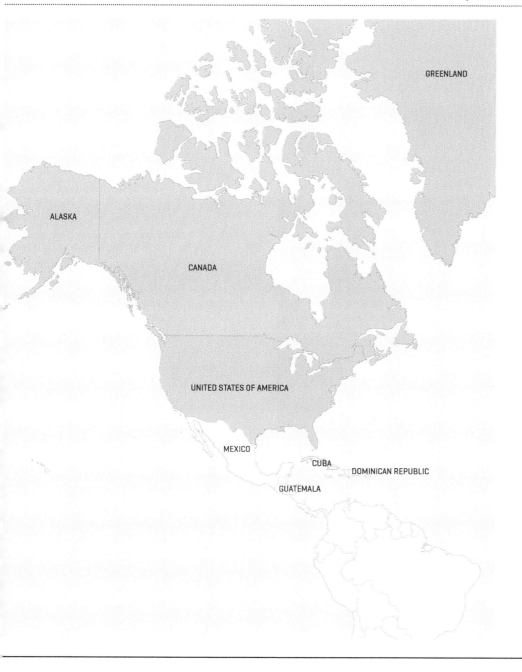

CHRONOLOGY OF THE LIBERATION PERIOD
1945-1948

1945

FEBRUARY 4-11: Yalta Conference.

APRIL 12: Death of Franklin Roosevelt.

JULY 16-AUGUST 2: Potsdam Conference.

AUGUST 12: The Soviet army enters Korea.
15: Surrender of Japan to the Allied Powers. Liberation of Korea from Japanese rule.
17: The US Army's General Order No. 1 determines that on the Korean peninsula Japanese forces will surrender to the Americans south of the 38th parallel and to the Soviets north of the 38th parallel.
: Establishment of the Joseon Academy.
: Formation of the Committee for the Preparation of Korean Independence.
20: A committee to reestablish the Korean Communist Party is formed in Seoul.
26: Arrival of the first Soviet troops in Pyongyang.

SEPTEMBER 6: The Korean People's Republic is established in Seoul.
8: Arrival of US troops.
9: Founding of the Korean Democratic Party.
19: Kim Il Sung arrives at Wonsan from the Soviet Union.

OCTOBER 10-13: In the north, a North Korean Bureau of the Korean Communist Party is organized.
16: Return of Syngman Rhee.

NOVEMBER 11: Formation of the People's Party.
12: The Oriental Development Company's name is changed to the New Korea Company [Sin Han gongsa].
23: Return of Gim Gu and other leaders of the Korean Provisional Government.
: The newspaper *Joseon ilbo* resumes publication.
30: Return of over 450,000 Koreans from Japan.

DECEMBER 6: Issuance of USAMGIK Ordinance 33, which vested all Japanese property and financial assets in Korea in the Military Government of Korea as of September 25, 1945.
16-26: At the Moscow Conference of Foreign Ministers, the US and Soviet Union agree to set up a Joint Commission to administer Korea under a proposed four-year trusteeship.
29: Beginning of the anti-trusteeship movement in South Korea.
30: Assassination of Song Jinu.

1946

FEBRUARY 1: Formation of the Emergency National Council.
8: Establishment of the North Korean Provisional People's Committee. Formation of the National Society for the Rapid Realization of Korean Independence.
15: Formation of the Democratic National Front in the South.

MARCH 5: A land reform law is passed in North Korea.
20: The first round of US–USSR Joint Commission talks begins.

JUNE 3: In Jeongeup, Syngman Rhee advocates the creation of a separate southern government.
22: Return of Yi Beomseok and other members of the Gwangbok Army.

JULY 22: The Left–Right Coalition Committee holds its first meeting in Seoul. Law on gender equality is passed in North Korea.

AUGUST 10: Nationalization of key industries in the north.
22: Establishment of Seoul National University.

SEPTEMBER: A series of uprisings begins in Busan.
1: Founding of Kim Il Sung University.

OCTOBER: The Autumn Harvest Uprisings (October Rebellion) begin in Daegu.

NOVEMBER 23: The Workers' Party of South Korea is formed in Seoul through a merger of three parties.

DECEMBER 12: Opening of the South Korean Interim Legislative Assembly.

UNITED STATES

1933–1945: Franklin D. Roosevelt
1945–1953: Harry S. Truman
  1945, Oct.: Establishment of the
    United Nations
  1946, Feb. 26: George Kennan's
    "Long Telegram"

1947: Beginning of the
    Truman Doctrine
1948, April: Beginning of
    the Marshall Plan
1948, June: Beginning of the
    Berlin blockade and airlift

JAPAN

1945: Prince Higashikuni
1945–1946: Kijūrō Shidehara
1946–1947: Shigeru Yoshida
1947–1948: Tetsu Katayama
1948: Hitoshi Ashida

1947

FEBRUARY 5: An Jaehong is appointed as Civil Administrator.
  17–20: Elections of representatives to the North Korean People's Committee.
  22: Founding of the North Korean People's Committee.

MARCH 1: Leftist and rightist groups clash near Namdaemun after holding separate commemorations of the March First Movement.

APRIL 19: Seo Yunbok wins the Boston Marathon.

MAY 21: The second round of US–USSR Joint Commission talks opens.
  24: Yeo Unhyeong forms the Worker-People's Party.

JULY: Tenancy disputes are frequent.
  19: Assassination of Yeo Unhyeong.

AUGUST 14: Arrest of around 1,000 leftist figures in the South, including Heo Heon.
  26: General Albert Wedemeyer visits Korea as a special envoy.

SEPTEMBER 21: Formation of the Daedong Youth Corps.

OCTOBER: US–USSR Joint Commission talks are adjourned indefinitely.

NOVEMBER 14: The UN establishes the United Nations Temporary Commission on Korea to oversee nationwide elections.

DECEMBER 2: Assassination of Jang Deoksu.

1948

FEBRUARY 8: Founding of the Korean People's Army in North Korea.

MARCH 10: The UN Temporary Commission sets the voting age at twenty-one.
  12: Gim Gu, Gim Gyusik, and five other politicians sign a statement announcing their decision not to participate in the upcoming elections.
  14: Throughout the North, over 200,000 people protest the holding of separate elections in the south.
  27–30: Second Congress of the Workers' Party of Korea.

APRIL 3: Beginning of the Jeju Island uprising.
  19–30: First round of the North–South joint conference is held in Pyongyang.

MAY 10: UN-sponsored elections are held in South Korea.
  14: North Korea cuts off provision of electricity to the South.
  29: Dissolution of the Interim Legislative Assembly.

AUGUST 1: Yi Beomseok is appointed as the first prime minister of South Korea.
  15: End of the US military government in the South. Establishment of the Republic of Korea.
  25: Elections to the Supreme People's Assembly are held in North Korea.

SEPTEMBER 2: First meeting of the Supreme People's Assembly.
  7: Passage of the law for the Punishment of Anti-Nationalist Activities in South Korea.
  9: Establishment of the Democratic People's Republic of Korea.
  28: All commerce between the two Koreas is terminated.

OCTOBER: The Soviet Union withdraws its troops from North Korea.
  20: Outbreak of the Yeosu and Suncheon rebellions.

NOVEMBER: Beginning of guerrilla warfare in the South.

DECEMBER 1: The anticommunist National Security Law is introduced.

1949

APRIL: Increase of military clashes along the 38th parallel.

MAY 4: Intense battle in the Gaeseong region.
  : Beginning of months of border fighting between North and South Korean forces.
  18: Beginning of the National Assembly Fraktsiya Incident.
  20: The US announces the withdrawal of its troops from South Korea.

JUNE 26: Assassination of Gim Gu.
  29: US forces complete their withdrawal from South Korea.
  30: Merger of the Workers' Party of South Korea and the Workers' Party of North Korea.

AUGUST 6: Chiang Kai-shek pays an official visit to South Korea.

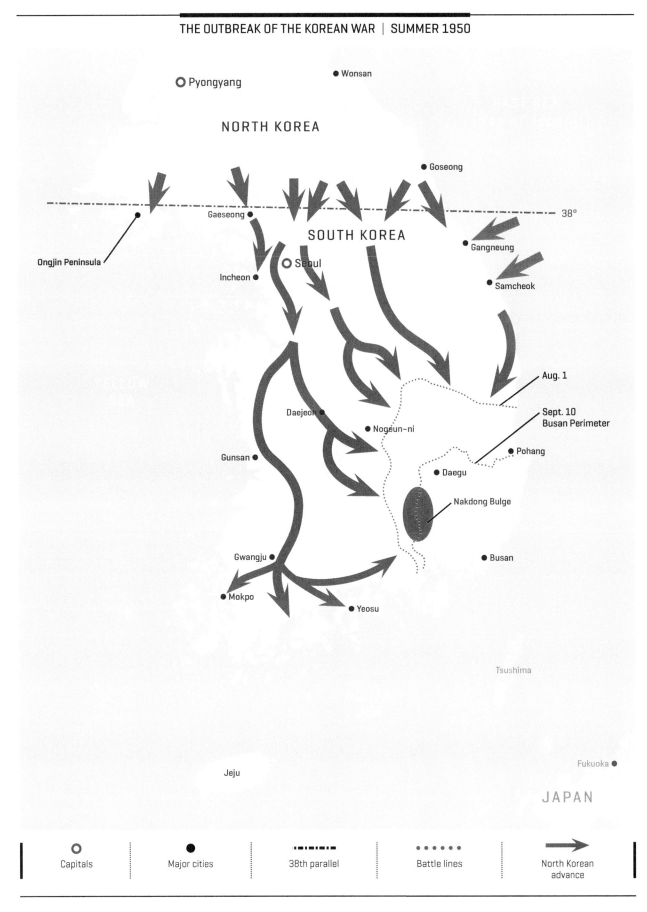

Pyongyang

Wonsan

NORTH KOREA

Goseong

38°

Gaeseong

SOUTH KOREA

Gangneung

Ongjin Peninsula

Seoul

Samcheok

Incheon

Aug. 1

Sept. 10
Busan Perimeter

Daejeon

Nogeun-ni

Pohang

Gunsan

Daegu

Nakdong Bulge

Gwangju

Busan

Mokpo

Yeosu

Tsushima

Jeju

Fukuoka

JAPAN

Capitals	Major cities	38th parallel	Battle lines	North Korean advance

THE KOREAN WAR

Photo of **children in front of an M-26 tank** taken in June 1951. [PD–US]

The Korean War began when North Korean forces crossed the thirty-eighth parallel early in the morning of June 25, 1950. In addition to the US and South Korea, UN forces consisted of troops from fifteen member countries, with others providing medical support. The initial North Korean offensive almost succeeded, driving UN forces to the southeastern corner of the peninsula. The Incheon landing, led by General Douglas MacArthur, reversed the tide of the war and forced North Korean troops to retreat. MacArthur's push to North Korea's northern border was halted when Chinese forces entered the war at the end of 1950. By mid-1951, the war reached a stalemate with no significant change in the battlefront for the next two years. Hostilities ended on July 27, 1953 with a ceasefire agreement that was signed by representatives of North Korea and the UN but not of South Korea. No peace treaty has been signed to this day. The Korean War was far shorter than the Vietnam War but generated a comparable number of casualties.

Forced to retreat because of successive defeats, the UN forces established a defensive line around the city of Busan. Fighting along the perimeter lasted from early August to mid-September. It marked the furthest southern advance of North Korean forces in the war. On September 15, 1950, UN forces began an amphibious operation at Incheon behind enemy lines. The landing was largely unopposed, but they engaged in fierce fighting with North Korean troops to recapture Seoul by the end of the month. It was the first major turning point in the war, forcing the North to retreat and giving the initiative to the UN side.

THE INCHEON LANDING
AND UN MARCH NORTH

O
Capitals

●
Major cities

⟶
UN advance

• • • • • •
Battle lines

Chinese Entry into the War | *Late 1950–Early 1951*

Soon after UN forces crossed the 38th parallel, troops from the People's Republic of China began secretly entering the Korean peninsula in October 1950. A few skirmishes with Chinese forces occurred in late October in places such as Unsan, but the major Chinese offensive did not begin until late November near the Cheongcheon River. The Chinese entry was the second major turning point of the war, forcing UN forces to retreat below the 38th parallel. The US X Corps were surrounded by Chinese forces at the Chosin Reservoir but managed to fight their way to Heungnam, where they were the last UN forces to be evacuated from North Korea.

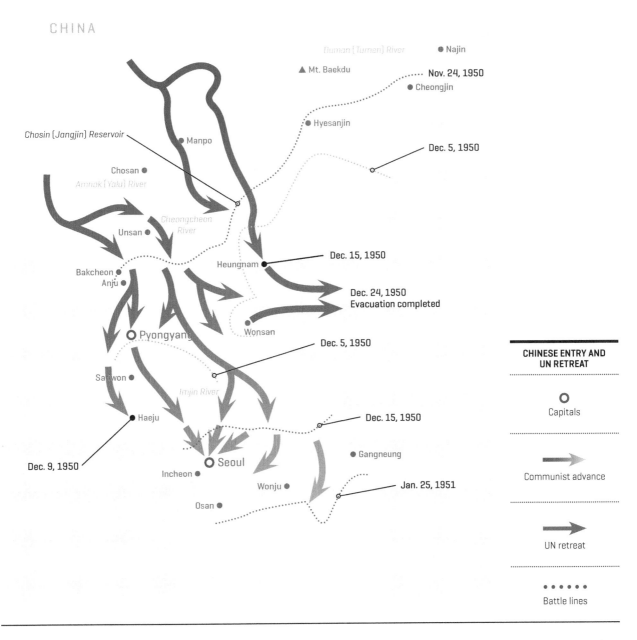

CHINA

Duman (Tumen) River   ● Najin

▲ Mt. Baekdu

Nov. 24, 1950
● Cheongjin

● Hyesanjin

Chosin (Jangjin) Reservoir   ● Manpo

Dec. 5, 1950

Chosan ●
Amnok (Yalu) River

Cheongcheon River

Unsan ●

Dec. 15, 1950

Bakcheon ●   Heungnam ●
Anju ●

Dec. 24, 1950
Evacuation completed

O Pyongyang

Wonsan ●

Dec. 5, 1950

Sariwon ●

Imjin River

● Haeju

Dec. 15, 1950

Dec. 9, 1950

O Seoul   ● Gangneung

Incheon ●

Wonju ●   Jan. 25, 1951

Osan ●

**CHINESE ENTRY AND
UN RETREAT**

O
Capitals

Communist advance

UN retreat

● ● ● ● ● ●
Battle lines

After UN forces retook Seoul, fighting stabilized in the middle of the peninsula by the late spring 1951. Though armistice talks began in summer 1951, the war continued for two more years as negotiations stalled over issues such as the repatriation of prisoners of war. Fighting resembled trench warfare with the battlefront moving back and forth over the same territory several times in some areas. Each side focused on establishing control over small areas of land to give their side an advantage in negotiations. Battles were fierce, many with high casualties; some of them are among the most well known in the West such as Heartbreak Ridge and Pork Chop Hill. Aerial bombing of North Korea continued through 1953, when important dams in the north were targeted.

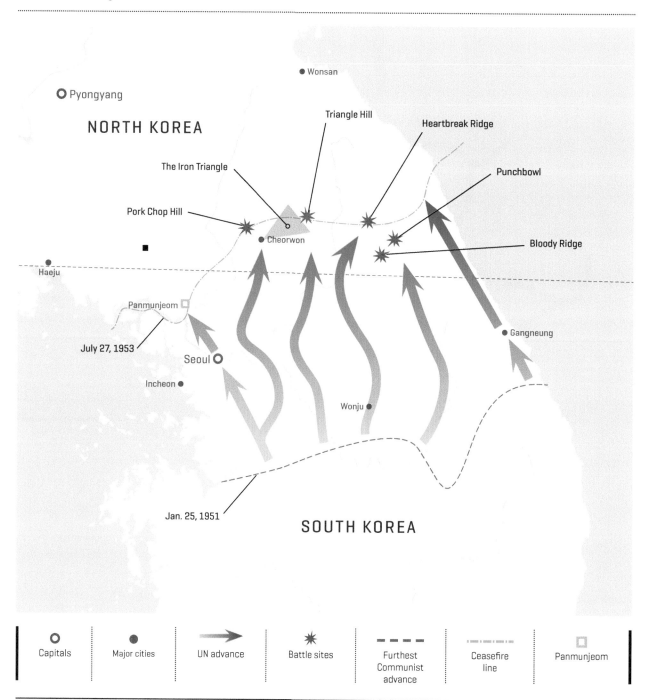

Statistics of the Korean War | *1950–1953*

Number of Troops and Casualties

UN FORCES [17 COUNTRIES]		
NAME OF COUNTRIES	NUMBER OF TROOPS	CASUALTIES
Republic of Korea, United States	1,789,000	621,479 [ROK] 137,250 [US]
United Kingdom	56,000	4,908
Canada	25,687	1,557
Turkey	14,936	3,216
Australia	8,407	1,584
The Philippines	7,420	398
Thailand	6.326	1,273
The Netherlands	5,322	768
Colombia	5,100	639
Greece	4,992	738
New Zealand	3,794	103
Ethiopia	3,518	657
Belgium	3,498	440
France	3,421	1,289
Republic of South Africa	826	43
Luxembourg	83	15
Denmark, India, Norway, Sweden, Italy	Provided medical support	

COMMUNIST FORCES [3 COUNTRIES]		
NAME OF COUNTRIES	NUMBER OF TROOPS	CASUALTIES
Democratic People's Republic of Korea		~2 million [1 million civilians]
People's Republic of China		~900,000
USSR		282 [killed]

Sources: ROK Ministry of National Defense; Xiaobing Li, *A History of the Modern Chinese Army* (Lexington: The University Press of Kentucky); G.F. Krivosheev, *Soviet Casualties and Combat Losses in the Twentieth Century* (London: Greenhill Books, 1997).

UN transport vehicles re-crossing the 38th parallel as they retreat from Pyongyang, January 1, 1951. [Getty Images]

Lt. General William K. Harrison and General Nam Il signing the armistice agreement at Panmunjeom on July 27, 1953. [Getty Images]

CHRONOLOGY OF THE KOREAN WAR
1950–1953

1950

JANUARY 12: Secretary of State Dean Acheson's Press Club speech.

APRIL: Kim Il Sung visits Moscow.

MAY: Kim Il Sung visits Beijing.

JUNE 18: John Foster Dulles visits the 38th parallel.
25: Hostilities break out between the two Koreas.
27: The government of the Republic of Korea moves to Daejeon.
The UN Security Council decides to send troops to the Korean peninsula.
27: Bodo League massacre begins
28: North Korean troops occupy Seoul.
29: American B-29 bombers attack Pyongyang for the first time.
30: North Korean troops cross the Han River.

JULY 1: Arrival of the first American forces [Task Force Smith].
7: General Douglas MacArthur is appointed as commander of the UN forces.
20: North Korean troops occupy Daejeon and capture US General William F. Dean.
26-28: The No Gun Ri incident.

AUGUST 4: The Battle of the Busan Perimeter begins.
18: The ROK government moves to Busan.

SEPTEMBER 2: North Korean troops begin an all-out assault along the Nakdong River.
15: The Incheon landing begins.
28: The recapture of Seoul by the UN forces.
20: President Truman signs National Security Council Report 68 [NSC 68].

OCTOBER 1: ROK troops cross the 38th parallel.
7: Establishment of the United Nations Commission for the Unification and Rehabilitation of Korea [UNCURK].
10: UN troops occupy the city of Wonsan.
19: UN troops occupy Pyongyang.
25: The Chinese People's Volunteer Army enters the war.
26: UN troops advance to the town of Chosan on the south bank of the Amnok [Yalu] River.

NOVEMBER 25: Mao Zedong's eldest son Anying, serving in the Chinese army in Korea, is killed in an air strike.
30: Truman does not rule out the use of nuclear weapons in Korea.

DECEMBER 1: General Assembly Resolution 410[V] establishes the United Nations Korean Reconstruction Agency [UNKRA].
5: Communist forces occupy Pyongyang.
13: The Battle of Chosin Reservoir [Jangjinho] ends.
23: General Walker, commander of the US Eighth Army, is killed in a road accident while inspecting the front.
24: UN forces and refugees complete their evacuation from Heungnam in South Hamgyeong province.
26: General Matthew Ridgway becomes commander of the US Eighth Army.
30: All UN troops retreat south of the 38th parallel.

1951

JANUARY 1: About 300,000 residents of Seoul flee the city.
4: UN troops withdraw from Seoul. The ROK government moves to Busan.

FEBRUARY 7: ROK forces massacre civilians in Hamyang and Sancheong in South Gyeongsang province.
11: Massacre of civilians at Geochang by the ROK army.

MARCH 7: UN forces begin Operation Ripper.
14: ROK forces recapture Seoul.
20: Peng Dehuai is appointed as commander of Chinese forces.
24: UN forces cross the 38th parallel again.
29: Revelation of embezzlement by high-ranking officers in South Korea's National Guard of military funds and supplies.

APRIL 11: General MacArthur is relieved of his post as supreme commander and replaced by General Matthew Ridgway.
22-25: Battle of the Imjin River.

JUNE 6: Intense fighting continues in the "Iron Triangle" of Cheorwon, Gimhwa, and Pyeonggang in Gangwon province.
23: Soviet representative Yakov Malik officially proposes armistice talks at the UN General Assembly.

JULY 1: Communist forces agree to the proposal for armistice talks.
10: The first day of armistice talks.
16: The US air force carries out the largest bombing raid of the war so far.

SOVIET UNION
1941–1953: Josef Stalin
1953–1964: Nikita Khrushchev

UNITED STATES
1945–1953: Harry S. Truman
    1951, Sept. 8: Signing of the San
       Francisco Peace Treaty
    1952, Nov. 1: First successful test of
       a hydrogen bomb

JAPAN
1948–1954: Yoshida Shigeru
    1951, Sept. 8: Signing of the Security
       Treaty Between the United States
       and Japan

1952

1953

AUGUST 18: Beginning of the Battle of Bloody Ridge.
31: Beginning of the Battle of the Punchbowl.

SEPTEMBER 5: End of the Battle of Bloody Ridge.
6: Establishment of the Women's Army of the ROK.
12: George Marshall resigns as the US Secretary of Defense.
13: Bombing of the port of Wonsan. Beginning of the Battle of Heartbreak Ridge.
21: Armistice talks are moved from Gaeseong to Panmunjeom.

OCTOBER 25: Ceasefire talks resume at Panmunjeom.
31: The communist side proposes that a military demarcation line and demilitarized zone be established on the basis of the current line of contact.

DECEMBER 18: The two sides exchange lists of POWs at Panmunjeom.
: General Mu Jeong is removed from his post.

JANUARY 10: Armistice talks are deadlocked.
18: The South Korean government announces the "Peace Line" demarking the area under its control in the East Sea (Sea of Japan).

FEBRUARY 18: Demonstration by prisoners at the POW camp on Geoje Island.

MARCH 15: Beijing claims that the US is engaging in germ warfare.

APRIL 28: General Mark W. Clark is appointed commander of UN forces.

MAY 7: Brigadier General Francis T. Dodd, commander of the Geoje Island POW camp, is taken hostage by prisoners.
10: General Dodd is released.

JUNE 25: Assassination attempt on Syngman Rhee.
29: UN forces reveal that they have destroyed thirteen of North Korea's hydroelectric plants.

JULY 3: At the armistice talks, the Communist side expresses approval for the UN proposal on the POW issue.

AUGUST 8: Syngman Rhee is reelected president of South Korea.

OCTOBER 14: Beginning of the Battle of Triangle Hill.
15: The Battle of White Horse ends.

DECEMBER 2: President-elect Dwight D. Eisenhower visits South Korea.
3: The UN General Assembly passes the "Indian Resolution."

MARCH 5: Death of Soviet leader Stalin.
9: General James Van Fleet, commander of the US Eighth Army, argues that nuclear weapons should be used in Korea.
23: South Korean forces use napalm bombs for the first time.

APRIL 8: 5,800 UN POWs are registered as wanting to be repatriated, while 600 Communist POWs want to be repatriated.
20: The beginning of eight rounds of exchanges of sick and wounded POWs.
29: Ceasefire talks resume at Panmunjeom.

MAY 7: The ROK government opposes the inclusion of Poland and Czechoslovakia among the five neutral nations.
8: Syngman Rhee announces his opposition to the armistice agreement.
13: Bombing of Doksan Dam.
24: The ROK government issues a statement opposing an armistice.

JUNE 8: An agreement is signed on POW exchanges.
18: Syngman Rhee releases anti-communist POWs.

JULY 13: Last major offensive by Communist forces.
21: South Korea announces that it will not send a representative to the armistice signing ceremony.
27: The ceasefire order is announced, and the armistice begins at 10:00 p.m. along the entire battlefront.

AUGUST 5: The exchange of POWs begins.
15: The South Korean government returns to Seoul.

SEPTEMBER 6: The exchange of POWs ends.

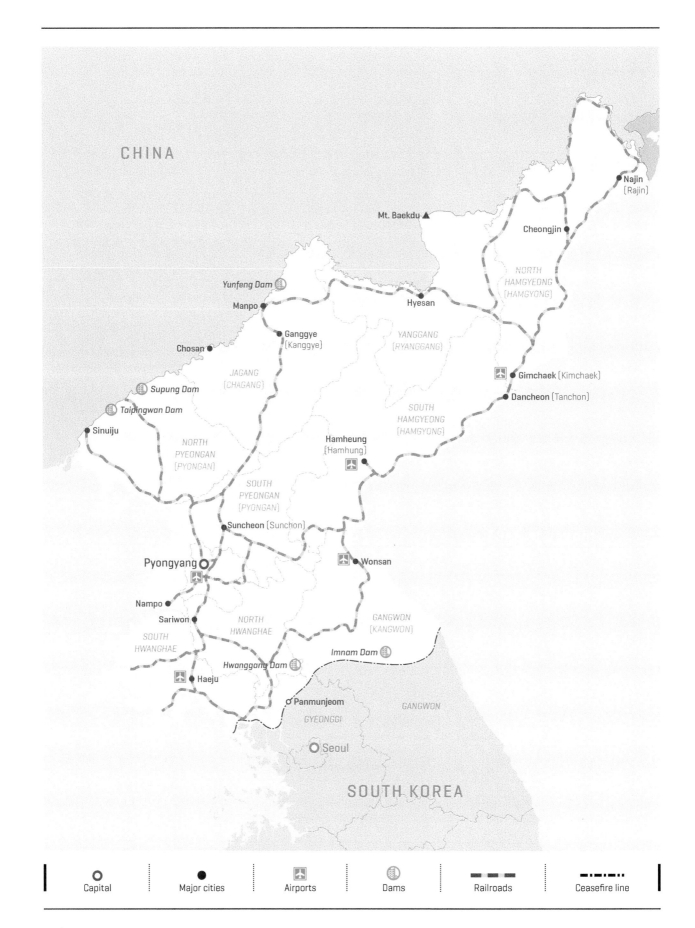

CHINA

Mt. Baekdu ▲

Najin [Rajin]

Cheongjin

NORTH HAMGYEONG [HAMGYONG]

Yunfeng Dam

Manpo

Hyesan

Ganggye [Kanggye]

YANGGANG [RYANGGANG]

Chosan

JAGANG [CHAGANG]

Gimchaek [Kimchaek]

Supung Dam

Dancheon [Tanchon]

SOUTH HAMGYEONG [HAMGYONG]

Taipingwan Dam

Sinuiju

NORTH PYEONGAN [PYONGAN]

Hamheung [Hamhung]

SOUTH PYEONGAN [PYONGAN]

Suncheon [Sunchon]

Pyongyang

Wonsan

Nampo

Sariwon

NORTH HWANGHAE

GANGWON [KANGWON]

SOUTH HWANGHAE

Imnam Dam

Hwanggang Dam

Haeju

Panmunjeom

GYEONGGI

GANGWON

Seoul

SOUTH KOREA

○ Capital   ● Major cities   ✈ Airports   ⊜ Dams   ▬ ▬ Railroads   ▬·▬·▬ Ceasefire line

10

NORTH KOREA

(DEMOCRATIC PEOPLE'S REPUBLIC OF KOREA)

Statue of Kim Il Sung on Mansudae Hill, Pyongyang. A statue of Kim Jong Il was added to the site in 2013. [Eric Lafforgue]

On September 9, 1948, the Democratic People's Republic of Korea was officially established, a day after Kim Il Sung was made chairman of the Supreme People's Assembly. It is one of three countries in the world with the term "people's republic" in its official name, along with China and Laos, and they are the oldest socialist states in Asia.

Monument to the Workers' Party Foundation. [Charlie Crane]

Economy

North Korea has a planned economy that is controlled by the state. Major industries were nationalized in 1946, and agriculture was collectivized after the Korean War. Though the means of production are owned by the state, individuals are allowed to own small plots of land for individual use. The Central People's Committee (CPC) sets broad economic goals, and the State Planning Committee creates more detailed plans and targets for each industrial sector. Regional committees exist at the provincial level. Recent constitutional revisions have given the cabinet and economic ministries more power and responsibilities. The economy is highly industrialized with an emphasis on heavy industry, including mining, machinery, chemicals, metal processing, and military weapons. Mining produces resources such as coal, graphite, gold ore, iron ore, zinc, molybdenum, magnesite, and tungsten. The country lacks oil and natural gas and is thus highly dependent on imports. It used to engage in trade with the Soviet Union and Eastern Europe, but now its main trade partners are China and South Korea. Industrial management is done according to the Cheongsan-ri Method and the Daean Work System. These systems put industrial and agricultural production under the control of party officials and encouraged them to make on-site inspections, to use incentives to increase production, and to provide technical guidance.

Culture

Juche became the official ideology of the country in 1972. Though the term is often translated as "self-reliance," it more accurately refers to the desire to be in control over one's own history. North Korean culture is a combination of Soviet, East Asian, and native influences. Folk rituals such as ancestor worship were discouraged in the 1950s, but the government allowed their revival in the 1970s. Family life remains strongly Confucian. The constitution guarantees freedom of religion, and the recognized religions are Buddhism, Christianity, and Cheondogyo, the descendant of the Donghak religion that was popular among the peasantry in the nineteenth century. Only Cheondogyo has political representation through the Young Friends' Party (Cheongudang). Cinema is the one of the most widespread forms of entertainment with urban residents seeing a relatively high number of films per year. It is estimated that about 40 percent of households have a television, and video players are beginning to be more common in Pyongyang. Radios and televisions are set so that they can only receive official channels. Some of the most important holidays in North Korea are political ones, such as the birthdays of Kim Il Sung and Kim Jong Il. The people also celebrate the traditional holidays of Lunar New Year, Chuseok, Dano, and Hansik.

Politics

Similar to other modern republics, the North Korean government is divided into executive, legislative, and judicial branches. The office of president (*juseok*) was created in 1972 and abolished in 1998 when Kim Il Sung became the "eternal president" four years after his death. The current head of the executive branch is the premier, and the cabinet consists of the premier, vice-premier, and the heads of each ministry and of some major institutions such as the Central Bank. The main executive decision-making organ is the Central People's Committee. The legislative branch is the Supreme People's Assembly (SPA) which has 687 seats and whose members serve five-year terms. The ruling party is the Korean Workers' Party (KWP), and though other parties exist, the government is effectively a single-party system. The Presidium of the SPA functions as the highest legislative organ when the SPA is not in session, and its head is called the President of the Presidium. The Central Court consists of judges elected by the SPA, and there are also the Provincial Court, municipal and county courts, and the Special Court.

The National Defense Commission has much authority over military affairs and is the highest organ of state power. The *de facto* leader of the country is Kim Jong Un, who is chairman of the National Defense Commission and First Secretary of the KWP. Though the party technically has control over it, the military is one of the most powerful forces in the government and is the fourth largest in the world. The DPRK is a socialist dynasty with a monolithic leadership structure similar to that for Stalin in the Soviet Union and Mao in China. The country is divided into nine provinces with two municipalities; each province has a people's committee and is headed by a Party Secretary.

Mangyeongdae. The birthplace of Kim Il Sung in Pyongyang. [Eckart Dege]

Buheung (Puhung) metro station, Pyongyang. [Charlie Crane]

Society

North Korea is a hierarchical society that, in its early years, was divided into three general groups according to their family background (*seongbun*). The highest group included people from worker families, former poor peasants, and party members; the lowest contained former rich peasants, former landlords, and Christian families. At the local level, people are organized into neighborhood associations (*inminban*), each consisting of twenty-five to fifty families. They handle many of the functions performed by municipal governments in Western societies. The country is highly urbanized with the majority of the population living in cities. The country has achieved virtually complete literacy. Education was compulsory for eleven years with one year of preschool, four years of primary school, and six years of secondary education; beginning in 2014, compulsory education is for twelve years with primary school increased to five years. About 20 percent of students advance to higher education; the most prestigious universities are generally in Pyongyang, headed by Kim Il Sung University. The military has a strong presence in people's lives, and military service is mandatory for males, lasting from two to ten years. In theory, women have equal rights to men, but they remain a minority in high status positions and certain workplaces. Mass media are generally owned and operated by the government. The main newspaper is the *Rodong Sinmun*, the official organ of the central committee of the Korean Workers' Party, which was established in 1945. The main television station is Korean Central Television, which began broadcasting in 1963; there are six hours of programming a day, beginning at 5:00 p.m., except on weekends and holidays.

Pyongyang | *The capital of North Korea*

The capital of North Korea is the largest city in the country with an estimated population of over three million. Large parts of the city were destroyed in the Korean War; few historical structures remain. In the process of modernization, the city has expanded to the north and west, as well as to the eastern side of the Daedong River.

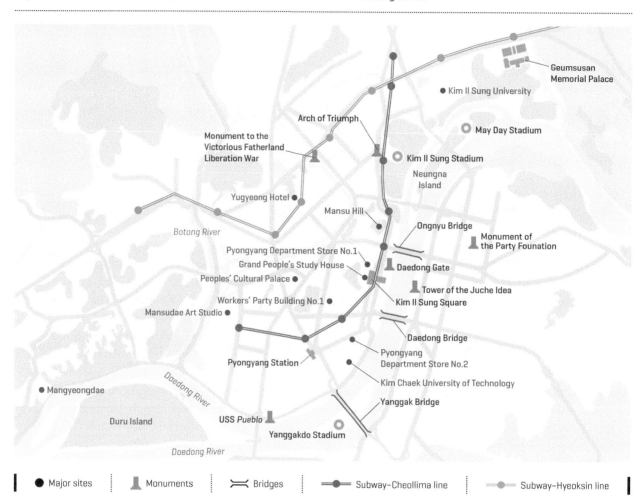

Geumsusan Memorial Palace

● Kim Il Sung University

○ May Day Stadium

Arch of Triumph

Monument to the Victorious Fatherland Liberation War

○ Kim Il Sung Stadium

Neungna Island

Yugyeong Hotel ●

Botong River

Mansu Hill

Ongnyu Bridge

Monument of the Party Founation

Pyongyang Department Store No.1

Grand People's Study House

Daedong Gate

Peoples' Cultural Palace ●

Tower of the Juche Idea

Workers' Party Building No.1 ●

Kim Il Sung Square

Mansudae Art Studio ●

Daedong Bridge

Pyongyang Department Store No.2

Pyongyang Station

Kim Chaek University of Technology

● Mangyeongdae

Daedong River

Yanggak Bridge

Duru Island

USS *Pueblo*

Yanggakdo Stadium ○

Daedong River

● Major sites   Monuments   ⨝ Bridges   Subway–Cheollima line   Subway–Hyeoksin line

Kim Il Sung Square, Pyongyang. Photo taken from the Juche Tower. [Kernbeisser]

The North Korean Nuclear Issue

The nuclear crisis began in the early 1990s when the US accused North Korea of building nuclear weapons and escalated in March 1993 when North Korea threatened to withdraw from the Nuclear Non–Proliferation Treaty. The two countries appeared to be headed toward armed conflict in 1994 until former US President Jimmy Carter made a visit to the North in June that began to defuse tensions. Negotiations led to the adoption of the Agreed Framework in October that was in effect until 2002.

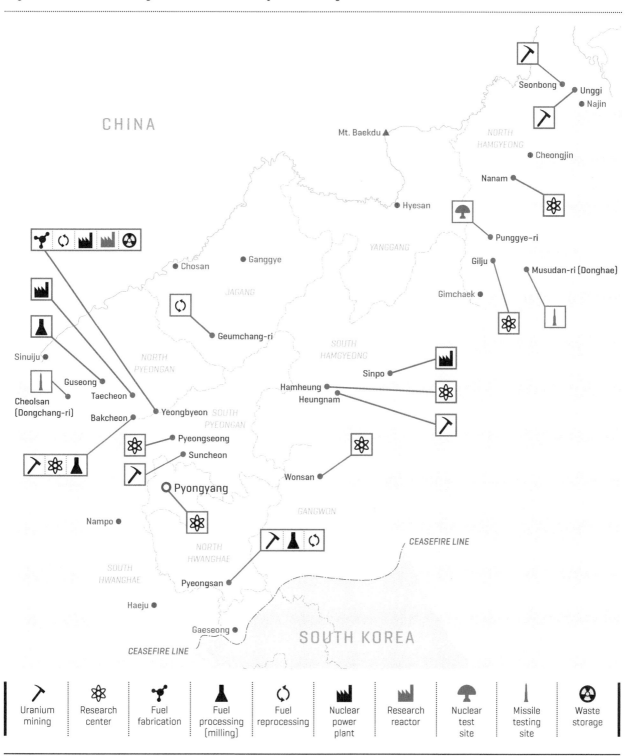

Statistics of North Korea | *1948–present*

Official name:
Democratic People's
Republic of Korea

Capital:
Pyongyang

National flag:
Gonghwagukgi

National flower:
Siebold's Magnolia
(Mongnan)

Area:
120,538 km²
(46,540 aquare miles)

Arable land:
22.4%

**Average annual
rainfall** (Pyongyang):
940 mm

Mean temperature
(Pyongyang):
5.6–15.7 °C

Life expectancy (2010):
70.3 years (female),
66.0 years (male)

Voting age:
17 years of age

Currency:
North Korean Won
Code: KPW (⊠)

Literacy rate:
~99%

Writing system:
Joseongeul

Time zone:
9 hours ahead of UTC

Military (active, 2010):
~1,190,000

Military (reserve, 2010):
~7,700,000

Armored vehicles (2010):
~2,100

Artillery (2010):
~8,500

Combat aircraft (2010):
~820

Warships (2010):
~420

Submarines (2010):
~70

Estimated population and Infant mortality
1946–2010

Year	Population		Infant morality (per 1,000 births)
	North Korea	Pyongyang	
1946	9,257,000	—	—
1949	9,622,000	—	—
1953	8,491,000	—	—
1956	9,359,000	—	—
1960	10,789,000	—	75.9
1965	12,408,000	—	66.9
1970	14,619,000	987,000	56.3
1975	15,986,000	1,348,000	44.1
1980	17,298,000	1,842,000	35.2
1985	18,792,000	2,195,000	29.9
1990	20,019,000	2,526,000	26.1
1991	20,495,000	—	—
1992	20,798,000	—	—
1993	21,103,000	—	—
1994	21,412,000	—	—
1995	21,715,000	2,749,000	24.3
1996	21,991,000	—	—
1997	22,208,000	—	—
1998	22,255,000	—	—
1999	22,507,000	—	—
2000	22,702,000	2,777,000	54.9
2005	23,561,000	2,805,000	28.5
2010	24,187,000	2,834,000	27.4

Source: Bank of Korea (ROK), Eberstadt and Banister (1990)

GDP, GNI per capita, economic growth rate
1960–2010

Year	Nominal GDP (millions US$)	GNI per capita (KRW ⊠)	Economic growth rate (%)
1960	1,520	—	—
1965	2,340	—	—
1970	3,980	—	—
1975	9,350	—	—
1980	13,550	—	—
1985	15,140	—	—
1990	23,100	81.1	-4.3
1991	22,900	81.8	-4.4
1992	21,100	79.1	-7.1
1993	20,500	77.9	-4.5
1994	21,200	79.5	-2.1
1995	22,300	79.1	-4.4
1996	21,400	78.5	-3.4
1997	17,700	75.7	-6.5
1998	12,600	78.7	-0.9
1999	15,800	83.3	6.1
2000	16,800	83.6	0.4
2005	—	105.2	3.8
2010	—	124.2	-0.5

Source: Bank of Korea (ROK); Yang Munsu, *Bukhan gyeongje ui gujo* (Seoul National University Press, 2001), pp. 26-27.

Trade with China, Japan and South Korea by share
2000–2010

Year	Share of trade (%)				Volume of trade (million US$)			
	China	Japan	Russia	South Korea	China	Japan	Russia	South Korea
2000	20.4	19.4	1.9	17.8	488	464	46	425
2002	25.4	12.7	2.8	22.1	738	370	81	642
2004	39.0	7.1	6.0	19.6	1,385	253	213	697
2006	39.1	2.8	4.8	31.1	1,580	122	211	1,350
2008	49.5	0.1	2.0	32.3	2,787	7.7	111	1,820
2010	56.9	0.0	1.8	31.4	3,466	0	111	1,912

Source: Statistics Korea

North Korean economy by sector
1946–1996

[units = million metric tons]

Year	Agriculture	Industry and construction	Services and other
1946	59.1	23.2	17.7
1949	40.6	42.8	16.6
1953	41.6	45.6	12.8
1956	26.6	52.4	21.0
1960	23.6	65.8	10.6
1962	21.3	70.1	8.6
1964	19.3	72.1	8.6
1970	18.3	73.2	8.5
1992	21.8	43.8	34.3
1993	22.4	45.3	32.3
1994	20.9	47.6	31.5
1995	17.4	47.2	35.4
1996	14.7	49.9	35.4

Source: Yang Munsu, *Bukhan gyeongje ui gujo*, p. 110.

Food shortages
1992–1999

[units = million metric tons]

Year	Domestic production	Imports	Demand	Shortfall
1990	5.48	0.86	6.50	-0.16
1991	4.81	1.27	6.47	-0.39
1992	4.43	0.92	6.50	-1.15
1993	4.27	1.09	6.58	-1.22
1994	3.88	0.60	6.67	-2.19
1995	4.13	0.89	6.72	-1.70
1996	3.45	1.05		
1997	3.69	1.63		
1998	3.49			
1999	3.89			

Source: Yang Munsu, p. 36; Unification Ministry (1999); Noland (2000), p. 173.

Food aid
1995–2010

[units = tons]

Year	USA	South Korea	Japan	China	EU	Australia	NGOs
1995	–	150,000	378,000	–	–	–	1,540
1996	22,196	2,754	137,521	100,000	–	3,099	33,543
1997	192,614	60,035	640	150,000	201,112	20,592	191,958
1998	231,361	48,455	67,000	151,105	103,687	2,319	107,794
1999	589,053	12,204	–	200,638	68,010	620	68,724
2000	351,253	351,703	99,999	280,026	70,504	26,673	33,634
2001	318,729	198,000	500,000	419,834	12,595	10,728	317
2002	222,153	457,800	–	329,606	11,606	11,600	7,007
2003	46,755	542,191	–	212,492	69,185	6,808	1,005
2004	105,030	406,510	80,803	132,319	10,989	11,337	317
2005	27,699	492,743	48,084	451,346	8,450	12,921	43
2006	–	79,500	–	207,251	–	985	–
2007	–	430,550	–	264,211	1,290	7,041	–
2008	171,110	58,605	–	–	38	511	–
2009	121,000	–	–	116,179	–	11,190	–
2010	1,470	22,994	–	–	–	6,065	–

Source: World Food Programme FAIS

Estimated deaths:
250,000–1.5 million

Chronically malnourished children (2002):
39.7%

Overall malnourished children (2002):
19.5%

Estimated number of refugees in China (2002):
10,000–300,000

Estimate of aid diverted to other purposes:
~30%

Aid organizations:

World Food Programme, Food and Agriculture Organization (UN), UNICEF, World Health Organization, United Nations Development Programme, Office for the Coordination of Humanitarian Affairs (UN), United Nations Population Fund

Other countries providing aid:

Austria, Canada, Cuba, Denmark, Finland, France, Germany, Greece, Holy See, India, Indonesia, Ireland, Italy, Liechtenstein, Luxembourg, the Netherlands, New Zealand, Mongolia, Norway, Pakistan, the Philippines, Poland, Romania, Russia, Saudi Arabia, South Africa, Sweden, Switzerland, Syria, Taiwan, Thailand, Turkey, United Kingdom, Vietnam

CHRONOLOGY OF NORTH KOREA
1948–PRESENT

CHINA

1949–1976: Mao Zedong
  1958–1962: Great Leap Forward
  1966–1976: Great Proletarian Cultural
    Revolution

1948, SEPTEMBER 9: Founding of the Democratic People's Republic of Korea.

1949: Beginning of the Two-Year Economic Plan.
JUNE 25 : Founding of the Democratic Front for the Reunification of the Fatherland.
JUNE 30: The Workers' Party of North Korea and the Workers' Party of South Korea are combined to form the Workers' Party of Korea.

1950, JUNE 25: The Korean War begins.

1952, DECEMBER: The Academy of Sciences is founded. Reorganization of the administrative districts of the country.

1953, AUGUST: Sixth plenum of the Workers' Party. Former members of the South Korean Workers' Party, including Bak Heonyeong, are purged.

1954–1956: The Three-Year Economic Plan for postwar recovery.

1955, APRIL 4: Promulgation of the "April Theses" on reunification and the construction of socialism.

1956, APRIL: Third Congress of the Workers' Party of Korea.
SUMMER: Execution of Bak Heonyeong.
AUGUST 8: The August Faction Incident.
DECEMBER: Beginning of the Chollima Movement.

1958, MARCH: First conference of the Workers' Party of Korea.
DECEMBER: Completion of the collectivization of agriculture.

1960: The first Five-Year Economic Plan, begun in 1957, is completed in four years.
FEBRUARY: The Chongsanri spirit and Chongsanri method of economic management are introduced.

1961–1970: The first Seven-Year Plan is implemented and extended by three years.

1961, SEPTEMBER: Fourth Congress of the Workers' Party of Korea.
DECEMBER: The Daean system of enterprise management is introduced.

1962, DECEMBER: The Four Military Guidelines are adopted.

1964, FEBRUARY: Promulgation of theses on socialist agriculture.

1966, OCTOBER: Second conference of the Workers' Party.

1967, MAY: The 15th plenum of the fourth Workers' Party Central Committee makes Kim Il Sung's power absolute. Purge of the Gapsan Faction.

1968, JANUARY: North Korean commandos attempt to raid the Blue House in Seoul. The USS *Pueblo* is captured by North Korean forces near Wonsan.

1970, NOVEMBER: Fifth Congress of the Workers' Party of Korea.

1971: Beginning of the Six-Year Economic Plan.

1972, JULY: The North–South Joint Statement is announced on the agreed principles for reunification.
DECEMBER: Promulgation of a revised constitution; *Juche* becomes the official ideology; the establishment of new government organs including the premiership.

1974, FEBRUARY: Sixth Plenum of the Korean Workers' Party central committee names Kim Jong Il as the successor to Kim Il Sung.

1976, JANUARY: North Korea becomes the first communist country to default on its foreign debt.
AUGUST: The ax murder incident in the Panmunjeom Joint Security Area of the DMZ.

1978: Beginning of the second Seven-Year Economic Plan.

1980, OCTOBER: Sixth Congress of the Workers' Party of Korea.

1984, APRIL: Successful test of a Scud-B ballistic missile (Hwasong-5).

1985, SEPTEMBER: The first reunions of separated families since the Korean War.

1987, AUGUST: The country defaults on its foreign loans.

1987–1993: The third Seven-Year Economic Plan is implemented.

	SOVIET UNION	**RUSSIA**
1978–1992: Deng Xiaoping	**1941–1953:** Josef Stalin	**1991–1999:** Boris Yeltsin
1993–2003: Jiang Zemin	**1953–1964:** Nikita Khrushchev	**2000–2008:** Vladimir Putin
2003–2013: Hu Jintao	**1964–1982:** Leonid Brezhnev	**2008–2012:** Dmitry Medvedev
2013– : Xi Jinping	**1985–1991:** Mikhail Gorbachev	**2012–** : Vladimir Putin

1990, APRIL 22: Elections are held for the Supreme People's Assembly.
JUNE: Successful test of a Scud-C missile [Hwasong-6].

1991, SEPTEMBER: North Korea becomes a member of the UN.
DECEMBER: The North–South Basic Agreement is adopted (Agreement on Reconciliation, Nonaggression, and Exchanges and Cooperation).

1993, MAY: Successful test of the Nodong-1 missile.

1994, MAY: North Korea removes 8,000 spent fuel rods from a nuclear reactor with IAEA inspectors present.
JULY: Death of Premier Kim Il Sung.
OCTOBER: The US–DPRK Agreed Framework is adopted in Geneva.

1995, AUGUST: Official request for humanitarian aid.

1996–1999: The beginning of severe food shortages caused by a series of natural disasters (the "Arduous March").

1997: The UN World Food Programme begins sending food aid to North Korea.

1998, JULY 26: Elections are held for the Supreme People's Assembly.
AUGUST: Unsuccessful attempt to use the three-stage Taepodong-1 missile to launch a satellite (Kwangmyongsong-1).
SEPTEMBER: Under a revision of the constitution, Kim Jong Il becomes chairman of the National Defense Commission.
OCTOBER: First appearance of the term "Military First policy."

2000, JANUARY: North Korea normalizes diplomatic relations with the countries of western Europe with the exception of France.
JUNE: The first Inter-Korean Summit takes place in Pyongyang.

2001, MAY: Kim Jong Nam, eldest son of Kim Jong Il, is detained in Japan on a trip to Tokyo Disneyland.

2002, JANUARY 29: In his State of the Union Address, President George W. Bush includes North Korea in the "Axis of Evil," along with Iran and Iraq.
JULY: The July 1st economic reform measures accept elements of a market economy.
OCTOBER: Assistant Secretary of State James Kelly visits North Korea.

2003, JANUARY: Withdrawal from the Nuclear Non-Proliferation Treaty.
AUGUST 3: Elections are held for the Supreme People's Assembly.
AUGUST: Six-party talks begin in Beijing on North Korea's nuclear program.

2004, JULY: Complex of Goguryeo (Koguryeo) tombs is inscribed in UNESCO's World Heritage List.
DECEMBER: Gaeseong Industrial Park opens with the participation of South Korean manufacturers.

2006, JULY: Unsuccessful test of the Taepodong-2 missile.
OCTOBER: First nuclear weapon test.

2007, OCTOBER: The second Inter-Korean Summit is held in Pyongyang.

2009, MARCH 8: Elections are held for the Supreme People's Assembly.
MAY: Second underground nuclear test.

2010, SEPTEMBER: at a conference of Workers' Party delegates, Kim Jong Un is named vice-chairman of the Central Military Commission and appointed to the party's Central Committee.
SEPTEMBER: Third conference of the Workers' Party.

2011, DECEMBER 17: Death of Kim Jong Il.

2012, APRIL 11: Fourth conference of the Workers' Party.
Kim Jong Un is appointed as First Secretary of the Workers' Party.

2012, APRIL 13: Kim Jong Un becomes the chairman of the National Defense Commission.

2013, JUNE: Historic monuments and sites in Gaeseong (Kaesong) are inscribed in UNESCO's World Heritage list.
DECEMBER 12: Execution of Jang Song Thaek (Jang Seongtaek).

2014, MARCH 9: Elections are held for the Supreme People's Assembly.

우리의것을 살려

North Korean poster promoting traditional culture with the slogan "Let's cherish what is ours." (David Heather)

NORTH KOREA

○ Pyongyang

GANGWON

SOUTH
HWANGHAE

CEASEFIRE LINE

🏛 Peace Dam   ● Sokcho

NORTHERN LIMIT LINE

○ Panmunjeom   ● Chuncheon

Paju ●   ● Uijeongbu   🛩 ● Gangneung

Incheon ◎ 🛩 ◎ Seoul   GANGWON

🛩 GYEONGGI

Suwon ●   ● Yongin   ● Wonju   ● Pyeongchang

Pyeongtaek ●   🏛 Chungju Dam   ⚛ Hanul (Uljin)

Cheonan ●   NORTH
CHUNGCHEONG

Asan ●

SOUTH
CHUNGCHEONG   🛩 ● Cheongju

Sejong ◎   ● Andong

◎ Daejeon   NORTH
GYEONGSANG

● Gumi   ● Pohang

● Jeonju   🛩   ● Gyeongju
Daegu ●

NORTH
JEOLLA   ⚛ Wolseong

⚛ Ulsan

Hanbit ⚛   SOUTH
GYEONGSANG   ⚛ Gori

[Yeonggwang]   🛩 🛩 ● Busan

🛩 ◎ Gwangju   Changwon ●

Jinju ●

SOUTH
JEOLLA

🛩 ● Mokpo   ● Yeosu   ● Geoje Island

KOREA STRAIT

Tsushima

🛩 ● Jeju City   ● Fukuoka

JEJU

JAPAN

Ulleung

Dok

○	●	◉	◎	🛩	⚛	- - -	▬ ▬ ▬
Capital	Major cities	Metropolitan cities	Special autonomous city	Airports	Nuclear power plant	Gyeongbu High Speed Railway	Honam High Speed Railway

11
SOUTH KOREA
(REPUBLIC OF KOREA)

Park Chung Hee.
President of the Republic of Korea, 1963–1979.
(Getty Images)

Kim Dae-jung.
President of the Republic of Korea, 1998–2003.
(The Kim Dae-jung Presidential Library)

The Republic of Korea was officially founded on August 15, 1948, three years after the end of Japanese rule. Since its founding, its constitution has been rewritten five times; the current government is under the Sixth Republic, which began in 1988. The history of South Korea since 1953 involves two main narratives – industrialization and the victory of the democracy movement over military dictatorship.

Funeral procession of Yi Hanyeol moving through the front gate of Yonsei University on July 9, 1987. He was a student at Yonsei who died on July 5 after being hit on the head a month earlier by a tear gas canister fired by riot police during a demonstration against the military dictatorship on June 9. [Corbis Images]

Society

The population of South Korea grew rapidly in the last half of the twentieth century, but now it has one of the lowest birth rates among industrialized countries. Another major development has been the rise of a middle class which was particularly noticeable from the 1980s. South Korea is one of the most urbanized countries in the world with around 80 percent of the population living in cities. The largest cities are Seoul, Busan, Daegu, Incheon, Gwangju, and Daejeon. The South Korean population is highly educated with virtually complete literacy. Education is compulsory for nine years, but a large number graduate from secondary school. The number of college graduates is also relatively high among OECD countries. Women have an increasing presence in higher education and the workplace but remain a minority in high-level positions. South Korea has a strong civil society with both students and labor organizations playing leading roles in the democracy movement. Mass media is a combination of state-run and private companies. There are four main daily newspapers – the *Chosun Ilbo*, the *Dong-a Ilbo*, the *JoongAng Ilbo*, and the *Hangyoreh*. There are three major public broadcasting companies – KBS (first broadcast in 1961), MBC (1969), and SBS (1991), as well as numerous regional and cable channels. In the internet age, it is also known to be one of the most wired countries in the world.

Culture

Though extended families are becoming increasingly rare, the Confucian family system remains strong. Confucian paternalism is also a prevalent feature of South Korean corporate management. The growth of Christianity has been rapid with over 25 percent of the population now identifying themselves as Christian. The main sects are Presbyterians, Methodists, and Catholics, and some of the largest churches in the world are located in Seoul. Buddhism remains popular, with the Jogye Order being the largest sect. The division of the country posed a challenge to the development of modern Korean literature, but a number of major writers emerged during this time such as Choe Inhun, Bak Gyeongni, and Jo Jeongnae. Western forms of entertainment have become very popular as popular culture underwent tremendous growth from the 1980s. Television has a penetration rate of virtually 100 percent, and most households have computers with high-speed internet access. The film industry experienced a boom from the mid-1990s, producing both box office hits and high-quality films that have won awards at major international film festivals. From the mid-1990s, Korean popular culture – including pop music, film, and television dramas – has become popular throughout Asia, a phenomenon known as the "Korean Wave."

Economy

South Korea has a modern industrial economy; it joined the Office for Economic Co-operation and Development in 1996 and is a member of the G-20. After its founding, the country underwent rapid industrialization. Agriculture as a share of GDP decreased from about 40 percent in the late 1950s to under 10 percent by the early 1990s. The economy developed in stages, moving from light industry to heavy industry and then to high-tech and service industries. Textiles and wigs were among the first major exports, and then came steel, shipbuilding, and automobiles; now companies have moved into electronics and other high-tech goods such as microchips. South Korean industrialization was based on export-led growth, with the United States as its major export market. The economy is dominated by large conglomerates called *chaebol* (*jaebeol*) such as Samsung and Hyundai. Unlike Japanese *zaibatsu*, they are generally family-owned and do not have their own banks. In 1992, the revenues of the top thirty conglomerates accounted for 80 percent of GDP. During the period of rapid growth in the 1960s and 1970s, the country had a planned economy. Beginning in 1961, the Economic Planning Board created a series of five-years plans that set the direction of industrial policy. Compared to other industrial countries, business has a close relation with the government in South Korea. The South Korean economy is dependent on imports for over 95 percent of its energy. It is one of the leading importers of coal, natural gas, and petroleum in the world, and nuclear power accounts for about 30 percent of its electricity generation.

50,000-won note with image of Sin Saimdang (1504-1551), the first woman to appear on a ROK banknote.

Hyundai car factory. Ulsan. [Daniel Brennwald]

Politics

Except for the Second Republic, the chief executive has been the president. From the beginning of the Sixth Republic, the president has been selected by direct election and serves a single five-year term. The president no longer has the authority to dissolve the legislature. There is a prime minister who is appointed by the president and must be confirmed by the legislature. The cabinet consists of the heads of the seventeen government ministries. Two foundations of the military dictatorship were the Korean Central Intelligence Agency (KCIA), founded in 1961, and the anti-communist National Security Law, which remains in effect today. South Korea has a unicameral legislature called the National Assembly. It must have at least 200 seats according to the constitution; at present, there are 299 seats. Members serve four-year terms, and there are no term limits. Most of the seats are filled by direct election, but some are allocated by proportional representation. To receive an allocation, a political party must receive at least 3 percent of the vote in a general election. A minimum of twenty members is necessary to constitute a negotiating group in the National Assembly. The Supreme Court has fourteen judges who serve six-year terms. The Chief Justice is selected by the president, subject to confirmation by the National Assembly, and serves a single term. The other justices can serve more than one term. There is also a Constitutional Court with nine judges who serve renewable six-year terms. The United States has maintained troops in South Korea since the end of the Korean War. There are currently about 28,000 troops on over forty army and air bases mostly located in the northern part of the country.

After suffering extensive damage during the Korean War, Seoul developed into one of the ten largest cities in the world by the end of the twentieth century with a population of over ten million. The capital is divided into twenty–five *gu* which are in turn divided into a total of 522 *dong*. It has expanded to the southern side of the Han River and is the political, economic, and cultural center of South Korea. With the construction of a number of satellite cities from the late 1980s, the Seoul metropolitan area contains over half the population of the country.

●	☐	◆	■		▧	- - - -	▬ ▬
Palace	Important buildings	Government office	Department store	Market	Newspaper offices	Tunnels	Railroad

Unjeong · Yangju · Uijeongbu · Namyangju

Ilsan · Goyang · Dobong-gu · Nowon-gu

▲▲ Mt. Bukhan

Eunpyeong-gu · Gangbuk-gu

Gimpo Bridge

Haengju Bridge

Jongno-gu · Seongbuk-gu · Jungnang-gu · Guri

Sungkyunkwan University

Gimpo · ● The Blue House · 🏛 Korea University

Cheongnyang-ri Station

● Gyeongbok Palace

Han River · Seodaemun-gu · Dongdaemun-gu

Myongji University 🏛 · Jung-gu · Han River

Yonsei University 🏛 🏛

Incheon · Gangseo-gu

✈ Gimpo Airport · Mapo-gu · Ewha Womans University · ⬡ Namsan Park

Gwangjin-gu · Gangdong-gu

National Assembly · Yongsan-gu · Seongdong-gu · Seongsu Bridge

SBS 📶 · KBS 📶 📶 · MBC

US Army Garrison · ⬡ Olympic Park · Hanam

Yangcheon-gu

Bucheon · National Museum of Korea

Jungdong · Guro-gu · Yeongdeungpo-gu · Dongjak-gu · Han River Bridge · Songpa-gu

Gangnam-gu

Guro Industrial Complex · Gwanak-gu · Seocho-gu

Incheon · 🏛 Seoul National University (main campus)

Gwangmyeong · ▲▲ Mt. Gwanak

Seongnam

Shiheung · Gwacheon · Gwangju

Anyang · Seongnam

Pangyo · Gwangju

Pyeongchon · Bundang

Sanbon

| Seoul | Gyeonggi | New town | Bridge | Broadcast 📶 | University 🏛 | Airport ✈ | Park ⬡ | Mountain ▲▲ |

The Growth of Seoul | 1395–1992

- 1395
- –1395
- 1936–1949
- 1949–1963
- 1963–1973
- 1973–1992
- ● Gyeongbok Palace

Bridges of Seoul

	Name of bridge		Name of bridge		Name of bridge
1	Gimpo	8	Mapo	15	Seongsu
2	Haengju	9	Wonhyo	16	Yeongdong
3	Banghwa	10	Hangang	17	Cheongdam
4	Gayang	11	Dongjak	18	Jamsil
5	Seongsan	12	Banpo	19	Olympic
6	Yanghwa	13	Hannam	20	Gwangjin
7	Seogang	14	Dongho	21	Gangdong

Industrial Development

South Korea underwent a compressed development that accomplished several stages of industrialization within a few decades. It first focused on light industry and then shifted to heavy industry and now to high-tech and service industries. During the period of military dictatorship, industrialization was concentrated in Gyeongsang and Gyeonggi provinces, where many of the elites in that era came from.

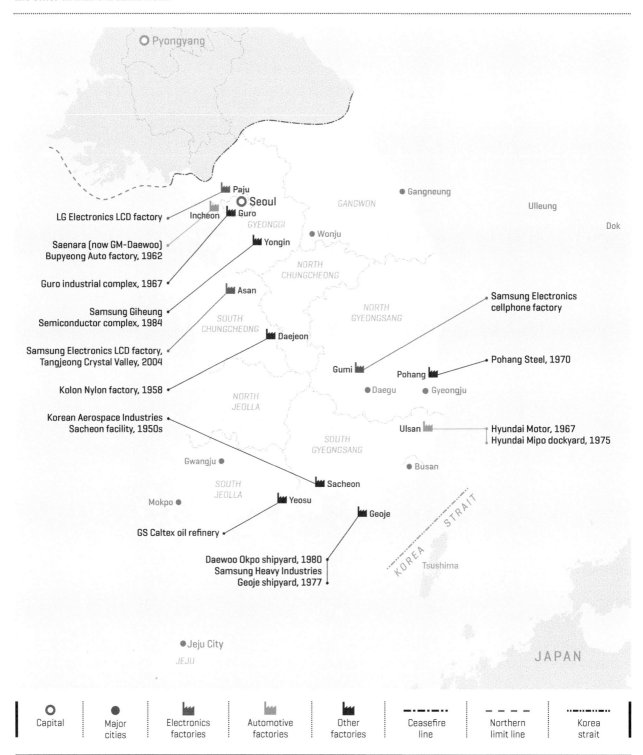

The Gwangju Democratic Uprising | *May 18–27, 1980*

Protests broke out all over South Korea in spring 1980 in opposition to General Chun Doo Hwan's efforts to seize power after Park Chung Hee's assassination in October 1979. They peaked in May, and when Chun sent troops to suppress the protests in Gwangju, they developed into a rebellion that took over the city for a few days before being suppressed.

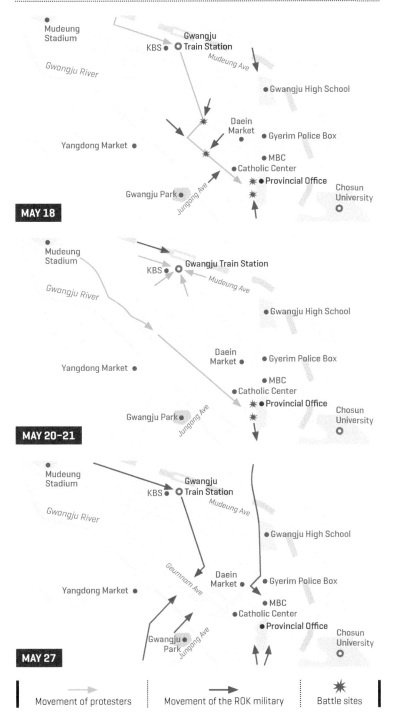

Movement of protesters | Movement of the ROK military | Battle sites

CHRONOLOGY OF THE UPRISING

MAY 14: Protests begin in Gwangju with demonstrations at Chonnam and Chosun Universities.

MAY 17: Arrest of opposition politician Kim Dae-jung.

MAY 18: The government imposes martial law over the entire country.
: Students gather at Chonnam National University; first clash with paratroopers.
: Students march to Geumnam Avenue in downtown Gwangju.
: Clashes lead to the arrest of over 500 people.
: The Martial Law Command announces that the curfew time will be moved to 9:00 p.m.

MAY 19: Reinforcements arrive in Gwangju very early in the morning.
: Death of Gim Gyeongcheol, the first known casualty of the uprising.
: Citizens begin gathering in downtown Gwangju.
: Clashes between citizens and paratroopers on Geumnam Avenue.
: An armored vehicle fires on the protestors near Gwangju High School.

MAY 20: Citizens continue to battle the paratroopers.
: Late in the afternoon, about 200 taxi drivers join the protest, driving from Mudeung Stadium to Geumnam Avenue.
: Protestors battle troops at MBC; in the evening, the building is set on fire.
: Soldiers fire on unarmed protestors near Gwangju Station.

MAY 21: In the early morning, telephone lines leading outside the city are cut off; the local KBS station is set on fire.
: Soldiers begin to fire on the protesters in front of the South Jeolla Provincial Office.
: Citizens take several military trucks and armored vehicles from the Asia Motors factory.
: The citizens' army, now armed, engage in pitched battles in the streets in front of the Provincial Government Office.
: In the afternoon, the army begins to retreat.

MAY 22: Formation of the Citizens' Settlement Committee.
: A citizens' assembly is held in the plaza in front of the Provincial Government Office.

MAY 23: The first All Citizens' Rally for the Protection of Democracy is held.

MAY 27: In the early hours of the morning, tanks enter the city, followed by troops.
: Government troops surround the Provincial Government Office and battle the citizens' army in the streets.
: The troops retake the Provincial Government Office and the rest of the downtown area.

Statistics of South Korea | *1948–2010*

Official name:
Republic of Korea

Capital:
Seoul

National flag:
Taegeukgi

National flower:
Rose of Sharon
(Mugunghwa)

Area:
99,828 km²
(38,544 square miles)

Arable land:
16.58%

Annual precipitation:
1,245 mm

Mean temperature
(Seoul):
8.2–16.9 °C
(maximum)

Life expectancy
(2009):
83.8 years (female)
77 years (male)

Voting age:
19 years of age

Religions:
Buddhism,
Protestantism,
Catholicism

Currency:
South Korean Won
Code: KRW (₩)

Literacy rate:
~97.9%

Writing system:
Hangeul

Drinking age:
20 years of age

Electricity:
220 volt

Time zone:
9 hours ahead of UTC

CO² emissions:
581.1 milion mt
(2010, 7th in the world)

Crude oil imports:
2.37 million bbl.day
(2012, 5th in the world)

Population of South Korea and Seoul
1944–2010

Year	Population			Birth rate
	South Korea	Seoul	Rural	
1944	—	988,537	—	—
1945	16,136,000	—	—	—
1949	20,189,000	1,446,019	—	—
1955	20,202,000	1,575,000	16,239,608	—
1960	25,012,374	2,445,000	17,992,495	—
1965	28,704,674	3,471,000	—	—
1970	32,240,827	5,433,198	18,504,312	4.53
1975	35,280,725	6,889,502	17,905,538	3.43
1980	38,123,775	8,364,379	15,997,362	2.82
1985	40,805,744	9,639,110	14,001,680	1.66
1990	42,869,283	10,612,577	11,100,319	1.57
1995	45,092,991	10,231,217	9,561,746	1.634
2000	47,008,111	9,895,217	9,342,841	1.467
2005	48,138,077	9,820,171	8,703,735	1.076
2010	48,875,000	9,794,304	—	1.22

Source: KOSIS

GDP of South Korea
1960–2010

Year	GDP current (Billion US $)	GNI per capita Atlas method current (US $)
1960	3.89	—
1965	3.02	130
1970	8.89	270
1975	21.46	630
1980	63.83	1,810
1985	96.62	2,330
1990	263.78	6,000
1995	517.12	10,770
2000	533.38	9,910
2005	844.86	16,900
2010	1,014.89	19,650

Source: World Bank Data Bank

Composition of economic output
1970–2010

(units = %)

Year	Agriculture, fisheries, and forestry	Mining	Manufacturing	Utilities	Construction	Service	Total
1970	29.1	1.7	18.5	1.3	5.1	44.3	100.0
1975	26.9	1.5	22.2	1.1	4.5	43.7	99.9
1980	16.0	1.4	24.6	2.1	7.9	48.0	100.0
1985	13.3	1.3	26.7	2.9	6.9	49.0	100.1
1990	8.7	0.8	26.6	2.1	10.4	51.5	100.1
1995	6.2	0.5	26.7	2.0	10.1	54.6	100.1
2000	4.6	0.3	28.3	2.5	6.9	57.3	99.9
2005	3.3	0.3	27.5	2.3	7.6	59.0	100.0
2010	2.6	0.2	30.3	2.0	6.3	58.5	99.9

Source: Bank of Korea

Economic growth rate of South Korea
1960–2010

(units = %)

Year	GDP growth rate	Economic growth rate	Year	GDP growth rate	Economic growth rate	Year	GDP growth rate	Economic growth rate
1960			1980	-1	-1.9	2000	8	8.8
1961	5		1981	6	7.4	2001	4	4
1962	2		1982	7	8.3	2002	7	7.2
1963	10		1983	11	12.2	2003	3	2.8
1964	8		1984	8	9.9	2004	5	4.8
1965	5		1985	7	7.5	2005	4	4
1966	13		1986	11	12.2	2006	5	5.2
1967	6		1987	11	12.3	2007	5	5.1
1968	12		1988	11	11.7	2008	2	2.3
1969	14		1989	7	6.8	2009	0	0.3
1970	8		1990	9	9.3	2010	6	6.3
1971	8	10.4	1991	9	9.7			
1972	4	6.5	1992	6	5.8			
1973	12	14.8	1993	6	6.3			
1974	7	9.4	1994	9	8.8			
1975	6	7.3	1995	9	8.9			
1976	11	13.5	1996	7	7.2			
1977	10	11.8	1997	5	5.8			
1978	9	10.3	1998	-7	-5.7			
1979	7	8.4	1999	9	10.7			

Sources: World Bank Data Bank, Bank of Korea.

Gini coefficient
1990–2010

Year	Gini coefficient	Relative poverty rate (%)	Year	Gini coefficient	Relative poverty rate (%)
1990	0.266	7.8	2000	0.279	10.4
1991	0.259	7.2	2001	0.29	11.3
1992	0.254	7.4	2002	0.293	11.1
1993	0.256	8.2	2003	0.283	12.1
1994	0.255	7.9	2004	0.293	12.8
1995	0.259	8.3	2005	0.298	13.6
1996	0.266	9.1	2006	0.305	13.8
1997	0.264	8.7	2007	0.316	14.9
1998	0.293	11.4	2008	0.319	14.7
1999	0.298	12.2	2009	0.32	15.4
			2010	0.315	14.9

KOSIS stats (urban, non-agricultural, more than 2 employees)

MEDIA AND INTERNET USAGE
(2010)

Internet users:
37 million

Internet usage rate
83.2% (male)
72.4% (female)
77.8% (total)

Average usage
14.7 hours (per week)

Internet access
81.6% (of households)

Broadband
95% (of households)

Mobile phone
96.6% (of households)

Desktop computer
81.4% (of households)

Mobile phone ownership
88.5% (male)
85.2% (female)
86.9% (total)

Average TV viewing time
16.3 hours (per week)

Newspaper readership
58.1% (non-internet)

Radio audience
50.2% (non-internet)

Source: Korea Internet and Security Agency

SOUTH KOREAN MILITARY
(2010)

Military :
~650,000 (active)

Military :
~3,200,000 (reserve)

Armored vehicles:
~2,600

Artillery:
~5,200

Combat aircraft:
~460

Warships:
~120

Submarines:
~10

CHRONOLOGY OF SOUTH KOREA
1948–PRESENT

1948, AUGUST 15: Founding of the Republic of Korea.

1949, JANUARY: South Korea's first application for UN membership is rejected.

1953, AUGUST 15: The South Korean government returns to Seoul.
OCTOBER 1: Signing of the Mutual Defense Treaty Between the United States and the Republic of Korea.

1954, JANUARY 30: Establishment of the Korean National Commission for UNESCO.
NOVEMBER 29: The government introduces a constitutional amendment that eliminates term limits for Syngman Rhee.

1955, AUGUST 8: Opening of the Seoul stock exchange.
AUGUST 26: South Korea joins the International Monetary Fund and IBRD.

1956, MAY 15: Reelection of Syngman Rhee as president.
JUNE 6: First observation of the Memorial Day holiday (Hyeonchungil).
NOVEMBER 10: Founding of the Progressive Party, with Jo Bongam as chairman.
28: Signing of the Friendship, Commerce, and Navigation Treaty with the US.

1957, SEPTEMBER 9: The Security Council rejects a Soviet proposal for joint admission of the two Koreas to UN membership.

1958, JANUARY 29: The US army begins to station nuclear weapons in South Korea.

1959, JULY 31: Execution of Jo Bongam.

1960, MARCH 15: Syngman Rhee is re-elected as president.
APRIL 19: Beginning of the April Revolution.
APRIL 26: Syngman Rhee resigns.
JUNE: Passage of the National Security Law.
JUNE 15: Beginning of the Second Republic.

1961, MAY 16: Park Chung Hee takes power in a coup d'état.
JUNE 13: Establishment of the Korean Central Intelligence Agency.
DECEMBER 31: KBS TV begins broadcasting.

1962, JANUARY 15: The first Five-Year Plan is announced.

1963, JANUARY: Busan becomes a "directly governed city" (jikhalsi).
OCTOBER 15: Election of Park Chung Hee as president.
DECEMBER 17: Beginning of the Third Republic.

1964, OCTOBER 31: South Korea agrees to send troops to Vietnam.

1965, JUNE 22: Normalization of relations between Japan and the Republic of Korea.

1966, JANUARY: Publication of the first issue of the journal *Changjak gwa bipyeong* (Creation and Criticism).
JULY: The Status of Forces Agreement (SOFA) is signed with the US.

1967, MAY 3: Reelection of Park Chung Hee as president.
OCTOBER 3: Construction begins on the Pohang steel plant.

1968, JANUARY 21: Attempted assassination of Park Chung Hee by North Korea.

1969, SEPTEMBER: The serialization of Bak Gyeongni's novel *Land* (Toji) begins.

1970, APRIL 22: Beginning of the Saemaul Movement for rural modernization.
NOVEMBER 13: Suicide by self-immolation of garment worker Jeon Taeil.

1971, FEBRUARY 9: The third Five-Year Economic Plan is announced.
APRIL 27: Park Chung Hee defeats Kim Dae-jung in a surprisingly close presidential election.

1972, AUGUST 30: The first round of Red Cross talks between North and South Korea opens in Pyongyang.
OCTOBER 17: Park Chung Hee declares martial law and dissolves the National Assembly.
NOVEMBER 21: Approval of the new authoritarian Yushin Constitution that eliminates presidential term limits.
DECEMBER 23: Park Chung Hee is reelected president.
DECEMBER 27: Beginning of the Fourth Republic.

1973, MARCH 14: The withdrawal of ROK troops from Vietnam.
AUGUST 8: Kim Dae-jung is kidnapped from a hotel in Tokyo by KCIA agents.

1974, JAN. 8: Promulgation of Emergency Decrees 1 and 2.
AUGUST 15: In a failed assassination attempt on Park, the First Lady is killed. Seoul's Subway Line 1 opens.
: Beginning of operation of Saemaeul-class trains.

1975, DECEMBER 31: Production begins of Korea's first domestically developed car.

1976: The Koreagate scandal.

1978, APRIL 29: South Korea's first nuclear power plant opens.
JULY 6: Reelection of Park Chung Hee as president.

US
1945–1953: Harry S. Truman
1953–1961: Dwight D. Eisenhower
1961–1963: John F. Kennedy
1963–1969: Lyndon B. Johnson
1969–1974: Richard Nixon
1974–1977: Gerald Ford

1977–1981: Jimmy Carter
1981–1989: Ronald Reagan
1989–1993: George H.W. Bush
1993–2001: Bill Clinton
2001–2009: George W. Bush
2009–   : Barack Obama

JAPAN
1926–1989: Shōwa period
    1955, Nov.: Formation of the
        Liberal Democratic Party (LDP)
    1964: Tokyo Olympics
1989–   : Heisei period

1979, AUGUST 8: Beginning of the YH Incident.
OCTOBER 26: Assassination of Park Chung Hee.
DECEMBER 12: Chun Doo-hwan carries out a coup d'état.

1980, MAY 17: Beginning of the Fifth Republic.
MAY 18: Beginning of the Gwangju Democratic Uprising.
SEPTEMBER 1: Chun Doo-hwan becomes president.
OCTOBER: Opening of Subway Line 2 in Seoul.

1982, MARCH 12: Protestors set fire to the American Cultural Service building in Busan.

1983, SEPTEMBER 1: Korean Airlines flight 007 is shot down by the Soviets near Sakhalin Island.
OCTOBER 9: Attempted assassination of Chun Doo-hwan in Myanmar (Burma).

1986, SEPTEMBER 20: The opening of the 10th Asian Games in Seoul.

1987, JANUARY 14: Death of SNU student Bak Jongcheol while being tortured by the police.
JUNE 9: Yonsei University student Yi Hanyeol is fatally injured during a demonstration.
JUNE 10: Beginning of the June Democracy Struggle.
JUNE 29: Presidential candidate Roh Tae-woo agrees to direct presidential elections and other democratic reforms.
DECEMBER 16: Roh Tae-woo is elected president.

1988, FEBRUARY 25: Beginning of the Sixth Republic.
SEPTEMBER 17: The 24th Olympic Games open in Seoul.

1990, SEPTEMBER 30: Establishment of diplomatic relations with the USSR.

1991, SEPTEMBER 17: Both South Korea and North Korea join the United Nations.

1992, AUGUST 23: Establishment of diplomatic relations with the People's Republic of China.
NOVEMBER: Part of the land occupied by the American garrison at Yongsan is returned to the city of Seoul.
DECEMBER 18: Election of Kim Young-sam as president.

1994, OCTOBER 21: Collapse of the Seongsu Bridge in Seoul.

1995, JANUARY: The government re-designates Busan, Daegu, Daejeon, Gwangju, and Incheon as Metropolitan Cities.
JUNE 29: Collapse of Sampoong Department Store in Seoul.
AUGUST 15: Beginning of the demolition of the former Government–General building in Seoul.
DECEMBER: Haein Temple, Jongmyo Shrine, and Seokguram Grotto/ Bulguk Temple are designated UNESCO World Heritage Sites.

1996: South Korea joins the OECD.
MARCH: Former presidents Chun Doo Hwan and Roh Tae Woo are tried for their roles in the 1979 coup and the suppression of the Gwangju Democratic Uprising in 1980.

1997: Ulsan becomes a Metropolitan City.
JULY: Beginning of the Asian financial crisis.
NOVEMBER: Formation of the Grand National Party (GNP).
DECEMBER 3: The International Monetary Fund agrees to a bailout of South Korea.
DECEMBER 18: Election of Kim Dae-jung as president.

2000, JUNE 13–15: The first North–South summit meeting is held in Pyongyang.
DECEMBER 10: President Kim Dae-jung is awarded the Nobel Peace Prize.

2002, MAY–JUNE: South Korea co-hosts the FIFA World Cup with Japan.
JUNE 13: Two thirteen-year-old schoolgirls are killed by an American armored vehicle in Uijeongbu.
DECEMBER 19: Election of Roh Moo-hyun as president.

2004, MARCH 12: The National Assembly votes to impeach the president.
APRIL: Start of high-speed rail service (KTX) between Seoul and Daegu.
MAY 14: The Constitutional Court overturns the impeachment vote.

2007, OCTOBER 2–4: The second inter-Korean summit meeting is held in Pyongyang.
DECEMBER 19: Election of Lee Myung-bak as president.

2008, FEBRUARY: Formation of the Democratic Party.
10: Sungnye Gate (Namdaemun) is destroyed by arson.

2009, MAY 23: Suicide of former president Roh Moo-hyun.
JULY: Opening of Subway Line 9 in Seoul.

2010, JUNE 26–27: Seoul hosts the fifth G-20 summit.
NOVEMBER 23: Yeonpyeong Island is attacked by North Korean artillery.

2011, NOVEMBER: The National Assembly ratifies the ROK-US Free Trade Agreement.

2012, DECEMBER 19: Election of Park Geun-hye as president.

2014, APRIL 16: The ferry Sewol sinks near Jin Island.

Contributors

Lee Injae, after receiving his undergraduate and graduate degrees from Yonsei University, has been teaching in the Department of History and Culture at Yonsei's Wonju campus since 1998. He has published numerous studies of the land system of the Unified Silla period and of Zen Buddhist thought in medieval Korea. He is also the head of a project to compile a reference book on the land system in Korea. At his university, he has served as Dean of Students and is currently Dean of the College of Liberal Arts. In 2011, he was the chair of the organizing committee for the Yeongwol-Yonsei Forum and served as the President of the Organization of Korean Historians.

Owen Miller is Lecturer in Korean Studies at SOAS, University of London where he teaches Korean history. He was previously a research associate at Robinson College, University of Cambridge. He received his PhD from SOAS in 2007 for a thesis on merchant-government relations in late nineteenth century Korea. His research interests include the social and economic history of 19th and 20th century Korea, urban history, Korean nationalist and Marxist historiographies, and the economic history of North Korea. He is a member of the council of the British Association for Korean Studies and a convenor of the Comparative Histories of Asia seminar at the Institute for Historical Research in London.

Park Jinhoon is currently an Associate Professor in the Department of History at Myongji University in Seoul. He received his Ph.D. from Yonsei University with a dissertation on government policy toward people of unfree status in the late Goryeo and early Joseon periods. Earlier in his career, he taught at Kookmin University, Catholic University of Korea, and Hankuk University of Foreign Studies and worked as a senior researcher at Kookmin University. His research focuses on the social status system in Goryeo and government policy and legal institutions on social class. He has also published an annotated translation of Jeong Dojeon's *Sambongjip* and is working on the restoration of the *Gyeongje ryukjeon*, a legal text from the early Joseon period. Some of his major articles include "Birth Registration and Census Registers in Goryeo," "Name Changing in the Goryeo Period," and "Discussion on the Law to Limit Possession of Private Unfree Laborers in the Early Joseon Period."

Michael D. Shin teaches Korean history at the University of Cambridge. He is the co-editor of *Landlords, Peasants, and Intellectuals in Modern Korea* (Cornell East Asia Series, 2005), editor and co-translator of *Everyday Life in Joseon-Era Korea: Economy and Society* by The Organization of Korean Historians (Global Oriental, 2014), and the author of the upcoming *The Specter of Yi Gwangsu: The March First Movement and the Nation under Colonial Rule*. His research focuses on the Japanese colonial period (1910-1945), and he has published a number of articles on the intellectual, literary, and social history of the early twentieth century.

Yi Hyunhae received her Ph.D. from Ewha Woman's University and has taught at Hallym University since 1988. Her research focuses on the society of the Samhan statelets in the first to third centuries and their development into the states of Silla and Baekje. She is the author of *The Formation of Samhan Society* (Iljogak, 1984) and *Production and Trade in Ancient Korea* (Iljogak, 1998), as well as numerous articles and co-authored volumes. She was the director of the University Museum at Hallym University from 2012-2014 and serves on the editorial boards of *Baekje yeongu* and of *Dongbuga yeoksa nonchong* and on the Cultural Heritage Committee in the Cultural Heritage Administration.

Joon Mo Kang (chief designer) was born in Seoul and is a graduate of the School of Visual Arts in New York City. He worked for many years as a graphic designer and illustrator in New York, doing illustrations that have won awards from AIGA, *American Illustration*, the Society of Publication Designers, and the Society for News Design, and the Society of Illustrators. He has also been an art director for *The New York Times*, *Newsweek*, and *Art Asia Pacific* magazine. He currently works in Seoul, Korea.

Chronology of The "Comfort Women" Issue

1921: The League of Nations agrees to the International Convention for the Suppression of the Traffic in Women and Children.

1931, SEPTEMBER 18: The Manchurian Incident.

1932, MARCH: Establishment of the first "comfort stations" in Shanghai.

1933, MARCH: First confirmed comfort station in northeast China.

1937, DECEMBER: The Nanjing Massacre.

1938, APRIL 1: Promulgation of the State Mobilization Law.

1941, DECEMBER 7: Japanese attacks Pearl Harbor. Beginning of the Pacific War.

1942: The Ministry of War takes charge of establishing military comfort stations.

1944, JANUARY: Announcement of plans for the Women's Volunteer Labor Corps (Joshi Rōdō Teishintai).
APRIL: Closure of comfort stations in Samarang (Java).
AUGUST: Promulgation of the Ordinance for the Women's Volunteer Labor Corps (Joshi Seishintai Kinrorei).

1948, FEBRUARY: The Batavia Temporary Court-Martial (aka the Batavia Military Tribunal) finds four officers and seven station operators guilty of war crimes, with one officer receiving the death penalty.

1990, NOVEMBER: Formation of Korean Council for the Women Drafted for Military Sexual Slavery by Japan (Jeongsindae munje daechaek hyeopuihoe).

1991, AUGUST: Gim Haksun (Kim Hak-soon) is the first former "comfort woman" in South Korea to give testimony using her real name and to go public with her story.

1992, JANUARY 8: The so-called "Wednesday protests" begin in front of Japanese embassy in Seoul.
JANUARY 11: The *Asahi shimbun* publishes documents found by Yoshimi Yoshiaki demonstrating that the Japanese military planned, built, and managed comfort stations.
JANUARY 14: For the first time, a Japanese Prime Minister, Kiichi Miyazawa, apologizes about the "comfort women" issue.

1992, OCTOBER: The Buddhist Jogye Order opens the House of Sharing (Nanum ui jip), a place for former "comfort women" to live together, in Seoul.

1993, AUGUST 4: The Kōno Statement. A statement issued by Yōhei Kōno, Chief Cabinet Secretary, acknowledges that coercion was used in the recruitment of "comfort women."

1994, JANUARY: The Netherlands government issues the "Report of a Study of Dutch Government Documents on the Forced Prostitution of Dutch Women in the Dutch East Indies during the Japanese Occupation."
AUGUST: Japanese Prime Minister Tomiichi Murayama apologizes about the "comfort women" issue.

1995, JUNE: The Japanese government establishes the Asian Women's Fund.
DECEMBER: The House of Sharing moves to its present location in Gwangju, Gyeonggi province.

1996, JANUARY: "Report on the mission to the Democratic People's Republic of Korea, the Republic of Korea, and Japan on the issue of military sexual slavery in wartime" submitted to the UN Commission on Human Rights.
JUNE: Japan's Ministry of Education approves seven junior high school textbooks with references to the "comfort women" issue; during a visit to South Korea, Japanese Prime Minister Ryūtarō Hashimoto gave an apology for the "comfort women" issue.

1997, DECEMBER 16: Death of Gim Haksun (Kim Hak-soon).

2000, SEPTEMBER 18: Former "comfort women" from South Korea, Taiwan, and the Philippines file a class action lawsuit in the US District Court in Washington, DC.
DECEMBER 8-12: The Women's International War Crimes Tribunal on Japan's Military Sexual Slavery is convened in Tokyo.

2001: Japanese Prime Minister Junichiro Koizumi sends a letter of apology, also signed by former prime ministers Ryutaro Hashimoto, Keizo Obuchi, and Yoshiro Mori, to former "comfort women" through the Asian Women's Fund.
JANUARY: NHK broadcasts a documentary on the "comfort women" entitled "How to Put War **ON TRIAL:** Wartime Sexual Violence Considered" (*Senso wo do sabaku ka: Towareru senji seiboryoku*).

JUNE: Publication of *New History Textbook* [Atarashi rekishi kyokasho] which does not mention the "comfort women" issue. Published by Fusōsha, it was written by the Japanese Society for History Textbook Reform [Atarashii Rekishi Kyōkasho o Tsukurukai].
OCTOBER 4: The US District Court dismisses the class action lawsuit.

2007, MARCH: Japanese Prime Minister Shinzō Abe states that there was no evidence that coercion was used to recruit the "comfort women."
- Closure of the Asian Women's Fund.
APRIL 3: The Congressional Research Service in the US issues a memorandum on the "Japanese military's 'comfort women' system."
JULY 30: Passage of US House of Representatives House Resolution 121, introduced by Mike Honda of California, asking for the Japanese government to apologize to the former "comfort women" and introduce the topic in school curricula.

NOVEMBER 28: The Canadian House of Commons passes a motion on the "comfort women" urging the Japanese government to take responbility for the issue and to offer an apology to the "comfort women" in the Diet.
DECEMBER 13: The European Parliament passes a Resolution [B60525/2007] on the comfort women, calling for the Japanese government "formally to acknowledge, apologize, accept historical and legal responsibility in a clear and unequivocal manner."

2010, OCTOBER: A small plaque honoring the memory of the Korean "comfort women" is erected in Palisades Park, New Jersey.

2011, AUGUST 30: The Constitutional Court of South Korea rules that it was unconstitutional for the ROK government to fail to address the claims of the former "comfort women" in the 1965 "Agreement on the Settlement of Problem

concerning Property and Claims and the Economic Cooperation between the Republic of Korea and Japan."
DECEMBER: A statue of a comfort woman is placed in front of the Japanese Embassy in Seoul.

2012, AUGUST: A few months before the general election, Abe hints that he may want to revise the Kōno Statement.

2013, MAY: Toru Hashimoto, the mayor of Osaka, says that the "comfort women" were necessary to provide relief to Japanese soldiers and to maintain discipline.
JULY: Glendale, CA puts a statue memorializing the former "comfort women" in its Central Park.

2014, FEBRUARY: Japanese Prime Minister Shinzō Abe indicates that his administration is considering revising the Kōno Statement.
JUNE 20: The Abe administration issues the results of a review of the Kono Statement by a committee that includes the historian Hata Ikuhiko.

LAWSUITS IN JAPANESE COURTS

Since the issue was made public, former "comfort women" have pursued their demands through the Japanese legal system. There were three cases involving former Korean "comfort women," and there were also lawsuits involving former Chinese, Filipino, and Taiwanese "comfort women."

1. LAWSUIT BY KOREAN VICTIMS OF THE ASIA-PACIFIC WAR.

Plaintiffs: 35, including three former "comfort women," later joined by six others.

1991, December 6: lawsuit filed in Tokyo District Court.

2001, March 26: Tokyo District Court dismisses the suit.

2003, July 22: Tokyo High Court rejects the appeal.

2004, November 29: The Supreme Court of Japan upholds the Tokyo High Court's ruling.

2. LAWSUIT BY FORMER "COMFORT WOMEN" AND FORMER WOMEN'S LABOR CORPS MEMBERS

Plaintiffs: 10, including three former "comfort women."

1992, December 25: lawsuit filed in Yamaguchi District Court [Shimonoseki Branch].

1998, April 27: The Yamaguchi District Court accepts a part of the claims by the former "comfort women."

2001, March 29: The Hiroshima High Court dismissed the Yamaguchi District Court's ruling.

2003, March 25: The Supreme Court of Japan rejects the appeal, nullifying the earlier ruling by the Yamaguchi District Court.

3. LAWSUIT BY SONG SINDO, A FORMER "COMFORT WOMAN" RESIDING IN JAPAN.

1993, April 3: lawsuit filed in Tokyo District Court.

1999, October 1: The Tokyo District Court dismisses the case.

2000, November 30: The Tokyo High Court rejects the appeal.

2003, March 28: The Supreme Court dismisses the appeal.

The Dok Island (Dokdo) Issue

Dok Island (Dokdo). (Northeast Asian History Foundation)

Dok Island actually consists of two small islets surrounded by a number of rock formations. It is also known as the Liancourt Rocks after the name of the French ship that charted it in 1849. There is a dispute between South Korea and Japan over who has sovereignty over the island. Regarding Dok Island to be the easternmost point of its territory, South Korea claims that it became part of Korean territory when the kingdom of Silla conquered the statelet of Usan in the year 512. On the other hand, Japan has asserted that it first discovered the island, which it has named Takeshima, in the seventeenth century and that it was uninhabited until February 1905 when Shimane Prefecture issued an edict incorporating it into its territory. Japan's claim is not generally based on cartographic evidence. Since Korea's liberation in 1945, South Korea has administered the island, and people began to reside permanently on the island from the year 1953. In many maps from the Joseon era, the location of Dok Island was incorrect; it appears to the southwest of Ulleung Island, rather than to the southeast. Since it was considered to be a part of Ulleung Island, the convention was for cartographers to place Dok Island to the Joseon side of Ulleung Island, and this was true of some Western maps as well.

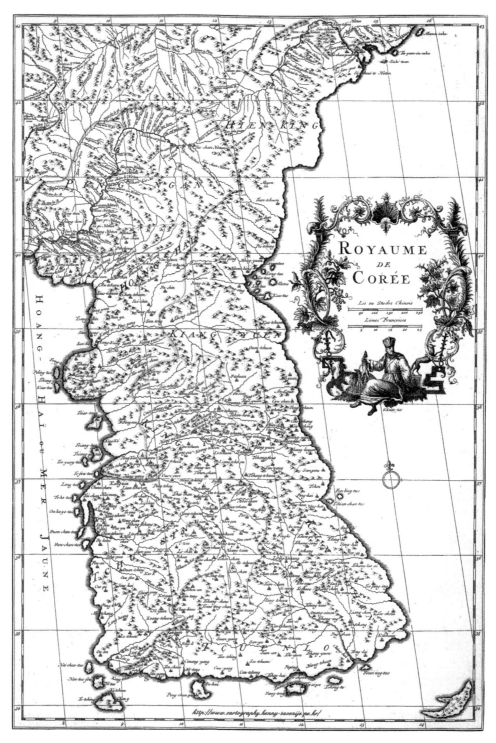

Detail of the map "Royaume de Corée" created by French cartographer Jean Baptiste
Bourguignon d'Anville in 1737. This was the first detailed Western map of the Korean peninsula
and was included in the book *Nouvel Atlas de la Chine*. Dok Island is called Tchian Chan Tao,
and Ulleung Island is Fang Ling Tao. (Henny Savenije)

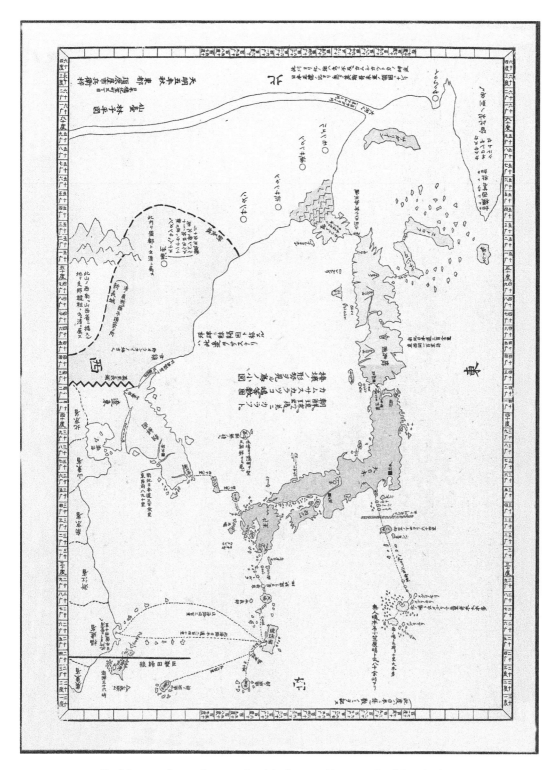

Detail of the map "Sangoku Setsujo Chizu" created by Hayashi Shihei for his book
Illustrated Description of Three Countries (*Sangoku Tsuran Zusetsu*) in 1785. The text next to the island
states that it belongs to Joseon (Korea). (Seoul Museum of History)

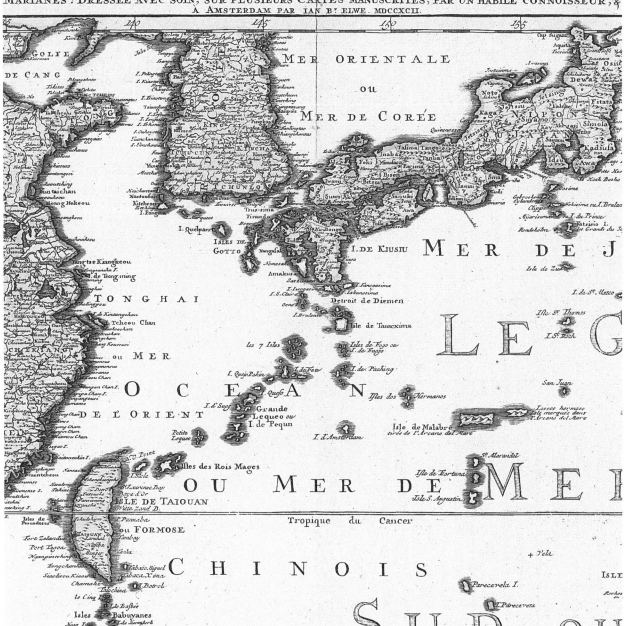

Detail of the map "Partie de la Nouvelle Grande Carte des Indes Orientales, Contenant les Empires de la Chine & de Japon, les Isles Philippines" by Jan B. Elwe. Published in the Netherlands in 1792. According to South Korea, Dok Island is indicated as Tchiangchantao, the pronunciation of the Chinese name for the island (Cheonsando in Korean) that refers to Usando, an old name for the island. The sea between Korea and Japan is called Mer de Corée (Sea of Korea). (Seoul Museum of History)

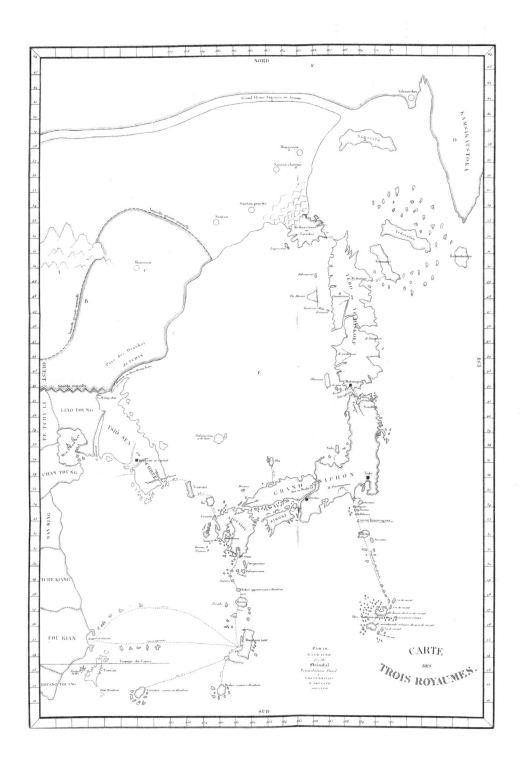

Detail of a map created by Julius Klaproth for the translation of Hayashi Shihei's
Illustrated Description of Three Countries that was published in Germany in 1832. Dok Island is labeled as
Takenosima, and the map indicates that it is Korean territory. (Seoul Museum of History)

CHRONOLOGY OF THE DOK ISLAND ISSUE

512: Silla conquers the country of Usan, which was located on Ulleung Island.

1693: Fisherman An Yongbok is kidnapped and taken to Japan.

1849: The French ship *Le Liancourt* passes near the island.

1900, OCTOBER: The Korean government issues Ordinance no. 41 which placed Seok Island (Dok Island) under the jurisdiction of Ulleung Island.

1905, FEBRUARY 22: Shimane Prefecture annexes the island.

1946, JANUARY: The Supreme Command for the Allied Powers issues an Instruction Note that excludes the island from Japanese territory (SCAPIN #677).
JUNE: The MacArthur Line excludes the island from Japanese territory (SCAPIN #1033).

1947: The US decides to use the island as a bombing range.

1951, SEPTEMBER: The San Francisco Peace Treaty leaves the issue of the island unresolved.

1952, JANUARY: Syngman Rhee includes the island in his "Peace Line."

1954, SEPTEMBER: Japan's proposal to bring the issue to the International Court of Justice is rejected by South Korea.

1965: The Treaty on Basic Relations between Japan and the Republic of Korea acknowledges the status quo with regard to South Korea's control over Dok Island.

1981: Choe Jongdeok becomes the first official resident of Dok Island.

1982: The South Korean government designates the island as Natural Monument no. 336.

2003, JANUARY: South Korea assigns Dok Island a postal code (799-805).

2005, MARCH: Shimane Prefecture proclaims February 22 to be "Takeshima Day."
MARCH 24: The South Korean governments relaxes restrictions on visiting the island.
AUGUST: For the first time, Japan's annual Defense White Paper mentions its claim to Dok Island.

2008, JULY 14: South Korea recalls its ambassador to Japan when the issue was included in curriculum guidelines for junior high schools in Japan.

2011, JUNE 15: Korean Air does a test flight of its new Airbus A380 jet over Dok Island; in response to this, the Japanese Foreign Ministry instructs its diplomats not to fly on Korean Air for one month.

2012, AUGUST 10: South Korean President Lee Myung-Bak visits the island.
: Japan again proposes to take the issue to the International Court of Justice.
DECEMBER: South Korea's Defense White Paper mentions its sovereignty over Dok Island for the first time.

Dok Island (Dokdo) Stamps.
Issued by South Korea in 1954.
(Northeast Asian History Foundation)

The Sexagenary Cycle

The sexagenary cycle is a method of recording years that was developed in ancient China and became widespread during the Han Dynasty. It is a set of sixty terms consisting of two Chinese characters each and generated according to a specific pattern. The first character of each term is taken from a group of ten known as the "heavenly stems" (*cheongan* in Korean); the second is taken from a group of twelve known as the "earthly branches" (*jiji* in Korean – Table 1). The first term is created by pairing the first "heavenly stem" with the first "earthly branch;" then the second "heavenly stem" is paired with the second "earthly branch." For the eleventh term, the first "heavenly stem" is paired with the eleventh "earthly branch," and the sequence continues. This method produces a set of sixty unique terms (Table 2) since sixty is the least common multiple of ten and twelve.

TABLE 1

THE TEN HEAVENLY STEMS AND
THE TWELVE EARTHLY BRANCHES

TABLE 2

THE SEXAGENARY CYCLE IN CHINESE AND KOREAN

TABLE 1 — THE TEN HEAVENLY STEMS AND THE TWELVE EARTHLY BRANCHES

THE TEN HEAVENLY STEMS	THE TWELVE EARTHLY BRANCHES
甲	子
乙	丑
丙	寅
丁	卯
戊	辰
己	巳
庚	午
辛	未
壬	申
癸	酉
	戌
	亥

TABLE 2 — THE SEXAGENARY CYCLE IN CHINESE AND KOREAN

CHINESE	KOREAN	ENGLISH	CHINESE	KOREAN	ENGLISH
甲子	갑자	Gapja	甲午	갑오	Gabo
乙丑	을축	Eulchuk	乙未	을미	Eulmi
丙寅	병인	Byeongin	丙申	병신	Byeongsin
丁卯	정묘	Jeongmyo	丁酉	정유	Jeongyu
戊辰	무진	Mujin	戊戌	무술	Musul
己巳	기사	Gisa	己亥	기해	Gihae
庚午	경오	Gyeongo	庚子	경자	Gyeongja
辛未	신미	Sinmi	辛丑	신축	Sinchuk
壬申	임신	Imsin	壬寅	임인	Imin
癸酉	계유	Gyeyu	癸卯	계묘	Gyemyo
甲戌	갑술	Gapsul	甲辰	갑진	Gapjin
乙亥	을해	Eulhae	乙巳	을사	Eulsa
丙子	병자	Byeongja	丙午	병오	Byeongo
丁丑	정축	Jeongchuk	丁未	정미	Jeongmi
戊寅	무인	Muin	戊申	무신	Musin
己卯	기묘	Gimyo	己酉	기유	Giyu
庚辰	경진	Gyeongjin	庚戌	경술	Gyeongsul
辛巳	신사	Sinsa	辛亥	신해	Sinhae
壬午	임오	Imo	壬子	임자	Imja
癸未	계미	Gyemi	癸丑	계축	Gyechuk
甲申	갑신	Gapsin	甲寅	갑인	Gabin
乙酉	을유	Eulyu	乙卯	을묘	Eulmyo
丙戌	병술	Byeongsul	丙辰	병진	Byeongjin
丁亥	정해	Jeonghae	丁巳	정사	Jeongsa
戊子	무자	Muja	戊午	무오	Muo
己丑	기축	Gichuk	己未	기미	Gimi
庚寅	경인	Gyeongin	庚申	경신	Gyeongsin
辛卯	신묘	Sinmyo	辛酉	신유	Sinyu
壬辰	임진	Imjin	壬戌	임술	Imsul
癸巳	계사	Gyesa	癸亥	계해	Gyehae

There are a number of ways of indicating the year in Korean historiography even though the Western calendar is now standard. The sexagenary cycle is still sometimes used to name significant past events. In academic writing, reign years are commonly used for premodern times. They are indicated by the name of the monarch and the year of the reign; for instance, the year 1420 can be represented as "Sejong 2." In the premodern era, there were some periods when kingdoms used their own reign names, as in Goguryeo, Silla, and the early years of Goryeo, but they are not generally used today. At the end of the Joseon period, the government began to use official reign names. As part of the Gabo Reforms of 1894, Joseon adopted the year name Gaeguk, with Gaeguk 1 being 1392, the year of Joseon's founding. When the Great Han Empire was founded in 1897, the government used its own reign years. During Gojong's reign, the year name was Gwangmu (光武); during Sunjong's reign, it was Yunghui (隆熙).

YEAR [BCE]	YEAR NAME	SILLA	GOGURYEO
57	Gapja	Hyeokgeose 1	
56	Eulchuk	2	
55	Byeongin	3	
54	Jeongmyo	4	
53	Mujin	5	
52	Gisa	6	
51	Gyeongo	7	
50	Sinmi	8	
49	Imsin	9	
48	Gyeyu	10	
47	Gapsul	11	
46	Eulhae	12	
45	Byeongja	13	
44	Jeongchuk	14	
43	Muin	15	
42	Gimyo	16	
41	Gyeongjin	17	
40	Sinsa	18	
39	Imo	19	
38	Gyemi	20	GOGURYEO
37	Gapsin	21	Dongmyeong 1
36	Eulyu	22	2
35	Byeongsul	23	3
34	Jeonghae	24	4
33	Muja	25	5
32	Gichuk	26	6
31	Gyeongin	27	7
30	Sinmyo	28	8

YEAR	YEAR NAME	SILLA	GOGURYEO	BAEKJE
29	Imjin	29	9	
28	Gyesa	30	10	
27	Gabo	31	11	
26	Eulmi	32	12	
25	Byeongsin	33	13	
24	Jeongyu	34	14	
23	Musul	35	15	
22	Gihae	36	16	
21	Gyeongja	37	17	
20	Sinchuk	38	18	
19	Imin	39	Yuri 1	BAEKJE
18	Gyemyo	40	2	Onjo 1
17	Gapjin	41	3	2
16	Eulsa	42	4	3
15	Byeongo	43	5	4
14	Jeongmi	44	6	5
13	Musin	45	7	6
12	Giyu	46	8	7
11	Gyeongsul	47	9	8
10	Sinhae	48	10	9
9	Imja	49	11	10
8	Gyechuk	50	12	11
7	Gabin	51	13	12
6	Eulmyo	52	14	13
5	Byeongjin	53	15	14
4	Jeongsa	54	16	15
3	Muo	55	17	16
2	Gimi	56	18	17

YEAR	YEAR NAME	SILLA	GOGURYEO	BAEKJE	YEAR	YEAR NAME	SILLA	GOGURYEO	BAEKJE
1	Gyeongsin	57	19	18	41	Sinchuk	15	24	14
(BCE)					42	Imin	16	25	15
1	Sinyu	58	20	19	43	Gyemyo	17	26	16
2	Imsul	59	21	20	44	Gapjin	18	Minjung 1	17
3	Gyehae	60	22	21	45	Eulsa	19	2	18
4	Gapja	Namhae 1	23	22	46	Byeongo	20	3	19
5	Eulchuk	2	24	23	47	Jeongmi	21	4	20
6	Byeongin	3	25	24	48	Musin	22	Mobon 1	21
7	Jeongmyo	4	26	25	49	Giyu	23	2	22
8	Mujin	5	27	26	50	Gyeongsul	24	3	23
9	Gisa	6	28	27	51	Sinhae	25	4	24
10	Gyeongo	7	29	28	52	Imja	26	5	25
11	Sinmi	8	30	29	53	Gyechuk	27	Taejo 1	26
12	Imsin	9	31	30	54	Gabin	28	2	27
13	Gyeyu	10	32	31	55	Eulmyo	29	3	28
14	Gapsul	11	33	32	56	Byeongjin	30	4	29
15	Eulhae	12	34	33	57	Jeongsa	Talhae 1	5	30
16	Byeongja	13	35	34	58	Muo	2	6	31
17	Jeongchuk	14	36	35	59	Gimi	3	7	32
18	Muin	15	Daemusin 1	36	60	Gyeongsin	4	8	33
19	Gimyo	16	2	37	61	Sinyu	5	9	34
20	Gyeongjin	17	3	38	62	Imsul	6	10	35
21	Sinsa	18	4	39	63	Gyehae	7	11	36
22	Imo	19	5	40	64	Gapja	8	12	37
23	Gyemi	20	6	41	65	Eulchuk	9	13	38
24	Gapsin	21	7	42	66	Byeongin	10	14	39
25	Eulyu	22	8	43	67	Jeongmyo	11	15	40
26	Byeongsul	23	9	44	68	Mujin	12	16	41
27	Jeonghae	Yuri 1	10	45	69	Gisa	13	17	42
28	Muja	2	11	Daru 1	70	Gyeongo	14	18	43
29	Gichuk	3	12	2	71	Sinmi	15	19	44
30	Gyeongin	4	13	3	72	Imsin	16	20	45
31	Sinmyo	5	14	4	73	Gyeyu	17	21	46
32	Imjin	6	15	5	74	Gapsul	18	22	47
33	Gyesa	7	16	6	75	Eulhae	19	23	48
34	Gabo	8	17	7	76	Byeongja	20	24	49
35	Eulmi	9	18	8	77	Jeongchuk	21	25	Giru 1
36	Byeongsin	10	19	9	78	Muin	22	26	2
37	Jeongyu	11	20	10	79	Gimyo	23	27	3
38	Musul	12	21	11	80	Gyeongjin	Pasa 1	28	4
39	Gihae	13	22	12	81	Sinsa	2	29	5
40	Gyeongja	14	23	13	82	Imo	3	30	6

YEAR	YEAR NAME	SILLA	GOGURYEO	BAEKJE
83	Gyemi	4	31	7
84	Gapsin	5	32	8
85	Eulyu	6	33	9
86	Byeongsul	7	34	10
87	Jeonghae	8	35	11
88	Muja	9	36	12
89	Gichuk	10	37	13
90	Gyeongin	11	38	14
91	Sinmyo	12	39	15
92	Imjin	13	40	16
93	Gyesa	14	41	17
94	Gabo	15	42	18
95	Eulmi	16	43	19
96	Byeongsin	17	44	20
97	Jeongyu	18	45	21
98	Musul	19	46	22
99	Gihae	20	47	23
100	Gyeongja	21	48	24
101	Sinchuk	22	49	25
102	Imin	23	50	26
103	Gyemyo	24	51	27
104	Gapjin	25	52	28
105	Eulsa	26	53	29
106	Byeongo	27	54	30
107	Jeongmi	28	55	31
108	Musin	29	56	32
109	Giyu	30	57	33
110	Gyeongsul	31	58	34
111	Sinhae	32	59	35
112	Imja	Jima 1	60	36
113	Gyechuk	2	61	37
114	Gabin	3	62	38
115	Eulmyo	4	63	39
116	Byeongjin	5	64	40
117	Jeongsa	6	65	41
118	Muo	7	66	42
119	Gimi	8	67	43
120	Gyeongsin	9	68	44
121	Sinyu	10	69	45
122	Imsul	11	70	46
123	Gyehae	12	71	47
124	Gapja	13	72	48

YEAR	YEAR NAME	SILLA	GOGURYEO	BAEKJE
125	Eulchuk	14	73	49
126	Byeongin	15	74	50
127	Jeongmyo	16	75	51
128	Mujin	17	76	Gaeru 1
129	Gisa	18	77	2
130	Gyeongo	19	78	3
131	Sinmi	20	79	4
132	Imsin	21	80	5
133	Gyeyu	22	81	6
134	Gapsul	Ilseong 1	82	7
135	Eulhae	2	83	8
136	Byeongja	3	84	9
137	Jeongchuk	4	85	10
138	Muin	5	86	11
139	Gimyo	6	87	12
140	Gyeongjin	7	88	13
141	Sinsa	8	89	14
142	Imo	9	90	15
143	Gyemi	10	91	16
144	Gapsin	11	92	17
145	Eulyu	12	93	18
146	Byeongsul	13	Chadae 1	19
147	Jeonghae	14	2	20
148	Muja	15	3	21
149	Gichuk	16	4	22
150	Gyeongin	17	5	23
151	Sinmyo	18	6	24
152	Imjin	19	7	25
153	Gyesa	20	8	26
154	Gabo	Adalla 1	9	27
155	Eulmi	2	10	28
156	Byeongsin	3	11	29
157	Jeongyu	4	12	30
158	Musul	5	13	31
159	Gihae	6	14	32
160	Gyeongja	7	15	33
161	Sinchuk	8	16	34
162	Imin	9	17	35
163	Gyemyo	10	18	36
164	Gapjin	11	19	37
165	Eulsa	12	Sindae 1	38
166	Byeongo	13	2	Chogo 1

YEAR	YEAR NAME	SILLA	GOGURYEO	BAEKJE	YEAR	YEAR NAME	SILLA	GOGURYEO	BAEKJE
167	Jeongmi	14	3	2	209	Gichuk	14	13	44
168	Musin	15	4	3	210	Gyeongin	15	14	45
169	Giyu	16	5	4	211	Sinmyo	16	15	46
170	Gyeongsul	17	6	5	212	Imjin	17	16	47
171	Sinhae	18	7	6	213	Gyesa	18	17	48
172	Imja	19	8	7	214	Gabo	19	18	Gusu 1
173	Gyechuk	20	9	8	215	Eulmi	20	19	2
174	Gabin	21	10	9	216	Byeongsin	21	20	3
175	Eulmyo	22	11	10	217	Jeongyu	22	21	4
176	Byeongjin	23	12	11	218	Musul	23	22	5
177	Jeongsa	24	13	12	219	Gihae	24	23	6
178	Muo	25	14	13	220	Gyeongja	25	24	7
179	Gimi	26	Gogukcheon 1	14	221	Sinchuk	26	25	8
180	Gyeongsin	27	2	15	222	Imin	27	26	9
181	Sinyu	28	3	16	223	Gyemyo	28	27	10
182	Imsul	29	4	17	224	Gapjin	29	28	11
183	Gyehae	30	5	18	225	Eulsa	30	29	12
184	Gapja	Beolhyu 1	6	19	226	Byeongo	31	30	13
185	Eulchuk	2	7	20	227	Jeongmi	32	Dongcheon 1	14
186	Byeongin	3	8	21	228	Musin	33	2	15
187	Jeongmyo	4	9	22	229	Giyu	34	3	16
188	Mujin	5	10	23	230	Gyeongsul	Jobun 1	4	17
189	Gisa	6	11	24	231	Sinhae	2	5	18
190	Gyeongo	7	12	25	232	Imja	3	6	19
191	Sinmi	8	13	26	233	Gyechuk	4	7	20
192	Imsin	9	14	27	234	Gabin	5	8	Saban 1, Goi 1
193	Gyeyu	10	15	28	235	Eulmyo	6	9	2
194	Gapsul	11	16	29	236	Byeongjin	7	10	3
195	Eulhae	12	17	30	237	Jeongsa	8	11	4
196	Byeongja	Naehae 1	18	31	238	Muo	9	12	5
197	Jeongchuk	2	Sansang 1	32	239	Gimi	10	13	6
198	Muin	3	2	33	240	Gyeongsin	11	14	7
199	Gimyo	4	3	34	241	Sinyu	12	15	8
200	Gyeongjin	5	4	35	242	Imsul	13	16	9
201	Sinsa	6	5	36	243	Gyehae	14	17	10
202	Imo	7	6	37	244	Gapja	15	18	11
203	Gyemi	8	7	38	245	Eulchuk	16	19	12
204	Gapsin	9	8	39	246	Byeongin	17	20	13
205	Eulyu	10	9	40	247	Jeongmyo	Cheomhae 1	21	14
206	Byeongsul	11	10	41	248	Mujin	2	Jungcheon 1	15
207	Jeonghae	12	11	42	249	Gisa	3	2	16
208	Muja	13	12	43	250	Gyeongo	4	3	17

YEAR	YEAR NAME	SILLA	GOGURYEO	BAEKJE	YEAR	YEAR NAME	SILLA	GOGURYEO	BAEKJE
251	Sinmi	5	4	18	293	Gyechuk	10	2	8
252	Imsin	6	5	19	294	Gabin	11	3	9
253	Gyeyu	7	6	20	295	Eulmyo	12	4	10
254	Gapsul	8	7	21	296	Byeongjin	13	5	11
255	Eulhae	9	8	22	297	Jeongsa	14	6	12
256	Byeongja	10	9	23	298	Muo	Girim 1	7	Bunseo 1
257	Jeongchuk	11	10	24	299	Gimi	2	8	2
258	Muin	12	11	25	300	Gyeongsin	3	Micheon 1	3
259	Gimyo	13	12	26	301	Sinyu	4	2	4
260	Gyeongjin	14	13	27	302	Imsul	5	3	5
261	Sinsa	15	14	28	303	Gyehae	6	4	6
262	Imo	Michu 1	15	29	304	Gapja	7	5	Biryu 1
263	Gyemi	2	16	30	305	Eulchuk	8	6	2
264	Gapsin	3	17	31	306	Byeongin	9	7	3
265	Eulyu	4	18	32	307	Jeongmyo	10	8	4
266	Byeongsul	5	19	33	308	Mujin	11	9	5
267	Jeonghae	6	20	34	309	Gisa	12	10	6
268	Muja	7	21	35	310	Gyeongo	Heulhae 1	11	7
269	Gichuk	8	22	36	311	Sinmi	2	12	8
270	Gyeongin	9	Seocheon 1	37	312	Imsin	3	13	9
271	Sinmyo	10	2	38	313	Gyeyu	4	14	10
272	Imjin	11	3	39	314	Gapsul	5	15	11
273	Gyesa	12	4	40	315	Eulhae	6	16	12
274	Gabo	13	5	41	316	Byeongja	7	17	13
275	Eulmi	14	6	42	317	Jeongchuk	8	18	14
276	Byeongsin	15	7	43	318	Muin	9	19	15
277	Jeongyu	16	8	44	319	Gimyo	10	20	16
278	Musul	17	9	45	320	Gyeongjin	11	21	17
279	Gihae	18	10	46	321	Sinsa	12	22	18
280	Gyeongja	19	11	47	322	Imo	13	23	19
281	Sinchuk	20	12	48	323	Gyemi	14	24	20
282	Imin	21	13	49	324	Gapsin	15	25	21
283	Gyemyo	22	14	50	325	Eulyu	16	26	22
284	Gapjin	Yurye 1	15	51	326	Byeongsul	17	27	23
285	Eulsa	2	16	52	327	Jeonghae	18	28	24
286	Byeongo	3	17	Chaekgye 1	328	Muja	19	29	25
287	Jeongmi	4	18	2	329	Gichuk	20	30	26
288	Musin	5	19	3	330	Gyeongin	21	31	27
289	Giyu	6	20	4	331	Sinmyo	22	Gogugwon 1	28
290	Gyeongsul	7	21	5	332	Imjin	23	2	29
291	Sinhae	8	22	6	333	Gyesa	24	3	30
292	Imja	9	Bongsang 1	7	334	Gabo	25	4	31

YEAR	YEAR NAME	SILLA	GOGURYEO	BAEKJE	YEAR	YEAR NAME	SILLA	GOGURYEO	BAEKJE
335	Eulmi	26	5	32	377	Jeongchuk	22	7	3
336	Byeongsin	27	6	33	378	Muin	23	8	4
337	Jeongyu	29	7	34	379	Gimyo	24	9	5
338	Musul	30	8	35	380	Gyeongjin	25	10	6
339	Gihae	31	9	36	381	Sinsa	26	11	7
340	Gyeongja	32	10	37	382	Imo	27	12	8
341	Sinchuk	33	11	38	383	Gyemi	28	13	9
342	Imin	34	12	39	384	Gapsin	29	Gogugyang 1	Chimnyu 1
343	Gyemyo	35	13	40	385	Eulyu	30	2	Jinsa 1
344	Gapjin	36	14	Gye 1	386	Byeongsul	31	3	2
345	Eulsa	37	15	2	387	Jeonghae	32	4	3
346	Byeongo	38	16	Geunchogo 1	388	Muja	33	5	4
347	Jeongmi	39	17	2	389	Gichuk	34	6	5
348	Musin	40	18	3	390	Gyeongin	35	7	6
349	Giyu	41	19	4	391	Sinmyo	36	Gwanggaeto 1	7
350	Gyeongsul	42	20	5	392	Imjin	37	2	Asin 1
351	Sinhae	43	21	6	393	Gyesa	38	3	2
352	Imja	44	22	7	394	Gabo	39	4	3
353	Gyechuk	45	23	8	395	Eulmi	40	5	4
354	Gabin	46	24	9	396	Byeongsin	41	6	5
355	Eulmyo	47	25	10	397	Jeongyu	42	7	6
356	Byeongjin	Naemul 1	26	11	398	Musul	43	8	7
357	Jeongsa	2	27	12	399	Gihae	44	9	8
358	Muo	3	28	13	400	Gyeongja	45	10	9
359	Gimi	4	29	14	401	Sinchuk	46	11	10
360	Gyeongsin	5	30	15	402	Imin	Silseong 1	12	11
361	Sinyu	6	31	16	403	Gyemyo	2	13	12
362	Imsul	7	32	17	404	Gapjin	3	14	13
363	Gyehae	8	33	18	405	Eulsa	4	15	Jeonji 1
364	Gapja	9	34	19	406	Byeongo	5	16	2
365	Eulchuk	10	35	20	407	Jeongmi	6	17	3
366	Byeongin	11	36	21	408	Musin	7	18	4
367	Jeongmyo	12	37	22	409	Giyu	8	19	5
368	Mujin	13	38	23	410	Gyeongsul	9	20	6
369	Gisa	14	39	24	411	Sinhae	10	21	7
370	Gyeongo	15	40	25	412	Imja	12	22	8
371	Sinmi	16	Sosurim 1	26	413	Gyechuk	13	Jangsu 1	9
372	Imsin	17	2	27	414	Gabin	14	2	10
373	Gyeyu	18	3	28	415	Eulmyo	15	3	11
374	Gapsul	19	4	29	416	Byeongjin	16	4	12
375	Eulhae	20	5	Geungusu 1	417	Jeongsa	Nulji 1	5	13
376	Byeongja	21	6	2	418	Muo	2	6	14

YEAR	YEAR NAME	SILLA	GOGURYEO	BAEKJE	YEAR	YEAR NAME	SILLA	GOGURYEO	BAEKJE
419	Gimi	3	7	15	461	Sinchuk	4	49	7
420	Gyeongsin	4	8	Guisin 1	462	Imin	5	50	8
421	Sinyu	5	9	2	463	Gyemyo	6	51	9
422	Imsul	6	10	3	464	Gapjin	7	52	10
423	Gyehae	7	11	4	465	Eulsa	8	53	11
424	Gapja	8	12	5	466	Byeongo	9	54	12
425	Eulchuk	9	13	6	467	Jeongmi	10	55	13
426	Byeongin	10	14	7	468	Musin	11	56	14
427	Jeongmyo	11	15	Biyu 1	469	Giyu	12	57	15
428	Mujin	12	16	2	470	Gyeongsul	13	58	16
429	Gisa	13	17	3	471	Sinhae	14	59	17
430	Gyeongo	14	18	4	472	Imja	15	60	18
431	Sinmi	15	19	5	473	Gyechuk	16	61	19
432	Imsin	16	20	6	474	Gabin	17	62	20
433	Gyeyu	17	21	7	475	Eulmyo	18	63	Munji 1
434	Gapsul	18	22	8	476	Byeongjin	19	64	2
435	Eulhae	19	23	9	477	Jeongsa	20	65	Samgeun 1
436	Byeongja	20	24	10	478	Muo	21	66	2
437	Jeongchuk	21	25	11	479	Gimi	Soji 1	67	Dongseong 1
438	Muin	22	26	12	480	Gyeongsin	2	68	2
439	Gimyo	23	27	13	481	Sinyu	3	69	3
440	Gyeongjin	24	28	14	482	Imsul	4	70	4
441	Sinsa	25	29	15	483	Gyehae	5	71	5
442	Imo	26	30	16	484	Gapja	6	72	6
443	Gyemi	27	31	17	485	Eulchuk	7	73	7
444	Gapsin	28	32	18	486	Byeongin	8	74	8
445	Eulyu	29	33	19	487	Jeongmyo	9	75	9
446	Byeongsul	30	34	20	488	Mujin	10	76	10
447	Jeonghae	31	35	21	489	Gisa	11	77	11
448	Muja	32	36	22	490	Gyeongo	12	78	12
449	Gichuk	33	37	23	491	Sinmi	13	79	13
450	Gyeongin	34	38	24	492	Imsin	14	Munjamyeong 1	14
451	Sinmyo	35	39	25	493	Gyeyu	15	2	15
452	Imjin	36	40	26	494	Gapsul	16	3	16
453	Gyesa	37	41	27	495	Eulhae	17	4	17
454	Gabo	38	42	28	496	Byeongja	18	5	18
455	Eulmi	39	43	Gaero 1	497	Jeongchuk	19	6	19
456	Byeongsin	40	44	2	498	Muin	20	7	20
457	Jeongyu	41	45	3	499	Gimyo	21	8	21
458	Musul	Jabi 1	46	4	500	Gyeongjin	Jijeung 1	9	22
459	Gihae	2	47	5	501	Sinsa	2	10	Muryeong 1
460	Gyeongja	3	48	6	502	Imo	3	11	2

YEAR	YEAR NAME	SILLA	GOGURYEO	BAEKJE
503	Gyemi	4	12	3
504	Gapsin	5	13	4
505	Eulyu	6	14	5
506	Byeongsul	7	15	6
507	Jeonghae	8	16	7
508	Muja	9	17	8
509	Gichuk	10	18	9
510	Gyeongin	11	19	10
511	Sinmyo	12	20	11
512	Imjin	13	21	12
513	Gyesa	14	22	13
514	Gabo	Beopheung 1	23	14
515	Eulmi	2	24	15
516	Byeongsin	3	25	16
517	Jeongyu	4	26	17
518	Musul	5	27	18
519	Gihae	6	Anjang 1	19
520	Gyeongja	7	2	20
521	Sinchuk	8	3	21
522	Imin	9	4	22
523	Gyemyo	10	5	Seong 1
524	Gapjin	11	6	2
525	Eulsa	12	7	3
526	Byeongo	13	8	4
527	Jeongmi	14	9	5
528	Musin	15	10	6
529	Giyu	16	11	7
530	Gyeongsul	17	12	8
531	Sinhae	18	Anwon 1	9
532	Imja	19	2	10
533	Gyechuk	20	3	11
534	Gabin	21	4	12
535	Eulmyo	22	5	13
536	Byeongjin	23	6	14
537	Jeongsa	24	7	15
538	Muo	25	8	16
539	Gimi	26	9	17
540	Gyeongsin	Jinheung 1	10	18
541	Sinyu	2	11	19
542	Imsul	3	12	20
543	Gyehae	4	13	21
544	Gapja	5	14	22

YEAR	YEAR NAME	SILLA	GOGURYEO	BAEKJE
545	Eulchuk	6	Yangwon 1	23
546	Byeongin	7	2	24
547	Jeongmyo	8	3	25
548	Mujin	9	4	26
549	Gisa	10	5	27
550	Gyeongo	11	6	28
551	Sinmi	12	7	29
552	Imsin	13	8	30
553	Gyeyu	14	9	31
554	Gapsul	15	10	Wideok 1
555	Eulhae	16	11	2
556	Byeongja	17	12	3
557	Jeongchuk	18	13	4
558	Muin	19	14	5
559	Gimyo	20	Pyeongwon 1	6
560	Gyeongjin	21	2	7
561	Sinsa	22	3	8
562	Imo	23	4	9
563	Gyemi	24	5	10
564	Gapsin	25	6	11
565	Eulyu	26	7	12
566	Byeongsul	27	8	13
567	Jeonghae	28	9	14
568	Muja	29	10	15
569	Gichuk	30	11	16
570	Gyeongin	31	12	17
571	Sinmyo	32	13	18
572	Imjin	33	14	19
573	Gyesa	34	15	20
574	Gabo	35	16	21
575	Eulmi	36	17	22
576	Byeongsin	Jinji 1	18	23
577	Jeongyu	2	19	24
578	Musul	3	20	25
579	Gihae	Jinpyeong 1	21	26
580	Gyeongja	2	22	27
581	Sinchuk	3	23	28
582	Imin	4	24	29
583	Gyemyo	5	25	30
584	Gapjin	6	26	31
585	Eulsa	7	27	32
586	Byeongo	8	28	33

YEAR	YEAR NAME	SILLA	GOGURYEO	BAEKJE
587	Jeongmi	9	29	34
588	Musin	10	30	35
589	Giyu	11	31	36
590	Gyeongsul	12	Yeongyang 1	37
591	Sinhae	13	2	38
592	Imja	14	3	39
593	Gyechuk	15	4	40
594	Gabin	16	5	41
595	Eulmyo	17	6	42
596	Byeongjin	18	7	43
597	Jeongsa	19	8	44
598	Muo	20	9	Hye 1
599	Gimi	21	10	Beop 1
600	Gyeongsin	22	11	Mu 1
601	Sinyu	23	12	2
602	Imsul	24	13	3
603	Gyehae	25	14	4
604	Gapja	26	15	5
605	Eulchuk	27	16	6
606	Byeongin	28	17	7
607	Jeongmyo	29	18	8
608	Mujin	30	19	9
609	Gisa	31	20	10
610	Gyeongo	32	21	11
611	Sinmi	33	22	12
612	Imsin	34	23	13
613	Gyeyu	35	24	14
614	Gapsul	36	25	15
615	Eulhae	37	26	16
616	Byeongja	38	27	17
617	Jeongchuk	39	28	18
618	Muin	40	Yeongnyu 1	19
619	Gimyo	41	2	20
620	Gyeongjin	42	3	21
621	Sinsa	43	4	22
622	Imo	44	5	23
623	Gyemi	45	6	24
624	Gapsin	46	7	25
625	Eulyu	47	8	26
626	Byeongsul	48	9	27
627	Jeonghae	49	10	28
628	Muja	50	11	29

YEAR	YEAR NAME	SILLA	GOGURYEO	BAEKJE
629	Gichuk	51	12	30
630	Gyeongin	52	13	31
631	Sinmyo	53	14	32
632	Imjin	Seondeok 1	15	33
633	Gyesa	2	16	34
634	Gabo	3	17	35
635	Eulmi	4	18	36
636	Byeongsin	5	19	37
637	Jeongyu	6	20	38
638	Musul	7	21	39
639	Gihae	8	22	40
640	Gyeongja	9	23	41
641	Sinchuk	10	24	Uija 1
642	Imin	11	Bojang 1	2
643	Gyemyo	12	2	3
644	Gapjin	13	3	4
645	Eulsa	14	4	5
646	Byeongo	15	5	6
647	Jeongmi	Jindeok 1	6	7
648	Musin	2	7	8
649	Giyu	3	8	9
650	Gyeongsul	4	9	10
651	Sinhae	5	10	11
652	Imja	6	11	12
653	Gyechuk	7	12	13
654	Gabin	Muyeol 1	13	14
655	Eulmyo	2	14	15
656	Byeongjin	3	15	16
657	Jeongsa	4	16	17
658	Muo	5	17	18
659	Gimi	6	18	19
660	Gyeongsin	7	19	20
661	Sinyu	Munmu 1	20	
662	Imsul	2	21	
663	Gyehae	3	22	
664	Gapja	4	23	
665	Eulchuk	5	24	
666	Byeongin	6	25	
667	Jeongmyo	7	26	
668	Mujin	8	27	
669	Gisa	9		
670	Gyeongo	10		

YEAR	YEAR NAME	SILLA	YEAR	YEAR NAME	SILLA	YEAR	YEAR NAME	SILLA	YEAR	YEAR NAME	SILLA
671	Sinmi	11	713	Gyechuk	12	755	Eulmi	14	797	Jeongchuk	13
672	Imsin	12	714	Gabin	13	756	Byeongsin	15	798	Muin	14
673	Gyeyu	13	715	Eulmyo	14	757	Jeongyu	16	799	Gimyo	Soseong 1
674	Gapsul	14	716	Byeongjin	15	758	Musul	17	800	Gyeongjin	Aejang 1
675	Eulhae	15	717	Jeongsa	16	759	Gihae	18	801	Sinsa	2
676	Byeongja	16	718	Muo	17	760	Gyeongja	19	802	Imo	3
677	Jeongchuk	17	719	Gimi	18	761	Sinchuk	20	803	Gyemi	4
678	Muin	18	720	Gyeongsin	19	762	Imin	21	804	Gapsin	5
679	Gimyo	19	721	Sinyu	20	763	Gyemyo	22	805	Eulyu	6
680	Gyeongjin	20	722	Imsul	21	764	Gapjin	23	806	Byeongsul	7
681	Sinsa	Sinmun 1	723	Gyehae	22	765	Eulsa	Hyegong 1	807	Jeonghae	8
682	Imo	2	724	Gapja	23	766	Byeongo	2	808	Muja	9
683	Gyemi	3	725	Eulchuk	24	767	Jeongmi	3	809	Gichuk	Heondeok 1
684	Gapsin	4	726	Byeongin	25	768	Musin	4	810	Gyeongin	2
685	Eulyu	5	727	Jeongmyo	26	769	Giyu	5	811	Sinmyo	3
686	Byeongsul	6	728	Mujin	27	770	Gyeongsul	6	812	Imjin	4
687	Jeonghae	7	729	Gisa	28	771	Sinhae	7	813	Gyesa	5
688	Muja	8	730	Gyeongo	29	772	Imja	8	814	Gabo	6
689	Gichuk	9	731	Sinmi	30	773	Gyechuk	9	815	Eulmi	7
690	Gyeongin	10	732	Imsin	31	774	Gabin	10	816	Byeongsin	8
691	Sinmyo	11	733	Gyeyu	32	775	Eulmyo	11	817	Jeongyu	9
692	Imjin	Hyoso 1	734	Gapsul	33	776	Byeongjin	12	818	Musul	10
693	Gyesa	2	735	Eulhae	34	777	Jeongsa	13	819	Gihae	11
694	Gabo	3	736	Byeongja	35	778	Muo	14	820	Gyeongja	12
695	Eulmi	4	737	Jeongchuk	Hyoseong 1	779	Gimi	15	821	Sinchuk	13
696	Byeongsin	5	738	Muin	2	780	Gyeongsin	Seondeok 1	822	Imin	14
697	Jeongyu	6	739	Gimyo	3	781	Sinyu	2	823	Gyemyo	15
698	Musul	7	740	Gyeongjin	4	782	Imsul	3	824	Gapjin	16
699	Gihae	8	741	Sinsa	5	783	Gyehae	4	825	Eulsa	17
700	Gyeongja	9	742	Imo	Gyeongdeok 1	784	Gapja	5	826	Byeongo	Heungdeok 1
701	Sinchuk	10	743	Gyemi	2	785	Eulchuk	Wonseong 1	827	Jeongmi	2
702	Imin	Seongdeok 1	744	Gapsin	3	786	Byeongin	2	828	Musin	3
703	Gyemyo	2	745	Eulyu	4	787	Jeongmyo	3	829	Giyu	4
704	Gapjin	3	746	Byeongsul	5	788	Mujin	4	830	Gyeongsul	5
705	Eulsa	4	747	Jeonghae	6	789	Gisa	5	831	Sinhae	6
706	Byeongo	5	748	Muja	7	790	Gyeongo	6	832	Imja	7
707	Jeongmi	6	749	Gichuk	8	791	Sinmi	7	833	Gyechuk	8
708	Musin	7	750	Gyeongin	9	792	Imsin	8	834	Gabin	9
709	Giyu	8	751	Sinmyo	10	793	Gyeyu	9	835	Eulmyo	10
710	Gyeongsul	9	752	Imjin	11	794	Gapsul	10	836	Byeongjin	Huigang 1
711	Sinhae	10	753	Gyesa	12	795	Eulhae	11	837	Jeongsa	2
712	Imja	11	754	Gabo	13	796	Byeongja	12	838	Muo	Minae 1

YEAR	YEAR NAME	SILLA
839	Gimi	Sinmu 1, Munseong 1
840	Gyeongsin	2
841	Sinyu	3
842	Imsul	4
843	Gyehae	5
844	Gapja	6
845	Eulchuk	7
846	Byeongin	8
847	Jeongmyo	9
848	Mujin	10
849	Gisa	11
850	Gyeongo	12
851	Sinmi	13
852	Imsin	14
853	Gyeyu	15
854	Gapsul	16
855	Eulhae	17
856	Byeongja	18
857	Jeongchuk	Heonan 1
858	Muin	2
859	Gimyo	3
860	Gyeongjin	4
861	Sinsa	Gyeongmun 1
862	Imo	2
863	Gyemi	3
864	Gapsin	4
865	Eulyu	5
866	Byeongsul	6
867	Jeonghae	7
868	Muja	8
869	Gichuk	9
870	Gyeongin	10
871	Sinmyo	11
872	Imjin	12
873	Gyesa	13
874	Gabo	14
875	Eulmi	Heongang 1
876	Byeongsin	2
877	Jeongyu	3
878	Musul	4
879	Gihae	5

YEAR	YEAR NAME	SILLA	GORYEO
880	Gyeongja	6	
881	Sinchuk	7	
882	Imin	8	
883	Gyemyo	9	
884	Gapjin	10	
885	Eulsa	11	
886	Byeongo	Jeonggang 1	
887	Jeongmi	Jinseong 1	
888	Musin	2	
889	Giyu	3	
890	Gyeongsul	4	
891	Sinhae	5	
892	Imja	6	
893	Gyechuk	7	
894	Gabin	8	
895	Eulmyo	9	
896	Byeongjin	10	
897	Jeongsa	Hyogong 1	
898	Muo	2	
899	Gimi	3	
900	Gyeongsin	4	
901	Sinyu	5	
902	Imsul	6	
903	Gyehae	7	
904	Gapja	8	
905	Eulchuk	9	
906	Byeongin	10	
907	Jeongmyo	11	
908	Mujin	12	
909	Gisa	13	
910	Gyeongo	14	
911	Sinmi	15	
912	Imsin	Sindeok 1	
913	Gyeyu	2	
914	Gapsul	3	
915	Eulhae	4	
916	Byeongja	5	
917	Jeongchuk	Gyeongmyeong 1	GORYEO
918	Muin	2	Taejo 1
919	Gimyo	3	2
920	Gyeongjin	4	3
921	Sinsa	5	4

YEAR	YEAR NAME	SILLA	GORYEO
922	Imo	6	5
923	Gyemi	7	6
924	Gapsin	Gyeongae 1	7
925	Eulyu	2	8
926	Byeongsul	3	9
927	Jeonghae	Gyeongsun 1	10
928	Muja	2	11
929	Gichuk	3	12
930	Gyeongin	4	13
931	Sinmyo	5	14
932	Imjin	6	15
933	Gyesa	7	16
934	Gabo	8	17
935	Eulmi	9	18
936	Byeongsin		19
937	Jeongyu		20
938	Musul		21
939	Gihae		22
940	Gyeongja		23
941	Sinchuk		24
942	Imin		25
943	Gyemyo		26
944	Gapjin		Hyejong 1
945	Eulsa		2
946	Byeongo		Jeongjong 1
947	Jeongmi		2
948	Musin		3
949	Giyu		4
950	Gyeongsul		Gwangjong 1
951	Sinhae		2
952	Imja		3
953	Gyechuk		4
954	Gabin		5
955	Eulmyo		6
956	Byeongjin		7
957	Jeongsa		8
958	Muo		9
959	Gimi		10
960	Gyeongsin		11
961	Sinyu		12
962	Imsul		13
963	Gyehae		14

YEAR	YEAR NAME	GORYEO	YEAR	YEAR NAME	GORYEO	YEAR	YEAR NAME	GORYEO	YEAR	YEAR NAME	GORYEO
964	Gapja	15	1006	Byeongo	9	1048	Muja	2	1090	Gyeongo	7
965	Eulchuk	16	1007	Jeongmi	10	1049	Gichuk	3	1091	Sinmi	8
966	Byeongin	17	1008	Musin	11	1050	Gyeongin	4	1092	Imsin	9
967	Jeongmyo	18	1009	Giyu	12	1051	Sinmyo	5	1093	Gyeyu	10
968	Mujin	19	1010	Gyeongsul	Hyeonjong 1	1052	Imjin	6	1094	Gapsul	11
969	Gisa	20	1011	Sinhae	2	1053	Gyesa	7	1095	Eulhae	Heonjong 1
970	Gyeongo	21	1012	Imja	3	1054	Gabo	8	1096	Byeongja	Sukjong 1
971	Sinmi	22	1013	Gyechuk	4	1055	Eulmi	9	1097	Jeongchuk	2
972	Imsin	23	1014	Gabin	5	1056	Byeongsin	10	1098	Muin	3
973	Gyeyu	24	1015	Eulmyo	6	1057	Jeongyu	11	1099	Gimyo	4
974	Gapsul	25	1016	Byeongjin	7	1058	Musul	12	1100	Gyeongjin	5
975	Eulhae	26	1017	Jeongsa	8	1059	Gihae	13	1101	Sinsa	6
976	Byeongja	Gyeongjong 1	1018	Muo	9	1060	Gyeongja	14	1102	Imo	7
977	Jeongchuk	2	1019	Gimi	10	1061	Sinchuk	15	1103	Gyemi	8
978	Muin	3	1020	Gyeongsin	11	1062	Imin	16	1104	Gapsin	9
979	Gimyo	4	1021	Sinyu	12	1063	Gyemyo	17	1105	Eulyu	10
980	Gyeongjin	5	1022	Imsul	13	1064	Gapjin	18	1106	Byeongsul	Yejong 1
981	Sinsa	6	1023	Gyehae	14	1065	Eulsa	19	1107	Jeonghae	2
982	Imo	Seongjong 1	1024	Gapja	15	1066	Byeongo	20	1108	Muja	3
983	Gyemi	2	1025	Eulchuk	16	1067	Jeongmi	21	1109	Gichuk	4
984	Gapsin	3	1026	Byeongin	17	1068	Musin	22	1110	Gyeongin	5
985	Eulyu	4	1027	Jeongmyo	18	1069	Giyu	23	1111	Sinmyo	6
986	Byeongsul	5	1028	Mujin	19	1070	Gyeongsul	24	1112	Imjin	7
987	Jeonghae	6	1029	Gisa	20	1071	Sinhae	25	1113	Gyesa	8
988	Muja	7	1030	Gyeongo	21	1072	Imja	26	1114	Gabo	9
989	Gichuk	8	1031	Sinmi	22	1073	Gyechuk	27	1115	Eulmi	10
990	Gyeongin	9	1032	Imsin	Deokjong 1	1074	Gabin	28	1116	Byeongsin	11
991	Sinmyo	10	1033	Gyeyu	2	1075	Eulmyo	29	1117	Jeongyu	12
992	Imjin	11	1034	Gapsul	3	1076	Byeongjin	30	1118	Musul	13
993	Gyesa	12	1035	Eulhae	Jeongjong 1	1077	Jeongsa	31	1119	Gihae	14
994	Gabo	13	1036	Byeongja	2	1078	Muo	32	1120	Gyeongja	15
995	Eulmi	14	1037	Jeongchuk	3	1079	Gimi	33	1121	Sinchuk	16
996	Byeongsin	15	1038	Muin	4	1080	Gyeongsin	34	1122	Imin	17
997	Jeongyu	16	1039	Gimyo	5	1081	Sinyu	35	1123	Gyemyo	Injong 1
998	Musul	Mokjong 1	1040	Gyeongjin	6	1082	Imsul	36	1124	Gapjin	2
999	Gihae	2	1041	Sinsa	7	1083	Gyehae	Sunjong 1	1125	Eulsa	3
1000	Gyeongja	3	1042	Imo	8	1084	Gapja	Seonjong 1	1126	Byeongo	4
1001	Sinchuk	4	1043	Gyemi	9	1085	Eulchuk	2	1127	Jeongmi	5
1002	Imin	5	1044	Gapsin	10	1086	Byeongin	3	1128	Musin	6
1003	Gyemyo	6	1045	Eulyu	11	1087	Jeongmyo	4	1129	Giyu	7
1004	Gapjin	7	1046	Byeongsul	12	1088	Mujin	5	1130	Gyeongsul	8
1005	Eulsa	8	1047	Jeonghae	Munjong 1	1089	Gisa	6	1131	Sinhae	9

YEAR	YEAR NAME	GORYEO	YEAR	YEAR NAME	GORYEO	YEAR	YEAR NAME	GORYEO	YEAR	YEAR NAME	GORYEO
1132	Imja	10	1174	Gabo	4	1216	Byeongja	3	1258	Muo	45
1133	Gyechuk	11	1175	Eulmi	5	1217	Jeongchuk	4	1259	Gimi	46
1134	Gabin	12	1176	Byeongsin	6	1218	Muin	5	1260	Gyeongsin	Wonjong 1
1135	Eulmyo	13	1177	Jeongyu	7	1219	Gimyo	6	1261	Sinyu	2
1136	Byeongjin	14	1178	Musul	8	1220	Gyeongjin	7	1262	Imsul	3
1137	Jeongsa	15	1179	Gihae	9	1221	Sinsa	8	1263	Gyehae	4
1138	Muo	16	1180	Gyeongja	10	1222	Imo	9	1264	Gapja	5
1139	Gimi	17	1181	Sinchuk	11	1223	Gyemi	10	1265	Eulchuk	6
1140	Gyeongsin	18	1182	Imin	12	1224	Gapsin	11	1266	Byeongin	7
1141	Sinyu	19	1183	Gyemyo	13	1225	Eulyu	12	1267	Jeongmyo	8
1142	Imsul	20	1184	Gapjin	14	1226	Byeongsul	13	1268	Mujin	9
1143	Gyehae	21	1185	Eulsa	15	1227	Jeonghae	14	1269	Gisa	10
1144	Gapja	22	1186	Byeongo	16	1228	Muja	15	1270	Gyeongo	11
1145	Eulchuk	23	1187	Jeongmi	17	1229	Gichuk	16	1271	Sinmi	12
1146	Byeongin	24	1188	Musin	18	1230	Gyeongin	17	1272	Imsin	13
1147	Jeongmyo	Uijong 1	1189	Giyu	19	1231	Sinmyo	18	1273	Gyeyu	14
1148	Mujin	2	1190	Gyeongsul	20	1232	Imjin	19	1274	Gapsul	15
1149	Gisa	3	1191	Sinhae	21	1233	Gyesa	20	1275	Eulhae	Chungnyeol 1
1150	Gyeongo	4	1192	Imja	22	1234	Gabo	21	1276	Byeongja	2
1151	Sinmi	5	1193	Gyechuk	23	1235	Eulmi	22	1277	Jeongchuk	3
1152	Imsin	6	1194	Gabin	24	1236	Byeongsin	23	1278	Muin	4
1153	Gyeyu	7	1195	Eulmyo	25	1237	Jeongyu	24	1279	Gimyo	5
1154	Gapsul	8	1196	Byeongjin	26	1238	Musul	25	1280	Gyeongjin	6
1155	Eulhae	9	1197	Jeongsa	27	1239	Gihae	26	1281	Sinsa	7
1156	Byeongja	10	1198	Muo	Sinjong 1	1240	Gyeongja	27	1282	Imo	8
1157	Jeongchuk	11	1199	Gimi	2	1241	Sinchuk	28	1283	Gyemi	9
1158	Muin	12	1200	Gyeongsin	3	1242	Imin	29	1284	Gapsin	10
1159	Gimyo	13	1201	Sinyu	4	1243	Gyemyo	30	1285	Eulyu	11
1160	Gyeongjin	14	1202	Imsul	5	1244	Gapjin	31	1286	Byeongsul	12
1161	Sinsa	15	1203	Gyehae	6	1245	Eulsa	32	1287	Jeonghae	13
1162	Imo	16	1204	Gapja	7	1246	Byeongo	33	1288	Muja	14
1163	Gyemi	17	1205	Eulchuk	Huijong 1	1247	Jeongmi	34	1289	Gichuk	15
1164	Gapsin	18	1206	Byeongin	2	1248	Musin	35	1290	Gyeongin	16
1165	Eulyu	19	1207	Jeongmyo	3	1249	Giyu	36	1291	Sinmyo	17
1166	Byeongsul	20	1208	Mujin	4	1250	Gyeongsul	37	1292	Imjin	18
1167	Jeonghae	21	1209	Gisa	5	1251	Sinhae	38	1293	Gyesa	19
1168	Muja	22	1210	Gyeongo	6	1252	Imja	39	1294	Gabo	20
1169	Gichuk	23	1211	Sinmi	7	1253	Gyechuk	40	1295	Eulmi	21
1170	Gyeongin	24	1212	Imsin	Gangjong 1	1254	Gabin	41	1296	Byeongsin	22
1171	Sinmyo	Myeongjong 1	1213	Gyeyu	2	1255	Eulmyo	42	1297	Jeongyu	23
1172	Imjin	2	1214	Gapsul	Gojong 1	1256	Byeongjin	43	1298	Musul	24
1173	Gyesa	3	1215	Eulhae	2	1257	Jeongsa	44	1299	Gihae	25

YEAR	YEAR NAME	GORYEO	YEAR	YEAR NAME	GORYEO	YEAR	YEAR NAME	GORYEO
1300	Gyeongja	26	1342	Imo	3	1384	Gapja	10
1301	Sinchuk	27	1343	Gyemi	4	1385	Eulchuk	11
1302	Imin	28	1344	Gapsin	5	1386	Byeongin	12
1303	Gyemyo	29	1345	Eulyu	Chungmok 1	1387	Jeongmyo	13
1304	Gapjin	30	1346	Byeongsul	2	1388	Mujin	Chang 1
1305	Eulsa	31	1347	Jeonghae	3	1389	Gisa	Gongyang 1
1306	Byeongo	32	1348	Muja	4	1390	Gyeongo	2
1307	Jeongmi	33	1349	Gichuk	Chungjeong 1	1391	Sinmi	3	JOSEON
1308	Musin	34	1350	Gyeongin	2	1392	Imsin		Taejo 1
1309	Giyu	Chungseon 1	1351	Sinmyo	3	1393	Gyeyu		2
1310	Gyeongsul	2	1352	Imjin	Gongmin 1	1394	Gapsul		3
1311	Sinhae	3	1353	Gyesa	2	1395	Eulhae		4
1312	Imja	4	1354	Gabo	3	1396	Byeongja		5
1313	Gyechuk	5	1355	Eulmi	4	1397	Jeongchuk		6
1314	Gabin	Chungsuk 1	1356	Byeongsin	5	1398	Muin		7
1315	Eulmyo	2	1357	Jeongyu	6	1399	Gimyo		Jeongjong 1
1316	Byeongjin	3	1358	Musul	7	1400	Gyeongjin		2
1317	Jeongsa	4	1359	Gihae	8	1401	Sinsa		Taejong 1
1318	Muo	5	1360	Gyeongja	9	1402	Imo		2
1319	Gimi	6	1361	Sinchuk	10	1403	Gyemi		3
1320	Gyeongsin	7	1362	Imin	11	1404	Gapsin		4
1321	Sinyu	8	1363	Gyemyo	12	1405	Eulyu		5
1322	Imsul	9	1364	Gapjin	13	1406	Byeongsul		6
1323	Gyehae	10	1365	Eulsa	14	1407	Jeonghae		7
1324	Gapja	11	1366	Byeongo	15	1408	Muja		8
1325	Eulchuk	12	1367	Jeongmi	16	1409	Gichuk		9
1326	Byeongin	13	1368	Musin	17	1410	Gyeongin		10
1327	Jeongmyo	14	1369	Giyu	18	1411	Sinmyo		11
1328	Mujin	15	1370	Gyeongsul	19	1412	Imjin		12
1329	Gisa	16	1371	Sinhae	20	1413	Gyesa		13
1330	Gyeongo	17	1372	Imja	21	1414	Gabo		14
1331	Sinmi	Chunghye 1	1373	Gyechuk	22	1415	Eulmi		15
1332	Imsin	Chungsuk 1	1374	Gabin	23	1416	Byeongsin		16
1333	Gyeyu	2	1375	Eulmyo	U 1	1417	Jeongyu		17
1334	Gapsul	3	1376	Byeongjin	2	1418	Musul		18
1335	Eulhae	4	1377	Jeongsa	3	1419	Gihae		Sejong 1
1336	Byeongja	5	1378	Muo	4	1420	Gyeongja		2
1337	Jeongchuk	6	1379	Gimi	5	1421	Sinchuk		3
1338	Muin	7	1380	Gyeongsin	6	1422	Imin		4
1339	Gimyo	8	1381	Sinyu	7	1423	Gyemyo		5
1340	Gyeongjin	Chunghye 1	1382	Imsul	8	1424	Gapjin		6
1341	Sinsa	2	1383	Gyehae	9	1425	Eulsa		7

YEAR	YEAR NAME	JOSEON	YEAR	YEAR NAME	JOSEON	YEAR	YEAR NAME	JOSEON
1426	Byeongo	8	1468	Muja	14	1510	Gyeongo	5
1427	Jeongmi	9	1469	Gichuk	Yejong 1	1511	Sinmi	6
1428	Musin	10	1470	Gyeongin	Seongjong 1	1512	Imsin	7
1429	Giyu	11	1471	Sinmyo	2	1513	Gyeyu	8
1430	Gyeongsul	12	1472	Imjin	3	1514	Gapsul	9
1431	Sinhae	13	1473	Gyesa	4	1515	Eulhae	10
1432	Imja	14	1474	Gabo	5	1516	Byeongja	11
1433	Gyechuk	15	1475	Eulmi	6	1517	Jeongchuk	12
1434	Gabin	16	1476	Byeongsin	7	1518	Muin	13
1435	Eulmyo	17	1477	Jeongyu	8	1519	Gimyo	14
1436	Byeongjin	18	1478	Musul	9	1520	Gyeongjin	15
1437	Jeongsa	19	1479	Gihae	10	1521	Sinsa	16
1438	Muo	20	1480	Gyeongja	11	1522	Imo	17
1439	Gimi	21	1481	Sinchuk	12	1523	Gyemi	18
1440	Gyeongsin	22	1482	Imin	13	1524	Gapsin	19
1441	Sinyu	23	1483	Gyemyo	14	1525	Eulyu	20
1442	Imsul	24	1484	Gapjin	15	1526	Byeongsul	21
1443	Gyehae	25	1485	Eulsa	16	1527	Jeonghae	22
1444	Gapja	26	1486	Byeongo	17	1528	Muja	23
1445	Eulchuk	27	1487	Jeongmi	18	1529	Gichuk	24
1446	Byeongin	28	1488	Musin	19	1530	Gyeongin	25
1447	Jeongmyo	29	1489	Giyu	20	1531	Sinmyo	26
1448	Mujin	30	1490	Gyeongsul	21	1532	Imjin	27
1449	Gisa	31	1491	Sinhae	22	1533	Gyesa	28
1450	Gyeongo	32	1492	Imja	23	1534	Gabo	29
1451	Sinmi	Munjong 1	1493	Gyechuk	24	1535	Eulmi	30
1452	Imsin	2	1494	Gabin	25	1536	Byeongsin	31
1453	Gyeyu	Danjong 1	1495	Eulmyo	Yeonsangun 1	1537	Jeongyu	32
1454	Gapsul	2	1496	Byeongjin	2	1538	Musul	33
1455	Eulhae	Sejo 1	1497	Jeongsa	3	1539	Gihae	34
1456	Byeongja	2	1498	Muo	4	1540	Gyeongja	35
1457	Jeongchuk	3	1499	Gimi	5	1541	Sinchuk	36
1458	Muin	4	1500	Gyeongsin	6	1542	Imin	37
1459	Gimyo	5	1501	Sinyu	7	1543	Gyemyo	38
1460	Gyeongjin	6	1502	Imsul	8	1544	Gapjin	39
1461	Sinsa	7	1503	Gyehae	9	1545	Eulsa	Injong 1
1462	Imo	8	1504	Gapja	10	1546	Byeongo	Myeongjong 1
1463	Gyemi	9	1505	Eulchuk	11	1547	Jeongmi	2
1464	Gapsin	10	1506	Byeongin	Jungjong 1	1548	Musin	3
1465	Eulyu	11	1507	Jeongmyo	2	1549	Giyu	4
1466	Byeongsul	12	1508	Mujin	3	1550	Gyeongsul	5
1467	Jeonghae	13	1509	Gisa	4	1551	Sinhae	6

YEAR	YEAR NAME	JOSEON	YEAR	YEAR NAME	JOSEON	YEAR	YEAR NAME	JOSEON
1552	Imja	7	1594	Gabo	27	1636	Byeongja	14
1553	Gyechuk	8	1595	Eulmi	28	1637	Jeongchuk	15
1554	Gabin	9	1596	Byeongsin	29	1638	Muin	16
1555	Eulmyo	10	1597	Jeongyu	30	1639	Gimyo	17
1556	Byeongjin	11	1598	Musul	31	1640	Gyeongjin	18
1557	Jeongsa	12	1599	Gihae	32	1641	Sinsa	19
1558	Muo	13	1600	Gyeongja	33	1642	Imo	20
1559	Gimi	14	1601	Sinchuk	34	1643	Gyemi	21
1560	Gyeongsin	15	1602	Imin	35	1644	Gapsin	22
1561	Sinyu	16	1603	Gyemyo	36	1645	Eulyu	23
1562	Imsul	17	1604	Gapjin	37	1646	Byeongsul	24
1563	Gyehae	18	1605	Eulsa	38	1647	Jeonghae	25
1564	Gapja	19	1606	Byeongo	39	1648	Muja	26
1565	Eulchuk	20	1607	Jeongmi	40	1649	Gichuk	27
1566	Byeongin	21	1608	Musin	41	1650	Gyeongin	Hyojong 1
1567	Jeongmyo	22	1609	Giyu	Gwanghaegun 1	1651	Sinmyo	2
1568	Mujin	Seonjo 1	1610	Gyeongsul	2	1652	Imjin	3
1569	Gisa	2	1611	Sinhae	3	1653	Gyesa	4
1570	Gyeongo	3	1612	Imja	4	1654	Gabo	5
1571	Sinmi	4	1613	Gyechuk	5	1655	Eulmi	6
1572	Imsin	5	1614	Gabin	6	1656	Byeongsin	7
1573	Gyeyu	6	1615	Eulmyo	7	1657	Jeongyu	8
1574	Gapsul	7	1616	Byeongjin	8	1658	Musul	9
1575	Eulhae	8	1617	Jeongsa	9	1659	Gihae	10
1576	Byeongja	9	1618	Muo	10	1660	Gyeongja	Hyeonjong 1
1577	Jeongchuk	10	1619	Gimi	11	1661	Sinchuk	2
1578	Muin	11	1620	Gyeongsin	12	1662	Imin	3
1579	Gimyo	12	1621	Sinyu	13	1663	Gyemyo	4
1580	Gyeongjin	13	1622	Imsul	14	1664	Gapjin	5
1581	Sinsa	14	1623	Gyehae	Injo 1	1665	Eulsa	6
1582	Imo	15	1624	Gapja	2	1666	Byeongo	7
1583	Gyemi	16	1625	Eulchuk	3	1667	Jeongmi	8
1584	Gapsin	17	1626	Byeongin	4	1668	Musin	9
1585	Eulyu	18	1627	Jeongmyo	5	1669	Giyu	10
1586	Byeongsul	19	1628	Mujin	6	1670	Gyeongsul	11
1587	Jeonghae	20	1629	Gisa	7	1671	Sinhae	12
1588	Muja	21	1630	Gyeongo	8	1672	Imja	13
1589	Gichuk	22	1631	Sinmi	9	1673	Gyechuk	14
1590	Gyeongin	23	1632	Imsin	10	1674	Gabin	15
1591	Sinmyo	24	1633	Gyeyu	11	1675	Eulmyo	Sukjong 1
1592	Imjin	25	1634	Gapsul	12	1676	Byeongjin	2
1593	Gyesa	26	1635	Eulhae	13	1677	Jeongsa	3

YEAR	YEAR NAME	JOSEON	YEAR	YEAR NAME	JOSEON	YEAR	YEAR NAME	JOSEON
1678	Muo	4	1720	Gyeongja	46	1762	Imo	38
1679	Gimi	5	1721	Sinchuk	Gyeonjong 1	1763	Gyemi	39
1680	Gyeongsin	6	1722	Imin	2	1764	Gapsin	40
1681	Sinyu	7	1723	Gyemyo	3	1765	Eulyu	41
1682	Imsul	8	1724	Gapjin	4	1766	Byeongsul	42
1683	Gyehae	9	1725	Eulsa	Yeongjo 1	1767	Jeonghae	43
1684	Gapja	10	1726	Byeongo	2	1768	Muja	44
1685	Eulchuk	11	1727	Jeongmi	3	1769	Gichuk	45
1686	Byeongin	12	1728	Musin	4	1770	Gyeongin	46
1687	Jeongmyo	13	1729	Giyu	5	1771	Sinmyo	47
1688	Mujin	14	1730	Gyeongsul	6	1772	Imjin	48
1689	Gisa	15	1731	Sinhae	7	1773	Gyesa	49
1690	Gyeongo	16	1732	Imja	8	1774	Gabo	50
1691	Sinmi	17	1733	Gyechuk	9	1775	Eulmi	51
1692	Imsin	18	1734	Gabin	10	1776	Byeongsin	52
1693	Gyeyu	19	1735	Eulmyo	11	1777	Jeongyu	Jeongjo 1
1694	Gapsul	20	1736	Byeongjin	12	1778	Musul	2
1695	Eulhae	21	1737	Jeongsa	13	1779	Gihae	3
1696	Byeongja	22	1738	Muo	14	1780	Gyeongja	4
1697	Jeongchuk	23	1739	Gimi	15	1781	Sinchuk	5
1698	Muin	24	1740	Gyeongsin	16	1782	Imin	6
1699	Gimyo	25	1741	Sinyu	17	1783	Gyemyo	7
1700	Gyeongjin	26	1742	Imsul	18	1784	Gapjin	8
1701	Sinsa	27	1743	Gyehae	19	1785	Eulsa	9
1702	Imo	28	1744	Gapja	20	1786	Byeongo	10
1703	Gyemi	29	1745	Eulchuk	21	1787	Jeongmi	11
1704	Gapsin	30	1746	Byeongin	22	1788	Musin	12
1705	Eulyu	31	1747	Jeongmyo	23	1789	Giyu	13
1706	Byeongsul	32	1748	Mujin	24	1790	Gyeongsul	14
1707	Jeonghae	33	1749	Gisa	25	1791	Sinhae	15
1708	Muja	34	1750	Gyeongo	26	1792	Imja	16
1709	Gichuk	35	1751	Sinmi	27	1793	Gyechuk	17
1710	Gyeongin	36	1752	Imsin	28	1794	Gabin	18
1711	Sinmyo	37	1753	Gyeyu	29	1795	Eulmyo	19
1712	Imjin	38	1754	Gapsul	30	1796	Byeongjin	20
1713	Gyesa	39	1755	Eulhae	31	1797	Jeongsa	21
1714	Gabo	40	1756	Byeongja	32	1798	Muo	22
1715	Eulmi	41	1757	Jeongchuk	33	1799	Gimi	23
1716	Byeongsin	42	1758	Muin	34	1800	Gyeongsin	24
1717	Jeongyu	43	1759	Gimyo	35	1801	Sinyu	Sunjo 1
1718	Musul	44	1760	Gyeongjin	36	1802	Imsul	2
1719	Gihae	45	1761	Sinsa	37	1803	Gyehae	3

YEAR	YEAR NAME	JOSEON
1804	Gapja	4
1805	Eulchuk	5
1806	Byeongin	6
1807	Jeongmyo	7
1808	Mujin	8
1809	Gisa	9
1810	Gyeongo	10
1811	Sinmi	11
1812	Imsin	12
1813	Gyeyu	13
1814	Gapsul	14
1815	Eulhae	15
1816	Byeongja	16
1817	Jeongchuk	17
1818	Muin	18
1819	Gimyo	19
1820	Gyeongjin	20
1821	Sinsa	21
1822	Imo	22
1823	Gyemi	23
1824	Gapsin	24
1825	Eulyu	25
1826	Byeongsul	26
1827	Jeonghae	27
1828	Muja	28
1829	Gichuk	29
1830	Gyeongin	30
1831	Sinmyo	31
1832	Imjin	32
1833	Gyesa	33
1834	Gabo	34
1835	Eulmi	Heonjong 1
1836	Byeongsin	2
1837	Jeongyu	3
1838	Musul	4
1839	Gihae	5
1840	Gyeongja	6
1841	Sinchuk	7
1842	Imin	8
1843	Gyemyo	9
1844	Gapjin	10
1845	Eulsa	11

YEAR	YEAR NAME	JOSEON
1846	Byeongo	12
1847	Jeongmi	13
1848	Musin	14
1849	Giyu	15
1850	Gyeongsul	Cheoljong1
1851	Sinhae	2
1852	Imja	3
1853	Gyechuk	4
1854	Gabin	5
1855	Eulmyo	6
1856	Byeongjin	7
1857	Jeongsa	8
1858	Muo	9
1859	Gimi	10
1860	Gyeongsin	11
1861	Sinyu	12
1862	Imsul	13
1863	Gyehae	14
1864	Gapja	Gojong 1
1865	Eulchuk	2
1866	Byeongin	3
1867	Jeongmyo	4
1868	Mujin	5
1869	Gisa	6
1870	Gyeongo	7
1871	Sinmi	8
1872	Imsin	9
1873	Gyeyu	10
1874	Gapsul	11
1875	Eulhae	12
1876	Byeongja	13
1877	Jeongchuk	14
1878	Muin	15
1879	Gimyo	16
1880	Gyeongjin	17
1881	Sinsa	18
1882	Imo	19
1883	Gyemi	20
1884	Gapsin	21
1885	Eulyu	22
1886	Byeongsul	23
1887	Jeonghae	24

YEAR	YEAR NAME	JOSEON		GREAT HAN EMPIRE
1888	Muja	25		
1889	Gichuk	26		
1890	Gyeongin	27		
1891	Sinmyo	28		
1892	Imjin	29		
1893	Gyesa	30		
1894	Gabo	31	Gaeguk 503	
1895	Eulmi	32	504	
1896	Byeongsin	33	Geonyang 1	
1897	Jeongyu	34		Gwangmu 1
1898	Musul	35		2
1899	Gihae	36		3
1900	Gyeongja	37		4
1901	Sinchuk	38		5
1902	Imin	39		6
1903	Gyemyo	40		7
1904	Gapjin	41		8
1905	Eulsa	42		9
1906	Byeongo	43		10
1907	Jeongmi	Sunjong 1		Yunghui 1
1908	Musin	2		2
1909	Giyu	3		3
1910	Gyeongsul	4		4

Index